THE ARAB UPRISINGS

WHAT EVERYONE NEEDS TO KNOW

[redacted]

THE ARAB UPRISINGS

WHAT EVERYONE NEEDS TO KNOW

JAMES L. GELVIN

OXFORD
UNIVERSITY PRESS

OXFORD
UNIVERSITY PRESS

Oxford University Press, Inc., publishes works that further
Oxford University's objective of excellence
in research, scholarship, and education.

Oxford New York
Auckland Cape Town Dar es Salaam Hong Kong Karachi
Kuala Lumpur Madrid Melbourne Mexico City Nairobi
New Delhi Shanghai Taipei Toronto

With offices in
Argentina Austria Brazil Chile Czech Republic France Greece
Guatemala Hungary Italy Japan Poland Portugal Singapore
South Korea Switzerland Thailand Turkey Ukraine Vietnam

Published by Oxford University Press, Inc.
198 Madison Avenue, New York, New York 10016
www.oup.com

Library of Congress Cataloging-in-Publication Data
Gelvin, James L., 1951–
The Arab uprisings : what everyone needs to know / James L. Gelvin.
p. cm.
Includes bibliographical references and index.
ISBN 978-0-19-989177-1 (pbk. : alk. paper)—
ISBN 978-0-19-989175-7 (hardcover : alk. paper)
1. Protest movements–Arab countries–History—21st century.
2. Protest movement–Middle East–History—21st century. 3. Arab countries–Politics and government—21st century. 4. Middle East–Politics and government—21st century. 5. Protest movements–Middle East I. Title.
JQ1850.A91G37 2012
956.05'4—dc23
2011041925

1 3 5 7 9 8 6 4 2

Printed in the United States of America
on acid-free paper

CONTENTS

ACKNOWLEDGMENTS

This book, which might also be subtitled "How I Spent My Summer Vacation," came about as a result of two phenomena. First, the Libyan uprising. Having completed a project on Syrian history, I decided to turn my sights 1,336 miles to the west to look at Libya—specifically how the Italian invasion of Libya in 1911 affected the inhabitants of the Arab east. Since the process of obtaining a Libyan visa was long and, to put it mildly, quirky, I had begun making travel arrangements in the fall of 2010 for a research trip the following summer. Then came the uprising, the government's brutal attempt to suppress it, and a six-month civil war, which tilted in favor of the rebels only in August 2011. Discretion being the better part of valor, I decided to abandon my travel plans and find another way to practice my craft (history) during my vacation.

The second phenomenon has to do with Los Angeles being a communications hub abounding in educational institutions and civic associations. After the Egyptian uprising demonstrated that the Tunisian uprising was no fluke, I began receiving requests for interviews and media appearances from as near as the local affiliates of the major American networks and as far away as Brasilia and Beijing. I also received requests for presentations from institutions as diverse as Pomona College and the Santa Monica Rotary Club. As of this writing, I have done nearly sixty interviews and made some two dozen presentations. The requests for interviews and presentations forced me to think critically about what was going on in the Arab world, particularly how history informs what is going on there, and to hone a narrative that would be accessible to a variety of audiences. The result is this book.

A number of people have assisted me in this project. First off, I would like to thank those who helped me research it by discovering useful sources in four languages and by helping me keep daily logs of the course of the various uprisings: Omar Elkabti, Patricia Fisher, Carol Hakim, Kathryn Kizer, Hanna Petro, and Elizabeth Waraksa. Then there were those who generously shared their knowledge, kibitzed, pointed out missteps, provided inspiration, or did any combination of the four: Ziad Abu-Rish, Asli Bali, Joel Beinin, David Dean Commins, Kristen Hillaire Glasgow, Bassam Haddad, Toby Jones, David W. Lesch, Maya Mikdashi, Sarah Shields, and Susan Slyomovics. Finally, there is my editor at Oxford University Press, Nancy Toff, and her assistant, Sonia Tycko, who saw this project through from beginning to end.

As far as a dedication is concerned, the choice is obvious: to all those who are still searching for heroes, I would suggest they look to the Arab world. Since December 2010 (and in many cases before), tens of thousands of men, women, and children have faced death on a daily basis to end the nightmare of oppression that all too many outside observers had written off as their destiny. This book is dedicated to them.

THE ARAB UPRISINGS

WHAT EVERYONE NEEDS TO KNOW

1

A REVOLUTIONARY WAVE?

What is the Arab world?

The phrase *Arab world* might be defined in two ways. First, it refers to a geographical expanse that stretches from North Africa to the western border of Iran (west to east), and from the southern border of Turkey to the Horn of Africa (north to south). The Arab world includes twenty-one states: Algeria, Bahrain, Comoros, Djibouti, Egypt, Iraq, Jordan, Kuwait, Lebanon, Libya, Mauritania, Morocco, Oman, Qatar, Saudi Arabia, Somalia, Sudan, Syria, Tunisia, the United Arab Emirates, and Yemen. It also includes the Palestinian territories. The predominant language in the region is Arabic.

The phrase *Arab world* also refers to the cultural world in which the inhabitants of the region, and others who identify with that cultural world, live.

How homogeneous is the Arab world?

Most inhabitants of the Arab world are Arabic-speaking Muslims. Nevertheless, the term *Arab world* masks the fact that the inhabitants in the region are not homogeneous. For example, Muslims are divided into two main branches, Shi'is and Sunnis. The split between the two branches of Islam occurred early on in Islamic history over a dispute about who should lead the Islamic community after the death of the prophet Muhammad. Over time, each branch also developed its own sets of rituals, traditions, and beliefs. Most Arabs are Sunni, but two Arab countries (Iraq and Bahrain) have Shi'i majorities, and there are substantial numbers of Shi'is in Lebanon, Yemen, Kuwait, and Saudi Arabia. Since both rulers and their opponents in the Arab world sometimes exploit the Sunni-Shi'i divide for their own benefit, it is necessary to know that there is a difference between the two branches of Islam. Knowing the contrasting sets of rituals, traditions, and beliefs is irrelevant for understanding the uprisings.

In addition to Shi'is and Sunnis, there are other Muslim sects in the Arab world. For example, the ruling group in Syria draws from the Alawite sect, which comprises about 11 percent of the Syrian population. There is also a substantial Christian population in the Arab world, including Maronite Christians in Lebanon, Coptic Christians in Egypt, and Orthodox Christians throughout the region.

Linguistic and ethnic minorities also live in the Arab world. Berbers, for example, make up about half the population of Morocco and about a third of the population of Algeria. Tunisia and Libya host Berber communities as well. Kurds living in the Arab world inhabit Syria and Iraq. Both groups have their own languages. Discrimination (and worse) has increased the sense of Berber and Kurdish identity among members of each group.

Why do Arabs identify with one another?

One of the most interesting aspects of the Arab uprisings has been how the actions of Egyptians, for example, captured the imagination of the inhabitants of Algeria, Yemen, Syria, and elsewhere. Besides a shared language, a number of factors have increased the likelihood that the inhabitants of the region would identify with a broader Arab community. There is a sense of shared history and experiences that school systems and intellectuals encourage. There is poetry, (Egyptian) soap operas, and movies that Arabs throughout the region, and throughout the world, share. This is why the adage "Egyptians write books, Lebanese publish them, and Iraqis read them" rings true. There are regional associations, such as the Arab League and the Gulf Cooperation Council; regional development funds, such as the Arab Monetary Fund and the Arab Fund for Social and Economic Development; and a few lingering pan-Arab political parties, such as the ruling Baath Party of Syria, whose slogan remains "unity, freedom, socialism" (even if its actual commitment to unity is no more serious than its current commitment to socialism). There is the widespread opposition to American activities in the region, notably the 2003 invasion of Iraq and America's backing of Israel, which unite many of the inhabitants of the region, as well as the widespread support for the Palestinian cause. And there is the remarkable growth of Arabic-language media, such as the satellite television channel al-Jazeera, which began broadcasting in 1996 and remains the most popular source for news in the region. During the Egyptian uprising, more Egyptians got their news from the Qatar-based channel than from any other news source.

It is important to differentiate between, on the one hand, what might be called an "imagined Arab community" that exists in the heads of those who identify themselves as Arab and, on the other, Arab nationalism. Just because people might identify themselves as Arab does not mean they necessarily want to renounce their Egyptian or Lebanese citizenship, for example, in favor of citizenship in a pan-Arab state. As a matter of fact, the (pan-)Arab nationalism of the 1950s, which political leaders of the time encouraged mainly for strategic purposes, has for the most part dissipated over the decades as more and more people have come to identify with the states in which they live. As recent events in the region attest, however, an Arab identity has not dissipated. This is one reason the inhabitants of the region have followed the uprisings in neighboring countries with such interest and, in some cases, sought to emulate them.

What was political life in the Arab world like on the eve of the uprisings?

In 2000, the Regional Bureau for Arab States of the United Nations Development Programme commissioned a group of scholars and policy makers to assess the state of human development in the Arab world. It published the first *Arab Human Development Report* in 2002, then followed it up with four others.[1] Overall, the reports provide a scathing assessment of political, economic, and social conditions in the Arab world in the period leading up to the uprisings.

In terms of politics, the 2002 report begins its assessment in this manner:

> There is a substantial lag between Arab countries and other regions in terms of participatory governance. The wave of democracy that transformed governance in most of Latin America and East Asia in the 1980s and Eastern Europe and much of Central Asia in the late 1980s and early 1990s has barely reached the Arab States. This freedom deficit undermines human development and is one of the most painful manifestations of lagging political development.

The reports cite a number of characteristics political systems in the region held in common:

- When it came to civil liberties, political rights, and independence of media, only Jordan ranked above the international mean (Kuwait ranked exactly at the mean).
- When it came to the quality of public services and the bureaucracy and independence of civil service, only eight of the twenty Arab states surveyed ranked above the international mean.
- When it came to public perceptions of corruption (graft, bribery, cronyism), ten out of the seventeen Arab states surveyed ranked above the international mean.

- The 2004 report categorized almost all Arab states as "black-hole states," in which the executive branch of the government is so powerful that it "converts the surrounding social environment into a setting in which nothing moves and from which nothing escapes."
- In states in which there was no dynastic succession (Algeria, Tunisia, Egypt, and Yemen), presidents regularly modified constitutionally mandated term limits. In Syria, the rubber-stamp parliament amended the constitution so that the underage son of the former president might assume the presidency.
- To garner support, most Arab governments resorted to the "legitimacy of blackmail"; that is, most presented themselves as the only bulwark standing between the citizenry and Islamism or chaos. (The terms *Islamism* and *Islamic movements* embrace a grab bag of associations, parties, and governments that seek to order their societies according to what they consider to be Islamic principles. The term *Islamist* refers to those who profess those principles. Some Islamists choose to participate in politics to achieve this end; others do not. Some believe Islamic principles provide them with a strict roadmap to be followed without deviation; others treat those principles more gingerly.)
- Most Arab states tightly restricted the formation of political parties. For example, interior ministers or government committees in Egypt, Yemen, Tunisia, and Jordan had to authorize the formation of any new party. The Gulf states and Libya dealt with the issue of political parties simply by banning them.
- Seventeen of the nineteen Arab states surveyed required newspapers to be licensed; there was pre-censorship in eleven states.
- Syrians had been living under a state of emergency since 1963, Egyptians since 1981, Algerians since 1992, Iraqis since 2004, Palestinians since 2007, and Sudanese since

2008 (2005 in the Darfur region of the Sudan). A state of emergency strips citizens of such fundamental rights as habeas corpus and the right to assemble, authorizes extraordinary courts and suspension of constitutions, and expands even further the powers of the bloated executive branch of government. Although some constitutions guarantee such fundamental rights as the sanctity of the home and freedom of expression, most guarantees of this kind were empty promises. In some states, the constitution was ambiguous when it came to rights. Other constitutions delegated the definition of rights to the government. And still other constitutions subordinated rights to an official ideology (such as to the principles of Arab socialism) or national unity.

- In its 2008 report, the Arab Organization for Human Rights cited seven states—Iraq, Syria, Egypt, Saudi Arabia, Morocco, Jordan, Kuwait—and the governing authorities in the West Bank and Gaza for regularly torturing interned prisoners; the United Nations High Commission for Human Rights also threw in Algeria, Bahrain, Morocco, and Tunisia, for good measure.
- "State security courts," operating with unclear jurisdictional limits, imprecise procedural guidelines, and no oversight, existed in a number of Arab states. Not that it always mattered: eleven states (Bahrain, Egypt, Jordan, Lebanon, Libya, Mauritania, Saudi Arabia, Sudan, Syria, Tunisia, Yemen) allowed extrajudicial detentions.

Overall, on a scale measuring the quality of political and social life, not one Arab state provided a high "standard of human welfare" to its population. Seven small Arab states, representing 8.9 percent of the population of the seventeen countries surveyed, offered a medium standard of human welfare to their populations. The remainder, with 91.1 percent of the population of the seventeen Arab states surveyed, were marked by a low standard of human welfare among their populations.

Why have authoritarian governments been so common in the Arab world?

For years, historians and political scientists speculated about the cultural or social origins of authoritarianism in the Arab world. Some pointed to Islam, arguing that it was not compatible with democracy or human rights. Others looked to family structure, arguing that a state dominated by a single (male) figure simply reproduced the patriarchy of the typical Arab family.

Today, few historians and social scientists take these explanations, or any single explanation, seriously. There is no reason to assume that Islam is any more or less compatible with democracy and human rights than Christianity or Judaism, for example. There is also no reason to assume that all Muslims approach their Islam in the same way, read the same meanings into their Islam, or even apply at all principles derived from Islam in their daily lives. Then there are counterexamples, such as Indonesia (the world's most populous Muslim country) and Turkey; both are democracies, although with flaws. And a state is not simply a family writ large.

Although there is no single explanation for the prevalence of authoritarian governments in the Arab world, historians and political scientists have offered two partial explanations with which many experts agree. The first has to do with the Arab state's control over resources, the second with American foreign policy.

States in the Arab world are highly dependent on a source of revenue called by economists "rent." Economists define rent as income acquired by states from sources other than taxation. Some economists call states that are dependent on rent for a certain proportion of their income "rentier states"; others call them "allocation states" because the states distribute the rent they receive to favored clients and projects.

The most lucrative source for rent in the Arab world is, of course, oil. Some Arab states derive well over 90 percent of their revenues from oil. But even Arab states not usually associated with oil production, such as Egypt and Syria, have an inordinate dependence on rent. In 2010, rent accounted for 40 percent of Egypt's revenue and 50 percent of Syria's. In the case of the former, the sale of oil provided $11 billion to the national treasury, but there were other sources of rent as well. These included American aid (about $1.6 billion) and Suez Canal tolls (about $5 billion). Syria has traditionally derived rent both from oil and from other states that fear its ability to cause trouble in the region (or that wish to encourage this ability).

In no other region of the world are states as dependent on rent as they are in the Arab world. And access to rent not only means that the state does not have to go hat in hand to its citizens for revenue, it also ensures that the state will be the dominant economic actor. This enables the state to attach itself to the population through ties of patronage. It also enables the state to buy off dissent. It was thus not out of character when, in the wake of the uprisings in Tunisia and Egypt and unrest at home, other states in the Arab world attempted to bribe their populations by offering them social benefits, pay raises, or higher government subsidies on basic commodities in order to buy social peace. In sum, rent reinforces a relationship between the state and the citizens of the state that can be summed up in the phrase "benefits for compliance."

The second partial explanation for the prevalence of authoritarian rule in the Arab world is American foreign policy. The United States did not have much of a policy toward the region until the immediate post–World War II period. American engagement with the region thus coincided with the onset of the cold war, which defined American goals there. Throughout the cold war, the United States sought to attain six goals in the region: prevent the expansion of Soviet influence; ensure Western access to oil; secure the peaceful resolution of conflicts and the maintenance of a regional balance of power; promote stable, pro-Western states in the region;

preserve the independence and territorial integrity of the state of Israel; and protect the sea lanes, lines of communications, and the like connecting the United States and Europe with Asia. Authoritarian regimes were useful in achieving all these goals. For example, American policy makers believed only strong, authoritarian regimes could bring about the rapid economic development necessary to prevent their populations from "going communist." Only strong, authoritarian regimes such as that in Egypt could sign peace treaties with Israel in the face of popular opposition to those treaties. And only strong, authoritarian regimes that maintained a regional balance of power could ensure the uninterrupted supply of oil to the United States and its allies.

American support for autocrats was both direct and indirect. The United States directly and indirectly supported military officers who seized power in states throughout the region from the late 1940s through the 1960s. For example, the United States backed (some say sponsored) the first post-independence coup d'état in Syria—the first coup in the Arab world following World War II—which overthrew a democratically elected government. And, of course, the United States directly and indirectly supported a host of autocratic kings and emirs. This began even before the end of World War II, when Saudi Arabia became the only neutral state to receive Lend-Lease assistance.

When the cold war ended, the United States maintained five of its six policy goals in the region; containing the Soviet Union, which was dismantled in 1991, was, of course, no longer necessary. Hence, the United States maintained its support for authoritarian regimes as well. Thus it was that the United States headed the coalition liberating Kuwait from Iraq in 1991. And after 9/11, the United States added another policy goal that turned out to be a further boon to friendly autocrats: the United States declared a global war on terrorism. Autocrats such as Hosni Mubarak of Egypt, Ali Abdullah Saleh of

Yemen, and even Muammar al-Qaddafi of Libya managed to put themselves on the side of angels by agreeing to accept and interrogate under torture suspected terrorists (Mubarak), allow the United States to fight the war on terror on his country's soil (Saleh), and renounce weapons of mass destruction (Qaddafi). Although President George W. Bush announced his "freedom agenda" in 2003—a professed commitment to "drain the swamp where terrorism breeds" by promoting democratic change in the region—the United States stuck with Mubarak and Saleh well past their expiration date.

What was the state of the economy in the Arab world on the eve of the uprisings?

The Arab world includes states such as Qatar, which boasts an annual per capita income of $88,232 (for the 20–25 percent of the inhabitants who are citizens, not guest workers), and Yemen (whose population earns an annual per capita income that hovers around $1,000). Simply put, states in the Arab world run the gamut when it comes to wealth and poverty. Overall, oil exporters tend toward the wealthy side of the spectrum, while states whose primary source of income is not oil tend toward the poorer side. It is thus difficult to generalize about economic conditions. But it is also necessary to try, since the uprisings that have spread throughout the Arab world are about economic as well as political conditions. As a matter of fact, protests in Algeria, which is rich in oil and natural gas, began as an old-fashioned "bread riot"—protesters initially shouted "We want sugar!"—before shifting their focus to include political demands. Furthermore, in more than one state leaders have attempted to meet political demands by making economic concessions—a sure sign that they recognize the role played by economic issues in promoting dissatisfaction.

In his address on the uprisings in May 2011, President Barack Obama made the point that economic assistance to

Tunisia and Egypt would be necessary to ensure a smooth transition to democracy. He also stated that such assistance would be a topic at the upcoming meeting of eight industrialized countries (the G-8). In preparation for that meeting, the International Monetary Fund (IMF) put together a report on the state of the economies in the Middle East and North Africa.[2] The report paints a fairly bleak picture:

- Over the course of the previous three decades, the growth of the GDP in the region averaged 3 percent, while the GDP in the rest of the developing world grew at the rate of 4.5 percent. (GDP—or gross domestic product—is the total market value for finished goods and services produced within a state or territory.) Between 1980 and 2010, per capita GDP grew at a rate of 0.5 percent annually, well below that of the 3 percent growth that marked the rest of the developing world. To absorb the unemployed and new entrants to the job market, the annual GDP would have to grow at a rate of 7.5 percent.
- With the exception of oil and gas, exports have remained flat in recent decades. The remainder of the developing world has more than doubled its share of the international market since 1980. The situation looks even worse when exports from oil importers in the region are compared with exports from other regions. In 2009, exports reached only 28 percent of GDP, compared with 56 percent for the Asia Pacific region.
- Close to 60 percent of the region's exports go to Europe. This indicates two problems. First, the only comparative advantage the region has is its proximity to Europe. Second, the region is isolated from the global economy in general and from emerging markets such as China in particular. (Other sources assert that outside sub-Saharan Africa, the region is the least globalized in the world.)
- The number of jobs grew 2 percent annually between 2000 and 2007. Overall, unemployment in countries

for which data are available—Egypt, Jordan, Lebanon, Syria, and Tunisia—hovered between 10 and 12 percent (other sources put the unemployment rate as high as 15 percent).

- Overall, the report asserted that oil importing states would need foreign grants and loans to the tune of $160 billion during 2011–2013 to meet their obligations.

What benefits did Arab regimes originally promise their populations?

Most states in the Arab world received their independence at roughly the same time, during the post–World War II period. There was variation in government forms, of course. In many cases, although not all, this had to do with the identity of the colonial power that had been present before independence. The British, the preeminent power in Egypt, Jordan, Iraq, and the Gulf, generally left behind monarchies (Egypt was a kingdom until 1953, Iraq until 1958). The French, the preeminent power in North Africa, Syria, and Lebanon, generally left behind republics. In spite of the variation in government forms, however, the ruling bargains states struck with their populations were roughly the same. (The term *ruling bargain* is a metaphor used by political scientists to refer to the accommodation reached between states and the citizens they govern.) States played a major role in the economy. They did this to force-march economic development, expand employment opportunities, reward favored elements of the population, and gain control over strategic industries. States also provided a wide array of social benefits for their populations, including employment guarantees, health care, and education. In addition, states subsidized consumer goods.

There were a number of reasons states in the region—and, indeed, throughout the developing world—adopted these policies. The United States encouraged them to do so, believing that a combination of economic development and welfare would create stable, pro-Western states. So did international financial institutions, such as the World Bank and the IMF, and a legion of development experts who passed on cookie-cutter policies wherever they went. These policies fit the economic paradigm popular at the time, one that gave pride of place to full employment and rising standards of living as the two indicators of economic success. Governments, it was believed, could guide resources to ensure both goals were reached more effectively in environments where markets were not well developed.

A third factor leading to the adoption of these economic policies was the logic of decolonization. Before independence, imperial powers set economic policy, mainly for their own benefit. With independence, states asserted their economic rights to make up for lost time and attempted to win support through the redistribution of national wealth. Some states—Egypt, post-independence Algeria, Libya, Iraq, Syria at various times, and others—justified their policies using a populist discourse that extolled anticolonialism and the virtues of the revolutionary masses. In those states, the old regime that young military officers replaced represented collaboration with imperialists, feudalism, and corruption. Other states—Jordan and Saudi Arabia, for example—appealed to tradition or efficiency. Whether "revolutionary" or reactionary, however, Middle Eastern governments came to the same destination, although via different routes.

The case of Egypt was most dramatic, but not atypical. Using resources derived from widespread nationalizations (including the nationalization of the Suez Canal in 1956), a $42.5 million loan from the IMF, and $660 million in aid packages from the United States, Egypt adopted a program its leader, Gamal Abd al-Nasser, called "Arab socialism." Under Arab socialism, the state became the engine of the economy. By the mid-1960s, the Egyptian government owned and ran banks, insurance companies, textile mills, sugar-refining and food-processing facilities, air and sea transport, public utilities, urban mass transit, cinemas, theaters, department stores, agricultural credit institutions, fertilizer producers, and construction companies.

If measured by profit, state control over so much of the economy was highly inefficient. But the success or failure of Arab socialism cannot be measured in terms of efficiency alone. By administering so many productive and commercial establishments, the Egyptian state (and other states that went down a similar path) was able to allocate resources for its own purposes and gain control over industries it deemed vital for national development. Furthermore, the Egyptian government significantly reduced the ranks of the unemployed—even if the government had to hire many of the unemployed itself. For example, in 1961 the Egyptian government passed the Public Employment Guarantee Scheme, which, as the name says, guaranteed every university graduate a job in the public sector. The scheme was amended three years later to include all graduates of secondary technical schools. The result was as one might expect: the Egyptian bureaucracy, never a pretty sight, swelled from 350,000 in 1952 to 1.2 million in 1970. Although the government repealed the bill in 1990 after IMF prodding, the bureaucracy continued to grow. As of 2008, the government employed approximately 5 million Egyptians.

The Egyptian government used economic incentives to gain the compliance of the citizenry and reward those sectors of society it claimed to represent. Declaring an education to be a right for every citizen, for example, Nasser eliminated fees at Cairo University, after which enrollment skyrocketed (and standards declined, as they did when health care was nationalized). The state also attempted to keep household commodities affordable by furnishing subsidies for many of them, including basic foodstuffs, petroleum products, electricity, and water. As of 2009–10, subsidies, along with social benefits such as health care and education, still represented close to

42 percent of Egyptian government expenditures. Subsidies on household commodities alone accounted for about 23 percent.

Within this context, Arab policy makers came up with new definitions for democracy and democratic rights. Nasser, for example, differentiated between something he called "reactionary democracy" and his own "integral democracy." For Nasser, the reactionary democracy of the old regime was hopelessly flawed; although it promised political rights for all, the wealthy and powerful found ways to manipulate the system for their own ends. The result was rule by the few and economic exploitation of the many. Nasser's integral democracy, on the other hand, equated freedom with economic justice. And since the state was the expression of the "popular will" of the "progressive classes," it was up to the state to guarantee this economic justice. For Nasser, then, political pluralism was incompatible with the developmental and social justice goals of an activist Egyptian state.

In Egypt and throughout the Arab world, populations embraced the part of the ruling bargain that covered the state's responsibility for ensuring their welfare (this is not to say they necessarily embraced the second part of the bargain, which stipulated unquestioned submission to the dictates of the state). The 2004 *Arab Human Development Report* cites polls taken in Jordan, Lebanon, Palestine, Morocco, and Algeria on what sorts of freedom the populations expected their states to guarantee. Alongside and sometimes topping such political freedoms as the "right to form political opposition groups" and the "choice of central government leaders through free and fair elections," respondents listed "freedom from hunger," or "freedom from inadequate income," and the like. But these freedoms came at a price: according to World Bank data, average growth in Egypt, for example, was 7.52 percent between 1959 and 1964. This was the period in which the Egyptian government was first taking on the obligations of Arab socialism. During the 1964–1973 period, when Arab socialism was at its height, growth declined to 2.85 percent.

Why and how did Arab regimes renege on the promises they had made to their populations?

Toward the end of the 1970s, governments in the Arab world began attempting to renegotiate the ruling bargain. They had to. After the price of oil spiked first in 1973 and then again in 1979, it plummeted. All Arab states had benefited from high oil prices, producers and nonproducers alike. Oil producers subsidized the ruling bargains of their less-fortunate brethren. They did this through grants and loans on the one hand, and by providing job opportunities to the populations of labor-rich, but oil-poor, Arab states on the other. When oil prices began their rapid descent in the 1980s, governments had to retrench. Two factors made matters even worse. First, a number of Arab states—Algeria, Egypt, Jordan, Syria, Morocco, Yemen, and the Sudan being the most prominent—had borrowed heavily in flush times when interest rates were low and then continued to borrow to pay debt service, maintain what they could of their increasingly tattered ruling bargain, or both. The debt burdens were so massive that one economist referred to the region as part of a "Mediterranean debt crescent."[3] Second, times had changed, and so too had the prevailing economic paradigm. State-guided economic development was out, as was public ownership of manufacturing and commercial ventures. Neoliberalism was in.

Neoliberalism is the name given to a market-driven approach to economics in which the role of the state is kept to a minimum. Although often identified with Ronald Reagan in the United States and Margaret Thatcher in the United Kingdom, the roots of neoliberalism go back to the early 1970s, when the United States took a combative approach to demands made by developing nations for greater control of the raw materials they produced, as well as for a greater role in deciding international economic policy. When in 1973 oil producers gained control of the pricing and ownership of oil—acts that led to higher oil prices and stagnant economies and inflation in the developed world—the United States pushed back, decrying any and all political interference with the market. The debt crisis of the 1980s, which affected much of the developing world, presented the United States with a golden opportunity to push the new paradigm: states that not so long before had asserted their economic rights were now begging international banking institutions for debt relief.

Debt relief was forthcoming—but at a price. In return for debt relief and access to fresh capital from international lenders such as the IMF and the World Bank, states had to undertake immediate steps to stabilize their economies, then longer-term measures to ensure fiscal health. IMF and World Bank experts demanded states cut expenditures, liberalize trade, balance their budgets, remove price controls, deregulate business, privatize public enterprises by selling them off to the highest bidder, and end across-the-board subsidies on consumer goods. In place of across-the-board subsidies, international lending institutions recommended that states grant subsidies "targeted" only to the very poor. In other words, governments were to shred the ruling bargains they had struck with their populations.

Neoliberal policies got their tentative start in the Arab world in December 1976, when Egypt negotiated a $450 million credit line with the IMF, which also gave Egypt the wherewithal to postpone $12 billion in foreign debt. In return, Egypt cut $123 million in commodity supports and $64 million from direct subsidies. The result was what one might imagine: two days of bloody rioting in which eighty to one hundred protesters died and twelve hundred were arrested. Similar "IMF riots" broke out in Morocco (1983), Tunisia (1984), Lebanon (1987), Algeria (1988), and Jordan (1989, 1996) after the IMF attempted to impose conditions on loans and loan guarantees.

Initially, states backpedaled. The IMF also modified its demands. States began to apply neoliberal policies in earnest only in the late 1980s, after a "lost decade" of virtually no growth. In Egypt, serious "economic reform" did not really begin until 2004 with the appointment of the "cabinet of businessmen." Libya began its first wave of privatizations in 2003 and followed them up with cuts in subsidies a year later. And it was not only the IMF that was responsible for the spread of neoliberalism in the region: Saudi Arabia and Syria, for example, voluntarily adopted measures associated with neoliberalism. Saudi Arabia did so in order to join the World Trade Organization; Syria, as part of its fruitless quest to join the Euro-Mediterranean Free Trade Area. The fact that such entry requirements existed in the first place demonstrates the global predominance of the neoliberal economic paradigm.

In most states, the overall effect of neoliberal policies was to overlay a jury-rigged market economy on top of an inefficient command economy. And some policies had effects different from their intentions. Privatization, for example, did not lead to capitalism but rather to crony capitalism, as regime loyalists took advantage of their access to the powerful to gain ownership of sold-off state assets. Thus it was that in Egypt a friend of the son of the president came to control 60 percent of the steel industry, while in Syria the first cousin of the president gained control over the mobile communications giant Syriatel, which, in turn, controlled 55 percent of the market. Both became popular symbols of regime corruption during the uprisings.

Even though states in the region enjoyed high growth rates during the past decade, they also experienced greater income inequalities. This, in part, explains the participation of large numbers of middle-class, professional youths in uprisings throughout the region. While states have stripped members of this cohort of the "middle-class welfare" benefits their parents had enjoyed and condemned many to fend for themselves in the ranks of the un- and underemployed, they are denied both benefits targeted to the very poor and entry into the ranks of the very privileged. It also explains the upsurge in labor activism in various places in the Arab world and the prominent role played by labor in the uprisings in such places as Tunisia and Egypt. Or, as the last pre-upsurge finance minister of Egypt put it, "We do not have a constituency for reform at the street level."[4]

How did the demography of the Arab states make them vulnerable to uprisings?

Approximately 60 percent of the population of the Arab world is under the age of thirty, and the broader Middle East and North African region is second only to sub-Saharan Africa in the percentage of youth within that bracket. Demographers call what has taken place in the region a "youth bulge." To a certain extent, the current youth bulge might be attributed to the successes of states in the region. Historically, youth bulges occur as a stage in the process of moving from a population characterized by high rates of fertility and mortality to a population characterized by low rates of fertility and mortality. This transformation most frequently accompanies a rise in the standard of living. If such a transformation takes place at an even rate, there will be no youth bulge. But most often it does not. Mortality has been steadily declining in the Arab world for decades, if not longer, in large measure as the result of improvements in health care, education, public health, and sanitation. Fertility, on the other hand, did not begin to decline until the decades of the 1960s and 1970s. Population growth thus peaked in the 1980s as those born in the sixties and seventies entered their childbearing years. The result is the current youth bulge.

There is another statistic, however, that is more telling about the current state of the Arab world than the percentage of those under the age of thirty: the percentage of those between fifteen and twenty-nine, the period during which youths begin entering the job market and, more commonly in the case of women, marriage.[5] Youths between fifteen and twenty-nine make up 29 percent of the population in Tunisia, 30 percent in Egypt, 32 percent in Algeria, and 34 percent in Libya. Across the region, youth makes up approximately 25 percent of the unemployed (30 percent among women). But even this statistic has to be taken with a grain of salt. As might be expected, the youth unemployment rate is much higher in states whose exports of oil are either minimal or nonexistent. Youth unemployment in Egypt is 43 percent, for example, and in Tunisia it is 30 percent. Furthermore, the statistics on employment do not include those who have given up on finding work (the "discouraged unemployed") and those who work part-time but who wish to work more hours. In Egypt, for example, almost 60 percent of youths eighteen to twenty-nine are out of the labor force (in the case of women it is 83 percent). And when it comes to employment, education affords little advantage. As a matter of fact, in Egypt young people with college degrees rank highest among the unemployed of any sector of youth, and in Syria a vast majority of college graduates spend at least four years looking for employment before landing a job.

The lack of employment opportunities for young people in the Arab world has given rise to a phenomenon one political scientist calls "waithood," a period in which youths "wait for (good) jobs, wait for marriage and intimacy, and wait for full participation in their societies."[6] Men in particular delay marriage until they become solvent enough to pay the customary expenses associated with marriage and can support a family. As a result, life is put on hold, and the average age for marriage among men in the Arab world is the highest of any region of the world.

None of this is to say that demography is destiny, or that frustrations about job or life prospects necessarily translate themselves into rebellion. A 2010 survey of youth around the world found that Egyptian youths, for example, with all their demographic baggage, rank alongside their cohort in Jordan,

Vietnam, Indonesia, and Russia as the *least* likely to participate in oppositional politics among youth populations globally. As of 2004, Vietnam had a youth unemployment rate of under 5 percent, and Russia a rapidly graying population—very different profiles from that of Egypt. Furthermore, youth was hardly the only segment of Arab populations that mobilized during the uprising. Nevertheless, by 2010 there was a cohort of youth throughout the Arab world with grievances. Under the proper circumstances, this cohort was available to be mobilized for oppositional politics.

How did a food crisis make Arab states vulnerable to uprisings?

In January 2011, the Japanese investment bank Nomura compiled a list of the twenty-five countries that would be "crushed" in a food crisis.[7] The Arab world was well represented on the list: Tunisia came in at number eighteen, with Libya at sixteen, Sudan at eight, Egypt at six, Lebanon at five, Algeria at three, and Morocco at two. To understand the full effects of these numbers, consider that the portion of household spending that goes to pay for food in the countries on the list ranges from an average of 34 percent in Lebanon to an average of 63 percent in Morocco. The average percentage of household spending that goes to pay for food in the United States is about 7 percent—a figure that includes eating as entertainment, that is, dining outside the home.

There are two main reasons for the vulnerability of states in the Arab world to a food crisis. First, even though the region contains two areas that have historically been associated with agricultural plenty—"Mesopotamia," the territory between the Tigris and Euphrates rivers in Iraq, and the Nile valley in Egypt—agricultural conditions throughout much of the region are harsh, populations are rising, and water tables have diminished. Only two countries in the Arab world had reached the level of food self-sufficiency before 2006: Syria and Saudi Arabia. Then four consecutive years of drought made Syria a food importer rather than the food exporter it had been. Investment in agriculture had enabled Saudi Arabia to become a food exporter, and for a brief period in the early 1990s Saudi Arabia was the world's sixth largest exporter of grain. After the outbreak of the Gulf War in 1991, however, the Saudi government began diverting much of the money it had spent to subsidize agriculture to military procurement. In 2008, the government abandoned its grain cultivation program entirely, and two years later it was contemplating building a new Red Sea port geared toward handling imports of wheat and barley. Now all Arab countries are net food importers, and Egypt is the world's largest importer of wheat.

The other factor that has contributed to making the region vulnerable to a food crisis is neoliberal economic policies. As governments strove to avoid intervening in markets to fix prices or manipulate the exchange rates of their currencies, populations had to face fluctuations in international food prices on their own. In addition, the neoliberal policies that compelled governments to abandon across-the-board subsidies on food and replace them with subsidies targeted to the very poor have diminished food security for a wide swath of the population. They have also fueled popular anger when food prices go up. In 2007, for example, when prices began to climb, bread riots spread throughout the region, from Morocco and Algeria to Yemen, Jordan, Lebanon, and Syria. Given a choice between facing the ire of their populations and the ire of the IMF, governments chose the latter and increased subsidies and raised public sector wages. Egypt alone spent $3 billion for subsidies on food.

The increase in the price of food that the region began experiencing in 2007 turned out not to be a fluke. Between 2007 and the beginning of 2011, the price of food doubled on international markets, and as of March 2011 food prices had risen for eight consecutive months. Economists have given a number of reasons for the price increases. There is the increased acreage American, European, and Brazilian farmers have given over to the production of biofuels. In the United States alone, more than one-quarter of the 2010 grain harvest went to biofuel. (Rather than offering Tunisians and Egyptians IMF and World Bank assistance to further neoliberal policies in their countries, which President Obama did in his May 2011 speech to the Arab world, he might have offered them a very different type of remedy to their plight: an end to federal subsidies for the cultivation of corn for biofuel in the United States.)

Climate change, which has had its most dramatic effect on Russia in 2010 has also affected food prices. As a result of a heat wave, the Russian wheat harvest declined by 40 percent and Russia halted its grain exports. Russia had been Egypt's largest supplier of wheat.

In addition, some economists cite the changing patterns of consumption in emerging economies, particularly China. As the standard of living in China has risen, so has meat consumption. And although estimates of how many pounds of corn are required to produce one pound of beef vary widely, there is no denying that the production of more beef requires more corn.

Finally, economists cite the effects of dollar inflation on food prices. As in the case of all internationally traded commodities, the price of grain is denominated in dollars, and with the value of the dollar declining in the wake of the economic crisis of 2008 the price of grain has risen.

Whatever the causes, however, the fact remains that at the point at which the uprisings began and spread throughout the Arab world, the question of the vulnerability of the region to such a crisis was no longer theoretical.

Why did populations wanting change in the Arab world have to take to the streets?

The first Arab uprising, which broke out in Tunisia, took place a little over two years after the onset of the economic crisis of 2008. The intervening period had not been a good one for governments throughout the world, which found themselves caught between bankers and economists recommending austerity on the one hand, and populations fearing the end of the welfare state they had come to know on the other.

As the Arab uprisings spread, populations in other regions continued to show their dissatisfaction with those who governed them. They voted out ruling parties in the United Kingdom, Greece, Ireland, Portugal, Spain, and Iceland, among other countries. The ruling party in France lost heavily in local elections and was looking ahead to presidential elections the year after with trepidation. The prime minister of Italy resigned in the face of a parliamentary rebellion. In the United States, elections first threw out a Republican president, then a Democratic congress. And throughout Europe protesters and rioters took to the streets to prevent governments from cutting workers' pay and unemployment benefits, increasing the retirement age and cutting pensions, and eliminating bonuses to families having children. Yet through it all, not one government was overthrown, nor were political institutions uprooted. Blame fell on politicians and parties and the policies they pushed.

Now turn to the Arab world, where political institutions are weak and the lines separating the ruler, the ruling party, and ruling institutions (from the party congresses and "parliaments" to the military and intelligence services) are often blurred, if they exist at all. In most cases, popular representatives cannot be turned out of office because there are no popular representatives. In those few cases where there are, their power is limited. This is why populations throughout the region have taken to the streets as their first option. This also explains why the most common slogan during the uprisings was "Down with the *nizam*" (regime, system, order), and not "Down with the government."

Can we pinpoint the factors that caused the uprisings?

Unilateral attempts by regimes to renegotiate ruling bargains, demographic challenges, a food crisis, and brittleness made autocracies in the Arab world vulnerable, but they did not cause the uprisings. To attribute the uprisings to these factors or to any others overlooks a key variable—the human element—that determines whether an uprising will or will not occur. It also makes it seem that once a set of conditions is met, people will automatically respond in determined ways.

In the past, for example, it was common for historians and political scientists to attempt to connect uprisings with changes in economic conditions. In some cases (as in the case of the French Revolution of 1789) they have tracked the increase in the price of bread during the years leading up to the revolution and argued that the increase led to (in other words, caused) the revolution. Others, demonstrating that you can argue almost anything in the social sciences and get away with it, have asserted just the opposite. Uprisings, they claim, take place when a sudden reversal disrupts a period of improving economic conditions, thereby frustrating popular expectations. The problem with both theories is that they cannot explain the countless times in which conditions for an uprising are met but no uprising occurs. For example, Americans did not rebel after the onset of the Great Depression in 1929 when the economy suddenly collapsed; nor did they rebel in 1937 when the economy again took a sharp nosedive after years of recovery. Nor can the theories account for the timing of uprisings, except with the telltale sentence, "After X years of hunger (or repression, or corruption), the people had had enough." The problem is that unemployment and bread prices, for example, are objective categories that are quantifiable; the sense of deprivation or injustice—not to mention the compulsion to translate that sense into action—is not. To make matters even more unpredictable, people's sense of deprivation changes as circumstances unfold. Thus they might suddenly discover a cause worth fighting for once their neighbors have taken to the streets.

Then there is the role played by unexpected events that people might latch on to (or not) to reinterpret their circumstances in new ways. As we shall see, the unforeseen departure of the presidents of Tunisia and Egypt in the wake of popular protests changed the course of ongoing protest movements in Algeria and Yemen; troops firing on peaceful protesters in Bahrain revitalized that protest; and the arrest and torture of schoolchildren in a provincial city in Syria, followed by the murder of irate parents and their neighbors by security forces firing into a crowd, touched off a rebellion that no one had anticipated.

All this raises the issue of the predictability of uprisings in general and the predictability of the Arab uprisings in particular. Although many observers of the Arab world had turned their attention to the problem of why authoritarian regimes in the region seemed so durable, others predicted their demise. They pointed out the many problems, particularly economic, that Arab regimes faced and asserted that in a post–cold war world in which democracy and human rights had taken on a new lease on life, autocracies were just outmoded. The problem with these predictions was that they rarely offered up a timetable for events, and none foresaw the type of popular movement that swept through the region. Instead of envisaging masses of demonstrators shouting "Peaceful, peaceful" and demanding democratic rights, those who claimed to foresee the demise of regimes in the Arab world predicted that Islamists or disgruntled members of the regime would supply the shock troops for rebellion. Their predictions were thus like the proverbial stopped clock that tells the right time twice a day—except you do not know when that is.

No one really predicted the uprisings, but then no one could have done so. All rebellions—the Arab uprisings included—are by their nature unpredictable, as are the courses they take.

What was the spark that ignited the Arab uprisings?

On December 17, 2010, a street vendor, Muhammad Bouazizi, set himself on fire in front of the local government building in Sidi Bouzid, a rural town in Tunisia. Earlier in the day, a policewoman had confiscated his wares and publicly humiliated him. He tried to complain at the local municipality, but to no avail.

The self-immolation touched off protests that reached Tunisia's capital by December 27. At first, President Zine al-Abidine Ben Ali, who had ruled for a quarter-century, tried to pacify the protesters. He promised three hundred thousand new jobs and new parliamentary elections. This did little to mollify them. On January 14, military and political leaders had enough, and with the army refusing to fire on the protesters Ben Ali fled the country, leaving it in the hands of a caretaker government.

The Tunisian uprising was the first in a series of cascading events that swept through the Arab world. About a week and a half after the departure of Ben Ali, young people, many of whom belonged to an organization called the "April 6 Movement," began their occupation of Tahrir Square in Cairo. The security forces and goons-for-hire failed to dislodge the protesters, and the army announced it would not fire on them. Strikes and antigovernment protests spread throughout Egypt. On February 11, the army took matters into its own hands. It deposed President Hosni Mubarak, who had ruled for thirty years, and established a new government under the Supreme Council of the Armed Forces.

Events in Tunisia and Egypt demonstrated that Tunisian-style protest movements were viable elsewhere, and protests similar to those that had taken place in Tunisia and Egypt broke out in other places in the Arab world. After Egypt, ongoing protests in Algeria and Yemen took a new turn as young people consciously adopted the Tunisian and Egyptian style of protests. In Bahrain, Jordan, Saudi Arabia, and Morocco, kings who had presented themselves as "reformers" now faced demands for constitutional monarchies. Organizers called for a "Day of Rage" in Libya after the arrest of a prominent human rights lawyer who represented families of the twelve hundred "disappeared" political prisoners who had been murdered in cold blood in a single incident in 1996. The regime met the protests with violence, precipitating a civil war between regime loyalists and self-designated "revolutionaries." A month later, it was Syria's turn. Although protests in the capital of Damascus modeled on those that had brought down autocrats in Tunisia and Egypt failed to gain traction, protests erupted throughout the country in the wake of ruthless regime violence.

Where did the demands for democracy and human rights come from?

One can only speculate why calls for democracy and human rights became the core political demands of the protests (it should not be forgotten that economic demands also played a major role). It just might be that this question, like the question of the causes of the uprisings, is unanswerable. It also might be that it was the initial successes of relatively small pro-democracy, pro-human rights movements in Tunisia and Egypt, rather than anything intrinsic to the causes these movements supported, that bolstered popular support for democracy and human rights. After all, only a year before the outbreak of the Egyptian uprising just 11 percent of Egyptian youths had thought participation in government decision making was a top priority and a mere 3 percent thought freedom of expression should accompany the exercise of democracy in Egypt.[8] Certainly, the claim that the uprisings confirm the historical inevitability of democratic transformation worldwide reflects little more than wishful thinking—particularly since the triumph of democracy anywhere in the Arab world is, as of this writing, by no means assured. Perhaps the answer to the question lies in one or more of three possibilities.

First, there was the transformation of mainstream Islamic movements. As mentioned earlier, before the uprisings most analysts monitoring events in the Arab world looked to Islamic groups as the most likely source for change in the region. After the wave of Islamist violence of the 1980s—a wave that resulted in the brutal repression, and in some cases elimination, of Islamist groups throughout the region—many Islamists in mainstream organizations such as the Muslim Brotherhood of Egypt turned away from politics altogether or pledged their allegiance to working within the system. (Just how much political capital they lost by, in effect, endorsing regimes seen as corrupt and autocratic by so many of their citizens is anyone's guess.) During the ensuing decades, Islamist parties won elections or made significant inroads among voters throughout the region, from Algeria through Jordan. By running in elections, Islamist parties in effect put their seal of approval on the democratic process. Simultaneously, by doing so (or by rejecting politics altogether) they removed themselves from effective leadership of any movement that sought radical change through extralegal means.

The second possible explanation for why democracy and human rights have played such a prominent role in the demands of protesters throughout the region is the broadening and deepening of human rights as an international norm and the proliferation of international, regional, and local institutions to monitor the observance of those rights. Although the concept of human rights is as old as the eighteenth century, and the Universal Declaration of Human Rights was ratified by the United Nations in 1948, the human rights movement really came into its own in the 1970s. Since that time, international human rights law has evolved, international human rights institutions have emerged, and the mandates of those institutions have broadened. For example, the International Criminal Court, which indicted Libyan leader Muammar al-Qaddafi for crimes against humanity, was founded only in 2002. Furthermore, groups founded to monitor human rights violations have but recently proliferated. The oldest such group, Amnesty International, was founded in 1961, and Human Rights Watch dates back just to 1978.

Trends in the Arab world reflected broader trends, although they came a bit later and, while perhaps establishing regional precedents, did not affect government policy much, if at all. For example, the Arab League adopted the Arab Charter on Human Rights at the Tunis summit in 2004. The charter affirmed a number of rights, including freedom of assembly, freedom from torture, and equality before the law. The Tunis meeting came in the wake of a conference held two months before in Beirut, where representatives from fifty-two nongovernmental Arab human rights and pro-democracy organizations signed a document called the Second Declaration of Independence, which outlined demands for political change. (For those who would attribute a starring role for the United States in the Arab drama, the declaration explicitly rejected meddlesome interference from abroad.)

Finally, there is a provocative theory proposed by anthropologist Maya Mikdashi:[9] it is possible that the Arab uprisings both constituted a rejection of neoliberalism and were constituted by it. Neoliberal economic policies not only presume the ability of free markets to regulate themselves, they also presume that only a certain type of individual can participate in and take advantage of those markets. This individual is rational, autonomous, freedom-seeking, and endowed with legal rights that enable him or her to participate without fear of repercussions. In other words, neoliberalism both encourages democracy and human rights and is responsible for the construction of an environment in which individuals come to view themselves as rational, autonomous, etc. Although this theory endows neoliberalism with a greater influence than it may actually have, there just might be something to it.

How appropriate is the word wave *to describe the spread of protests throughout the Arab world?*

It has become very common to describe what has been occurring in the Arab world in terms of a "wave of protests," a "revolutionary wave," or even a "pro-democracy wave." The use of the wave metaphor is not a new one; historians have written about the "revolutionary wave" that engulfed Europe in 1848 and the one that engulfed the world in 1968 so often that it has become a cliché. Similarly, political scientist Samuel Huntington discussed three "waves of democratization" in a 1993 book: a nineteenth-century wave, a second wave that took place between 1945 and the 1960s and 1970s, and a third wave that began in the mid-1970s and continued through the 1990s.[10] Some observers cite events in the Arab world as evidence that this third wave has continued, while others view it as the beginning of a fourth wave.

It is important to remember that in all these contexts "wave" serves as a metaphor, and like any metaphor it has advantages and disadvantages. On the one hand, there is no denying that later Arab uprisings borrowed techniques of mobilization and even symbols from earlier ones. Town squares that became the sites of protest throughout the Arab world were renamed "Tahrir" square after the main site of protest in Cairo, and the habit of garnering enthusiasm and relaying marching orders by renaming days of the week "Day of Rage" or "Day of Steadfastness" also came from the Egyptian model. Then there is the highly touted use of social networking sites for the purpose of mobilization. On the other hand, the use of the wave metaphor obscures the fact that goals and styles of the uprisings have varied widely from country to country. In terms of the former, some protests have demanded reform, others the overthrow of the regime. In terms of the latter, there have been times when protests were predominantly peaceful and other times when they took a violent turn. More important, however, the wave metaphor lends an air of inevitability to what has been taking place in the Arab world. It was not inevitable. There are places in the Arab world, for example, that have not been affected. Most significantly, however, the air of inevitability connoted by the wave metaphor makes us lose sight of the tens of thousands of individual decisions made by people who joined the uprisings, and it takes away from the heroism of those who got up in the morning and decided, "Today I am going to face the full power of the state."

Where did the phrase "Arab Spring" come from, and how appropriate is it to describe events in the Arab world?

Springtime has always been associated with renewal, so perhaps it was inevitable that the Arab uprisings would earn the title "Arab Spring." This is not the first time commentators have invoked the term *spring* to describe political events. The raft of revolutions that advocated liberalism and nationalism in Europe in 1848 earned the title "Springtime of Nations," and the brief period in 1968 when Czechoslovakia flirted with liberal reform before Soviet tanks crushed Czech aspirations will forever be the "Prague Spring."

Nor is this the first time commentators have invoked the phrase "Arab Spring." Commentators used the phrase in 2005 to refer to events in the Arab world that occurred in the wake of (and, according to some, as a result of) the American invasion of Iraq in 2003 and President George W. Bush's "freedom agenda"—the idea that spreading democracy would "drain the swamp [terrorists] live in," as former Secretary of Defense Donald Rumsfeld put it.[11] Included among those events were the overthrow of Saddam Hussein's government and the first real elections in Iraq's recent history, and the so-called Cedar Revolution in Lebanon, when popular pressure brought down a pro-Syrian government and, in conjunction with international pressure, forced Syria to remove its troops from the country. In addition, Saudi Arabia held municipal elections, women in Kuwait marched for the right to vote, and Hosni Mubarak pledged that there would be free presidential elections in Egypt.

Unfortunately, the fulfillment of the promise of that Arab Spring proved elusive. In 2006, sectarian violence raged in Iraq, and Lebanese politics became hopelessly stalemated. Although the first municipal elections were held in Saudi

Arabia in 2005, the next round in 2009 was postponed. And, of course, Mubarak's pledge proved hollow. The only success story was women's suffrage in Kuwait.

Considering the track record of that Arab Spring, why would anyone want to burden the Arab uprisings with this title? And there are two other reasons to discourage its use. First, the term *spring* implies a positive outcome for the uprisings, which has yet to be achieved. Second, only one of the uprisings—in Syria—actually broke out in that season (if one includes all of March in spring). The others began in the dead of winter, a season hardly appropriate for an uplifting title.

2

THE BEGINNING

TUNISIA AND EGYPT

What characteristics do Tunisia and Egypt hold in common?

At first glance, it would seem that no two countries in the Arab world differ from each other more than Tunisia and Egypt. Egypt is the Arab world's most populous country, with an official population of 81 million and an estimated population of up to 100 million (because of conscription, not all families register the births of their sons). Tunisia, on the other hand, has a population of about 10.5 million. There is no comparison in terms of surface area either: Egypt is six times larger. On the other hand, Tunisians, on average, are wealthier (their per capita income is almost twice as high as Egyptians'), and the World Bank classifies more than 80 percent of the population as "middle class." In Egypt, by contrast, about 40 percent of the population lives on less than two dollars a day. Tunisia also is more urbanized (67 percent of the population as opposed to Egypt's 43 percent) and "more European." The slogan Tunisians shouted at their president during the uprising was "Dégage!" ("Get out!" in French). Egyptians, on the other hand, shouted "Irhal!" ("Get out!"—this time in Arabic).

In spite of their differences, however, Tunisia and Egypt share a number of key characteristics. These characteristics have a bearing on both the origin and the evolution of the uprisings in the two countries. For example, Tunisia and Egypt are relatively homogeneous. Approximately 98 percent of the population of Tunisia is Sunni Arab. About 90 percent of the population of Egypt is as well (the remainder is mainly Coptic Christian). Because of the relative homogeneity of the two states, political activists could not attempt to seize control by appealing to their followers' sectarian loyalties, nor could rulers of either state attempt to garner support by claiming that if he fell, the sect to which he and the core of his supporters belonged would be endangered (as rulers in Syria and Bahrain have done).

In addition, although neoliberal economic policies affected all states in the Arab world, Tunisia and Egypt held a special place in the hearts of those advocating economic reform. Egypt was the site of the first test of neoliberalism in the region, and the president of the World Bank once hailed Tunisia as the "best student . . . in the region" when it came to economic restructuring.[1] In both states, application of neoliberal policies exacerbated the divide between rich and poor, creating tensions that played out during the uprisings. Here's how *The Economist* described the Egyptian scene in 2008:

> Today, 44 percent of Egyptians still count as poor or extremely poor, with some 2.6m people so destitute that their entire income cannot cover basic food needs, let alone other expenses. Yet ranks of private jets clutter Cairo's airport. The flower arrangements at a recent posh wedding, where whisky flowed and the gowns fluttered in from Paris and Milan, were reputed to have cost $60,000 in a country where the average wage is less than $100 a month.[2]

Neoliberalism in general and privatization in particular have bred a new social class in Egypt, known as the "fat cats," or more colorfully "whales of the Nile"[3]—a small group of *über*-wealthy businessmen who live in gated communities on the edge of the desert, thus avoiding daily contact with the inhabitants of Cairo's slums.

Similarly, neoliberalism has exacerbated the traditional geographic divide in Tunisia that separates the relatively prosperous north and eastern coastline from the poorer inland region. The former area has benefited from an economy built on tourism; the latter, dependent in large measure on small-scale textile production and agriculture, has suffered as a result of the removal of protective trade barriers.

Tunisia and Egypt also share a history of state building that stretches back to the nineteenth century. This sets them apart from all other Arab states. Although Tunisia and Egypt belonged to the Ottoman Empire until 1881 and 1914, respectively, both enjoyed a great deal of autonomy. To protect that autonomy, local rulers embraced methods of governance and governing institutions modeled on those of European states, figuring that their domains could thus acquire the strengths of European states. So they "modernized" their militaries, constructed infrastructure, and adopted legal codes based on those of Europe. When the French made Tunisia a protectorate in 1881, they did nothing to reverse the processes of centralization and development, and when the British occupied Egypt (which nevertheless remained part of the Ottoman Empire) they imposed additional institutions and structures that fostered both as well (albeit for their own purposes). The process of centralization and development continued in Tunisia after it won its independence from France in 1956, as it did in Egypt after Gamal Abd al-Nasser and the "Free Officers" seized control in 1952 (although Egypt had received "conditional" independence in 1922, the British retained control of key institutions). This history of state building left a legacy in both states of strong national identities and administrative stability. These identities fostered the sense of solidarity that was so apparent in the uprisings—a sense that gave meaning to the ubiquitous slogan that began "the people want. . . ." And unlike in Libya and Syria, for example, no one predicted that the uprisings might lead to the fragmentation of either state. Strong institutions, such as the army, did not splinter, while others, such as those dealing with the economy and administration, remained in place to pick up the pieces even after rulers left the scene. On the other hand, the history of state building left a legacy of autocratic rule—a principal grievance of the protesters.

How entrenched were the autocracies ruling Tunisia and Egypt?

Strongmen ruling for long stretches of time have controlled Tunisia and Egypt for well over half a century. At the time of the uprising, Tunisians had known only two presidents since independence: Habib Bourguiba, who ruled for thirty years (1957–1987), and Zine al-Abidine Ben Ali, who ruled for twenty-four (1987–2011). Since the 1952 Free Officers' coup in Egypt, from which Mubarak's regime directly descended, Egyptians had known only three presidents: Gamal Abd al-Nasser (1952–1970), Anwar al-Sadat (1970–1981), and Hosni Mubarak (1981–2011).

Bourguiba was the leader of the Tunisian independence movement. A year after Tunisia won its independence from France, he deposed its monarch and proclaimed Tunisia a republic. He won election as the first president of Tunisia in 1959, and then three times after that until he decided to do away with the façade of elections entirely. Thus, in 1974, he had the National Assembly amend the constitution to make him president for life. Unfortunately, that life lasted longer than Bourguiba's mental faculties. In 1987, Prime Minister Ben Ali, who had risen through the ranks of the military before starting his political career, had doctors proclaim Bourguiba mentally incompetent, and in accordance with the constitution he became president. In some of his first acts, he raised hopes of Tunisians by abolishing the presidency-for-life and having the constitution amended to limit to three the number of terms a president could serve in office. Another amendment mandated the president to be under seventy-five when he takes office. In 2002, Ben Ali dashed those hopes by backing a phony referendum in which Tunisians repealed the amendments, making him eligible for more terms. Overall, he "won" reelection five times, garnering anywhere between 89 and 98 percent of the vote each time.

Like Bourguiba, Nasser abolished a monarchy to become Egypt's first president. The end of the monarchy brought Egypt's so-called liberal age to a close. During that era (1922–1952), Egypt had not only a king but a parliament in which seats were contested, political parties that competed with each other, and a press that was relatively free. It was hardly a golden age, unless one associates a golden age with plutocracy. Nevertheless, it was less despotic than what would succeed it and the population could enjoy a modicum of political freedom. Nasser did away with the trappings that characterized the liberal age, establishing one-man, one-party rule. After Nasser's death, Sadat, the hand-picked vice president, became president. It is possible to glean Sadat's concept of democracy from a confrontation he once had with a foreign reporter. When the reporter asked him a question he did not like, Sadat snapped, "In other times I would have shot you, but it is democracy I am suffering from." When an Islamist assassinated Sadat in 1981, his vice president, Mubarak, assumed the presidency. Like Nasser and Sadat, Mubarak came up through the military (in this case, the air force). He "won" the presidency three times. It was not all that difficult: the Egyptian constitution raised so many obstacles for candidates that he had few rivals. Before the uprising, Mubarak did promise that the 2011 elections would, however, be "freer" than those that had preceded it.

Were there political parties in Tunisia and Egypt?

In both Tunisia and Egypt, governing parties whose initial purpose had been to connect the state with the population became hollow shells whose sole purpose was to dispense patronage. Whereas the Neo-Destour party of Tunisia had once been the main arm of the independence movement and the roots of the National Democratic Party (NDP) of Egypt go back to the tellingly named "Arab Socialist Union" created by Nasser, by the time of the uprisings neither the heir to the Neo-Destour party nor the NDP served a representative purpose and neither was identified with an ideology. Each was more like a club whose board was composed of political and economic elites who divided political and economic spoils among themselves.

How did the regimes in Tunisia and Egypt attempt to control their populations?

In both Tunisia and Egypt, the state put in place an all-pervasive security apparatus to monitor, frighten, and repress the population. The term *security apparatus* covers a variety of formal and informal groups with overlapping and often ill-defined jurisdictions. For example, because Ben Ali was not satisfied with entrusting the entirety of his security needs to the minister of the interior and the military, he used his own "sovereignty fund" to set up a parallel security force over which he had direct control. Mubarak was even more ambitious when it came to his security forces: an estimated two million Egyptians participated at any given time in Egypt's security apparatus. They ran the gamut from ministry officials to agents in the field to hired thugs to common snitches. Some were attached to the interior ministry. Others, such as those in the Central Security Services, acted as Mubarak's private army. Then there were those in the Intelligence Services, a branch of the military. Each branch operated independently.

During the 1980s, government officials, members of the NDP, and private businessmen began to outsource their security needs to local hoodlums, known among Egyptians as *baltagiya*. The term was originally a Turkish word meaning "hatchet man." The baltagiya were drug runners, common criminals, gang members, former prisoners, or unemployed or underemployed slum dwellers whom the government, politicians, and businessmen hired to terrorize neighborhoods and political opponents, break up demonstrations, bust strikes, and in general contribute to creating a menacing atmosphere to cow the population.

How widespread was corruption in Tunisia and Egypt?

In both Tunisia and Egypt, tales of corruption took on almost mythic proportions. The inhabitants of both are used to dealing with policemen and civil servants with their hands out (because salaries are low, bribery is effectively written into the economic system). But during the uprisings, protesters vented their rage on corruption at the top. Take, for example, the system of crony capitalism that neoliberal reform engendered. In both Tunisia and Egypt, privatization of government-owned assets fed the corruption; those who had connections with, for example, the ruling party, or more important the president's family, were most successful in acquiring public enterprises, usually at bargain-basement rates. Thus the story of privatization in Tunisia contains a hefty subplot involving the family of Ben Ali's wife, Leila Trabelsi, while that of privatization in Egypt revolves around Gamal Mubarak, Hosni Mubarak's son.

There was, however, more to corruption than that bred by privatization, and there was a reason one of the most popular chants among protesters in Tunisia was "No, no to the Trabelsis who looted the budget" (it sounds better in Arabic). Thanks to WikiLeaks, which obtained and posted on the web cables sent by the American ambassador to Tunisia, details of the doings of the former hairdresser-turned-first-lady, whom the press called "the Marie Antoinette of Tunisia," or the "Imelda Marcos of Tunisia" (after another profligate spender), are widely known. So are the doings of her kin, who are called "the Family," with all its mafia connotations, in the cables. "Seemingly half of the Tunisian business community can claim a Ben Ali connection through marriage, and many of these relations are reported to have made the most of their lineage," one cable, titled "Corruption in Tunisia: What's Yours Is Mine," reported.[4] That cable and others describe boundless kleptomania and conspicuous consumption: the Trabelsi clan, for example, owned the only private radio station in the country, the largest airline, several hotel companies, extensive real estate holdings, car assembly plants, a for-profit school, etc., all of which they obtained through insider dealings, bribery, expropriation, and outright theft. Two members of the family stole the yacht of a prominent French businessman and had it repainted to avoid detection. Another bought 17 percent of the shares of a state bank scheduled for privatization, which enabled him to gain control since the government put only 35 percent of the bank's shares up for sale anyway. And the list goes on. Few were surprised, then, that when Leila Trabelsi fled the country she had $56 million in gold bullion stashed aboard her plane.

While less colorful, corruption among the ruling elite of Egypt was no less impressive. Although protesters chanted, "O Mubarak, tell us where you get $70 billion!" that figure was an exaggeration. Nevertheless, the American state department did estimate that over the course of his presidency Mubarak had managed to accumulate $2–3 billion—not a bad haul. But more serious than presidential theft was the nexus of NDP leadership, cabinet or parliamentary membership, and economic opportunity. Ahmad Ezz, who came to control 60 percent of the Egyptian steel industry, was a close friend of Gamal Mubarak, an "enforcer" for the NDP, and a member of parliament who used his connections to become "the emperor of steel." After the uprising, Ezz was indicted for allegedly blocking a 2008 law that would have forced him to divest from his monopoly. Then there is a former minister of agriculture, Amin Abaza, whose company was the largest exporter of Egyptian cotton, and a former minister of tourism, Zuhair Garrana, whose holding company owned luxury hotels and cruise ships. This list, too, can go on. Like Ezz, many of those on it have been indicted, had their passports revoked, or both.

How did the Tunisian uprising play out?

Two rumors have dogged the story of Muhammad Bouazizi, the twenty-six-year-old produce vendor whose humiliation and self-immolation provided the spark for the Tunisian uprising. The first is that the policewoman who confiscated his wares slapped Bouazizi in the market in front of others. She may have, but she was later acquitted of all charges arising from the incident, including that one. The second is that Bouazizi was a university graduate. He was not. Whatever their validity, however, the rumors might seem true to many Tunisians because they reaffirm two features of daily life they confronted: the daily abuse of power by those who could lord it over their compatriots, and the lack of economic opportunities, particularly for educated youths. The lack of economic opportunities was acutely felt in Bouazizi's hometown of Sidi Bouzid, which had a 30 percent unemployment rate.

The events that took place between Bouazizi's suicide on December 17, 2010, and the departure of Tunisian president Ben Ali close to a month later are straightforward. The day after the suicide, a crowd made up of fellow vendors, youths, labor activists, lawyers, and even some politicians began demonstrating in front of the local municipal building. Some in the crowd videotaped the demonstrations and posted the videos on Facebook, where al-Jazeera picked them up and broadcast them back into Tunisia. When the government cut Internet connections, demonstrators sent cell phone images directly to the satellite TV channel. About three weeks later, unemployed graduates and students in the nearby town of Thala clashed with police, who shot five of the protesters.

The first reaction of the government in Tunis to events was to offer both carrots and sticks. As the first carrot, Ben Ali promised the protesters fifty thousand new jobs, enough for only about a third of the estimated number of unemployed university graduates. Over the course of the uprising, he upped the ante by pledging parliamentary elections and an end to internet censorship, and by vowing that he would keep the constitutionally mandated age limit for president at seventy-five years, making him ineligible to run for another term. And as leaders of Egypt, Yemen, Bahrain and elsewhere would offer during subsequent uprisings, he proposed sitting down with the opposition and engaging in a "national dialogue" about the country's future. But, warning that protests were scaring off foreign investment and tourism, he ordered all schools and universities closed to prevent students from massing—in the process ensuring that a steady supply of students with time on their hands would feed the protests. He then dispatched security forces and the army to put down the uprising. In the first encounter with protesters, the army unit he dispatched refused to open fire.

A few days after the carnage at Thala, the uprising, which had previously been concerned primarily with economic demands, took a decidedly political turn. In the town of Kasserine in western Tunisia, where twenty-one died at the hands of government snipers, infuriated protesters turned their sights on those responsible, demanding the immediate departure of President Ben Ali. The stakes had risen dramatically and quickly. Fueled by new media (such as text messaging), old media (such as al-Jazeera), and word of mouth, the uprising spread throughout the country. When it reached Tunis on January 13, the chief of staff of the Tunisian armed forces told the army to stand down. Ben Ali fled to Saudi Arabia the next day (the role played by the army in his flight is still not clear). This was the first time in the modern history of the Arab world a popular uprising forced the ouster of a ruler.

Was the uprising in Egypt like that of Tunisia?

The Tunisian uprising left an immediate and powerful impression on many people in Egypt. More than a dozen Egyptians, for example, copied Muhammad Bouazizi's suicide-by-fire, a type of protest (repeated elsewhere) that had rarely before taken place in the Arab world. More productively, the Tunisian uprising demonstrated to the disaffected in Egypt and elsewhere that broad-based movements such as those that brought down the Tunisian government were viable. Those who planned the January 25, 2011, protests in Cairo and other Egyptian cities, for example—the opening salvo of the Egyptian uprising—have attributed their tactics, principal slogan ("The regime must go"), and ultimate goal (realization of that slogan) to their counterparts in Tunisia. And as in Tunisia, many of those who planned the January 25 protests and mobilized others for them were young and technology-savvy, so some of the similarities between events in the two countries were hardly coincidental. Thus, for example, their widespread use of social media. But even when events spun out of their control, there were important aspects of the Egyptian uprising that closely resembled those of the Tunisian one. Among them was the way in which the uprising fed off spontaneity, its leaderlessness, its rapid spread, and its nonreligious and largely nonviolent orientation. Like protesters in Tunisia, those in Egypt linked demands for political rights with economic justice and thus linked youths and labor activists in a common cause. And as in the case of the Tunisian uprising, the military in Egypt played a pivotal role, ensuring the speedy departure of the ruler.

There were several groups calling for protests on January 25. One included activists from the youth wings of political parties and the Muslim Brotherhood, along with labor organizers.

Another consisted of the administrators of the Facebook page "We are all Khaled Said." And there was Asmaa Mahfouz, a founder of a group called the April 6 Movement, who posted a video in which she taunted, "I, a girl, am going down to Tahrir Square and I will stand alone . . . and I'll hold up a banner, perhaps [other] people will show some honor." Organizers chose January 25 because it coincided with National Police Day—a newly proclaimed national holiday that celebrated its widely despised namesake. The irony was not lost on the organizers. It was for fear of being branded unpatriotic, however, that a number of organized political groupings chose not to participate.

In Cairo, the police stopped most of the demonstrators before they could converge on Tahrir Square, the site designated to be the epicenter of the protest. But because the police were so scattered, they were unable to stop one group that had rallied in a working-class neighborhood. By the time that group had reached the square, its ranks had swelled to thousands. Others joined the protesters while they marched to Tahrir Square or at the square, until they numbered an estimated ten thousand. Borrowing a slogan from Tunisia, the crowd chanted, "The people want the fall of the regime." Toward evening the police moved in and, after skirmishing with the protesters, fired tear gas and cleared most from the square.

Because most journalists in Egypt were based in Cairo, protests that occurred elsewhere were, by and large, consigned to the inner pages of newspapers or ignored entirely. This distorted the view of how the revolution unfolded. For example, on January 25 protesters held demonstrations in twelve of Egypt's twenty-seven provinces and in most of the principal cities of the country. Outside of Cairo, in cities such as Suez and Alexandria, protests were more violent. In the latter city, police reportedly killed three protesters. In the southern city of Asyut, riot police with batons attacked protesters. Even bedouin in the Sinai desert engaged in running firefights with police that lasted throughout the uprising. Also outside of Cairo, the profile of the protesters differed from that of the young, English-speaking professionals interviewed on American news. In Alexandria, the residents of some of the poorest neighborhoods joined the protests. In Mahalla al-Kubra, the site of the Egypt Spinning and Weaving Plant—the largest manufacturing plant in the Middle East—workers dominated the protests. They had been engaged in labor actions since 2006, drawing the attention of some of the youthful organizers who forged an alliance with strikers two years later. This is how the April 6 Movement had cut its teeth in organizing.

Having seen that the demand for the resignation of Mubarak resonated widely with Egyptians, organizers called for another round of protests to be held three days later. In Cairo, scattered crowds of protesters converged once again on Tahrir Square, battling police who fired tear gas and beat protesters with truncheons. Late in the day, as the tide of battle swung in favor of the protesters, Mubarak allegedly ordered his interior minister to authorize the police to use live ammunition. When the minister's deputy refused the order, Mubarak deployed the army. Furious that he had been pushed out of the loop, the interior minister ordered the police off the streets of Cairo, hours before the army arrived. This was all the time needed for protesters to take firm control of the square, which became the symbolic center of the Egyptian rebellion. Protesters stayed in the square for the remainder of the uprising. Others fanned out throughout the city, attacking the Ministry of Interior building and the state-run television station and setting the headquarters of the NDP and a number of police stations on fire. Similar scenes were repeated in Suez and other major cities. In Alexandria, protesters drove the police off the streets altogether and seized control of the city until the army restored government authority.

The events of January 28 might be seen as the beginning of the end for the Mubarak regime. Mubarak remained defiant: the government brought in goons on horseback and camelback in an unsuccessful attempt to dislodge the protesters from Tahrir Square, for example, and up until he announced his resignation Mubarak vowed to remain in office. Nevertheless, the army's announcement soon after taking control of the streets that it would not fire on the protesters ultimately tipped the balance in their favor. And just when it appeared that the protests might be running out of steam, they received a shot in the arm: Wael Ghonim, the founder of the Facebook page "We are all Khaled Said" (and, as American media constantly reminded their audience, an executive with Google) appeared on national television and gave an emotional interview about his kidnapping and imprisonment by the government ten days earlier. Ghonim's interview reanimated the protest movement. Two days later, tens of thousands of Egyptian workers went on strike demanding wage increases and Mubarak's resignation. On February 11, Omar Suleiman, Mubarak's recently appointed vice president (and designated successor), appeared on television and read this statement: "Taking into consideration the difficult circumstances the country is going through, President Mohammed Hosni Mubarak has decided to leave the post of president of the republic and has tasked the Supreme Council of the Armed Forces to manage the state's affairs." The army had had enough.

What did protest leaders in Egypt learn from earlier protests there?

During the period between the austerity riot of 1977, which came in response to the introduction of the first neoliberal policies into Egypt, and the strike wave that took place during the decade preceding the uprising, there were a number of protest movements in Egypt. They are important to the uprising of 2011 for several reasons: they made political, not just economic demands; they gave organizers tactical experience; and they generated organizations that participated in the uprising. Some social scientists have even asserted that they broke down the "barrier of fear" among Egyptians; that is, they enabled Egyptians increasingly to steel their nerve against the government. Such assertions are, of course, impossible to prove.

Three clusters of protests that broke out during the 1977–2011 period deserve mention. The first erupted in response to two events that took place outside Egypt. In 2000, Egyptians took to the streets in support of the second Palestinian uprising (*intifada*) against the Israeli occupation of the West Bank and Gaza Strip. They returned to the streets in 2003 in opposition to the American invasion and occupation of Iraq. During the latter demonstration, protesters symbolically reclaimed public spaces from the government, occupying Tahrir Square and chanting "The street is ours!" The Egyptian government, fearing the spread of the demonstrations should it move against the demonstrators, tolerated them.

The second cluster of protests broke out in 2004, shortly before the government held a referendum to confirm a fifth term for Mubarak. Among the groups founded at this time was one called Kefaya ("Enough!"), an amalgam of political currents ranging from nationalist to communist to Islamist that united around demands for electoral reform. It was the first group ever to call for Mubarak's resignation. Not only would Kefaya make demands echoed by activists in 2011, it pioneered tactics exploited during the uprising as well. For example, Kefaya defined itself as a loose movement rather than a tight party to ensure inclusiveness, used social media to organize demonstrations, mobilized in working class neighborhoods to broaden the movement's base, and asserted popular control over public spaces by organizing "flash mobs" to take them over for demonstrations. That Kefaya's demands and tactics matched those used during the uprising is not surprising: although Kefaya had faded years before the uprising, one of the founders of the April 6 Movement, which had a principal role in organizing the January 2011 protests, came from Kefaya's youth movement.

The third cluster of protests began among judges who refused to certify the results of the 2005 parliamentary elections, as the constitution mandates, citing massive electoral fraud. Their sit-in attracted international attention, and at the judges' disciplinary hearing protesters, including Kefaya members, chanted, "Judges, judges, save us from the tyrants!"

Why was one of the groups that organized the January 25 protests called "We are all Khaled Said"?

Tunisia had its Muhammad Bouazizi, an individual whose fate resonated widely there. Egypt had Khaled Said.

Said (pronounced Sa-*eed*) was a twenty-eight-year-old owner of a small import-export business in Alexandria. In June 2010, two plainclothes policemen dragged him from a cybercafé and beat him to death in the lobby of a nearby building. It is widely believed that they targeted him because he had posted on the web a video of the two policemen splitting up cash and drugs they had confiscated in a drug deal. The detectives claimed Said choked to death on drugs he had swallowed to avoid arrest for possession. A photograph of his mangled, bloodied face told a different story. Where that photograph came from is disputed. According to some accounts, his beating took place in front of witnesses, one of whom used his cell phone camera to photograph Said's face; other accounts assert that the family bribed a morgue technician to shoot the photograph. When prosecutors refused to take the case, Said's uncle began pushing the issue in press conferences, human rights advocates—including Muhammad El-Baradei, the former head of the International Atomic Energy Agency, who became a leading opponent of the regime—organized protests in Alexandria and Cairo; and Wael Ghonim co-created a Facebook page dedicated to Said, "We are all Khaled Said." Within a few weeks, 130,000 people joined the page, and by the time of the uprising it had 473,000 users. Although the powers attributed to the site are, no doubt, exaggerated, it did create a space in which like-minded individuals might come together as a community. The site also spread the word about the January 25 "Police Day" protests to a self-selecting group concerned about police brutality and human rights. In the meantime, the prosecutor reversed himself and brought the policemen to trial.

What was the role of social media in the Tunisian and Egyptian uprisings?

It was not long after the outbreak of the Tunisian uprising that Western media began to call the event a "Twitter Revolution" or a "Facebook Revolution," after two types of social media that the protesters used (protesters used other forms of "new media," such as cell phones and the blogosphere as well, but those did not seem to have the cachet of Twitter and Facebook). The terms were readily accessible to journalists; since 2004, it had become commonplace to name uprisings such as those in Moldova, Ukraine, and Iran after social media because participants had used them for one purpose or another. And after the outbreak of the Egyptian uprising (a second Facebook Revolution in a month!), journalists decided to abandon another term they had applied to the Tunisian uprising: the first "WikiLeaks Revolution," a title they had adopted that overemphasized the role played by the leaked American cables about corruption in provoking the protests.

The debate about the importance of social media in the Tunisian and Egyptian uprisings has involved two opposing camps, one made up of cyberphiles and the other of cyberskeptics. The cyberphile arguments underscore the essential role technology played in creating a community of protest in cyberspace (since real space was not available in Tunisia or Egypt for anti-regime activity); the rapid spread of social media in the region, which overwhelmed the ability of governments to respond effectively (between 2008 and 2010, Facebook memberships increased in the broader Middle East 360 percent to 3.5 million); and the calls made by Egyptian Facebook pages for the January 25 protests that initiated the uprising. As a matter of fact, the group behind one of those pages, the April 6 Movement, got its name from its call for a general strike on that day in 2008 in support of workers at Mahalla al-Kubra. According to cyberphiles, the call was the first demonstration of the revolutionary potential of social media in mobilizing protest in Egypt.

As cyberskeptics like to point out, however, the general strike of 2008 was a failure, as have been other uprisings in which social media purportedly played a central role (Moldova and Iran, 2009). So much for the near-magical potential of social media. Furthermore, attributing the Tunisian and Egyptian uprisings to social media underplays the role of groups that participated in them but were not as young or tech-savvy, and therefore not as photogenic, as, for example, the articulate young people in Tahrir Square. In addition, cyberskeptics argue that only 20 percent of Egyptians have internet access (to which cyberphiles might answer that fewer than a thousand Parisians stormed the Bastille in 1789), and that the government had already shut down internet connections before the pivotal events of January 28 (to which cyberphiles might answer that by then the uprising had already reached critical mass). The most convincing argument made by cyberskeptics, however, is that attributing the uprisings to social media transforms the true heroes of the uprisings—the participants—from protagonists into patsies who act not because they choose to but because they are somehow technologically compelled to. This was demonstrably false. According to the *Egypt Human Development Report* of 2010, there was no necessary link between internet usage and politics in Egypt before the uprising: 60 percent of youths on the internet spent their time chatting, 20 percent looked at pornography, 12 percent conducted business or research, and only 8 percent visited political sites.

The answer to the question about the importance of social media to the uprisings in Tunisia and Egypt probably lies between the positions staked out by the cyberphiles and cyberskeptics. Social media certainly played a role in the uprisings, but they did not *cause* the uprisings. Like the printing press and telegraph before them, social media performed two functions in the uprisings: they facilitated communication among the participants and would-be participants who elected to take part in the protests, and they broadened the range of tactical options (such as organizing demonstrations in "real time," for example) open to those participants.

Who led the Egyptian uprising in Cairo?

It is important to differentiate among three categories of political groups that played key roles in the uprising in Cairo. First, there were those who organized and participated in the initial protests of January 25. Second, there was the ad hoc assemblage of groups and individuals that came together in Tahrir Square on and after January 28. Although thrown together by circumstances, and of different backgrounds and political pedigrees, they managed to work out a division of labor among themselves: some took responsibility for defending the square or stood watch during prayers; others took charge of food distribution, manned first aid stations, or handled contacts with the media. The occupiers delegated planning and day-to-day decision making to a steering committee chosen on the spot. Their success is evident from the fact that they were able to remain in the square longer than Mubarak was able to remain in office. Finally, there was a category comprising organizations (such as the Muslim Brotherhood), established opposition parties (such as the previously moribund Kefaya), and established politicians (such as Muhammad El-Baradei) that joined the uprising soon after it broke out.

Over time, two important developments took place that allowed the disparate opposition groupings to maintain their cohesion. The first was that the April 6 Movement, Muhammad El-Baradei, and the Muslim Brotherhood emerged informally as the leadership of the opposition. Each was able to provide the uprising with something the others lacked.[5] The April 6 Movement made the demands for democracy and human rights credible and had initiated the protest movement in Cairo. On the other hand it did not have the standing among Egyptian and foreign movers and shakers El-Baradei was able to bring to the table, nor did it have the political muscle of the brotherhood. El-Baradei, on the other hand, had only recently arrived in Cairo from his IAEA stint abroad and had to be reintroduced to the Egyptian people. By backing him for transitional president, the April 6 Movement and the Muslim Brotherhood gave him "street cred." And when it came to advocacy for human rights, democracy, and even opposition to Mubarak, the Muslim Brotherhood's reputation could use burnishing by association with the April 6 Movement and El-Baradei.

The second development that enabled the opposition to maintain its cohesion was that it coalesced around a program acceptable to a broad swath of Egyptians: Mubarak had to go, a transitional government had to replace the NDP-dominated cabinet and parliament, emergency rule had to end, new elections had to be held, the constitution had to be amended to ensure term limits for the president and to open up the political process. They also agreed that their protests should remain peaceful.

Why did the Tahrir Square protesters and others adopt the tactic of nonviolent resistance?

Some of the most evocative images to come from the Egyptian uprising were of crowds of unarmed protesters standing toe-to-toe with army personnel or security forces chanting "Salmiyya, salmiyya!" ("Peaceful, peaceful"). Protesters reenacted this scene countless times as the uprisings spread throughout out the Arab world—but, alas, all too often without the same peaceful outcome. The tactic of peaceful resistance was a logical one: protesters could not come close to matching the government in firepower, unarmed protesters were less provocative than armed protesters, and violence proved to be ineffective when Islamist groups used it against the state in the 1980s. Most important, there was the success of groups committed to nonviolence in Tunisia, some of which had been collaborating with their Egyptian counterparts for several years.

But the choice of nonviolence had another source as well. The 2008 strike in Mahalla al-Kubra from which the April 6 Movement emerged had ended in violence, and police intervention crushed the general strike organizers had called. In the wake of the failed strikes, leaders of what would become the April 6 Movement sought out tactical pointers from others involved in struggles against authoritarian regimes. One of them, Muhammad Adel, traveled to Belgrade, Yugoslavia. There he enrolled in a one-week training program directed by the Center for Applied Non-Violent Action and Strategies (CANVAS), an organization founded by the nonviolent youth movement Otpor (Serbian for "Resistance"), which had spearheaded the uprising that brought down Serbian strongman Slobodan Milosevic. Adel was not alone; other pro-democracy advocates from Ukraine, Georgia, Zimbabwe, and Burma, for example, also received training in nonviolent resistance through CANVAS.

In the wake of the success of the Tunisian uprising, the April 6 Movement and allied organizations prepared for an uprising of their own, this time to be played by Otpor's rulebook. The tactics they employed were pure Otpor. For example, instead of attempting to organize a single march to Tahrir Square on January 25 that might easily be broken up by security forces (a "tactic of concentration"), they organized twenty-one separate marches from different locations. One march was kept secret from all but the small group of march organizers, who drifted into position in groups no larger than ten (a "tactic of dispersal"). The April 6 Movement even adopted the symbol of Otpor—a clenched fist—for its logo.

What was the role of labor in the two uprisings?

In both Tunisia and Egypt, labor activism has a venerable history, has long overlapped with political activism, and increased during the years building up to the uprisings. It should be no surprise, then, that labor activists in both places would put their skills in service to the uprisings.

In Tunisia, organized labor was at the forefront of the independence struggle, and after independence the trade union federation (the Union Générale Tunisienne du Travail, or UGTT) was one of two pillars upon which the new state rested (the other being Bourguiba's Neo-Destour Party). As a matter of fact, soon after independence there was a brief period in which it was impossible to determine whether the UGTT would become an affiliate of the party or the other way round. Since then, the UGTT had a checkered relationship with the regime, sometimes serving as a lapdog, sometimes standing in opposition to the regime's policies, particularly when they affected the federation's members. In 1977, for example, the UGTT called the first general strike in Tunisia's post-independence history, and in the mid-1980s relations between the federation and the regime got so bad that the regime clamped down hard on its rival. In addition, not all the trade unions represented in the federation march to the same drummer, nor have workers necessarily been compliant with their leadership, particularly when that leadership has aligned itself with the regime at their expense.

Labor activism in Egypt dates back to the turn of the twentieth century. Most recently, there has been an upsurge in labor activism, particularly as the Mubarak regime pushed ahead with a neoliberal agenda. Workers have found privatization and attempts to hold down wages and cut back benefits in the midst of inflation particularly offensive. Most link privatization with reductions in a firm's workforce and cutbacks in benefits guaranteed by public firms. Between the seating of the "cabinet of businessmen" in 2004 and the outbreak of the uprising, there were more than three thousand labor actions involving more than two million workers and their families. Labor activism spiked in the years 2006–2008, when it seemed that the entire textile industry and the communities that housed it had walked off the job and when the government was forced to recognize the first independent trade union since 1957. It would not be too far off the mark to say that labor activism became the primary form of resistance to the regime over the course of the decade that preceded the uprisings.

Labor thus came to play a key—and some would say pivotal—role in the Tunisian and Egyptian uprisings. In Tunisia, union activists exploited their talent for organizing early on to broaden the base of the protests, particularly among unemployed and underemployed youths. Professional associations (syndicates), such as those that represented lawyers and doctors, also joined the protests and were among the first to link economic grievances with political demands. Under mounting pressure from its rank and file, and with wildcat strikes breaking out throughout the country, the UGTT broke with the regime and threw its weight behind the uprising.

In Egypt, where protest leaders and the labor movement had an intertwined history, tens of thousands of workers from both the public and private sectors, including those from the petroleum, railroad, banking, retail, manufacturing, public transportation, health care, and heavy industry sectors, struck on February 10, 2011, and joined protesters on the streets of most major cities. In the volatile textile industry, eighteen thousand workers left their jobs, and walkouts shut down the Cairo airport and stock exchange. All this took place on the day before the army told Mubarak he had to go. It might have been coincidence, or it might have been that the strike wave had demonstrated to the military that Mubarak's position was untenable. There is no doubt, however, that the military was watching the strikes with trepidation: a few days after Mubarak's departure, the military sent out a text message to millions of Egyptian cell phone users reading, "The Supreme Council of the Armed Forces urges honest citizens to take part in efforts to reach a safe haven."—a not-very-subtle demand for them to get back to work.

What was the role of Islamic groups in the two uprisings?

The uprisings in the Arab world have sparked fears that they might lead to Islamist takeovers of various governments, much as happened in Iran in 1979. Some commentators have speculated that Islamists might gain control over the uprisings, while others assert that whatever their pro-democracy veneer, the uprisings themselves are little more than Islamist plots. In part, both groups of commentators are basing their conclusions on events that took place three decades ago, when violent Islamist movements proliferated throughout the Arab world. Since that time, most such movements seeking the overthrow of autocratic regimes have succumbed to state repression (al-Qaeda, a transnational organization with a very different structure and agenda, does not fit this pattern). Nevertheless, in most cases the state's overzealousness and inflexibility made its victory Pyrrhic.

As elsewhere, Tunisia and Egypt experienced a wave of Islamist violence in the 1980s that their rulers used as an excuse to justify repression and torture. In Tunisia, the government initially encouraged the Islamist movement, hoping it would serve as a counterweight to the UGTT. But when the Islamist party, Ennahda, demonstrated its popularity in the 1989 elections, the government clamped down hard, jailing members and driving its leader into exile. The party, which had vowed to work within the system, struck back with violence, calling for the overthrow of the government. Although the party was essentially destroyed in Tunisia, the government maintained its repressive apparatus even while much of the population became skeptical of its motives. Indeed, in the two decades preceding the uprising, the Tunisian government expanded and intensified repression to such an extent that Human Rights Watch declared Tunisia to be one of the most repressive states in the world—a world that, it should be remembered, includes Myanmar and Syria. It is partly for this reason that human rights became an issue of significance for Tunisians.

In Egypt, it was groups splintering off from the Egyptian Muslim Brotherhood or unaffiliated with the brotherhood that perpetrated the violence. The bloodletting climaxed with the 1997 massacre of sixty-three at the popular tourist destination of Luxor (the perpetrators wanted to bring down the Egyptian economy by targeting the lucrative tourism industry). As in Tunisia, the government responded to Islamist violence with heavy-handed repression. In the wake of the assassination of President Anwar al-Sadat, for example, the Egyptian government imposed an emergency law that entitled the state to restrict freedom of assembly, arrest and detain suspects without warrant, monitor and censor publications, establish exceptional courts to try those accused of violating presidential decrees, etc. Ending the state of emergency, which the government had once again extended for another two years in 2010, was one of the central demands of the protesters.

Although Ennahda received more than 40 percent of the vote in the election for the assembly charged with drafting Tunisia's post-uprising constitution, it did not guide or even participate in the uprising there. Such was the effectiveness of Ben Ali's repression. (The speed with which Ennahda regrouped after Ben Ali left, however, demonstrates it had not lost its appeal.) This was not the case in Egypt. In spite of the fact that the Egyptian Muslim Brotherhood officially refused to sanction the January 25 protest, members of the group's youth wing participated in its organization and played an important role in the uprising thereafter. After its late start, the Muslim Brotherhood did endorse the second round of protests on January 28 and a few days later backed Muhammad El-Baradei for transitional president.

None of this really explains anything about the role of Islamism in the Egyptian uprising, nor anything about its possible role in the future. The reason is that Islamic movements are not all the same, nor do they remain the same through time. Not only do their tactics and strategies change with time and circumstance, so do their ideologies.

The Egyptian Muslim Brotherhood was founded in 1928. Its last confirmed use of violence was in 1948, when its "secret apparatus" assassinated the Egyptian prime minister who had ordered the organization dissolved (Nasser accused the brotherhood of attempting to assassinate him in 1954, but this might have been a ploy to give him license to crush his rivals). Since that time, some within the brotherhood have periodically become radicalized (mainly in prison) and left the brotherhood to form their own organizations, while others acted as if they believed discretion to be the better part of valor. After years of repression, the "supreme guide" of the brotherhood renounced violence altogether in 1972, and his successor renewed the pledge in 1987 in return for permission to form a party so that the brotherhood might legally participate in the political process, such as it was. That permission was not forthcoming, but the organization did support candidates for parliament. In 2005, brotherhood-affiliated candidates won 20 percent of parliamentary seats. The government's response was massive electoral fraud in the parliamentary elections of 2010, which fed opposition to the regime.

Political scientist Carrie Rosefsky Wickham identifies three currents within the contemporary Egyptian Muslim Brotherhood.[6] The first consists of those who have foresworn political activity altogether in favor of preaching and pious activities. Their attitude seems to be that there is no point to imposing Islamic law over a society that is unprepared for and undeserving of it. The second faction, probably the largest, combines conservative religious views with political participation. They want to reassert Islamic law and what they consider to be Islamic values in the public sphere. Finally, there are those who have chosen to participate in politics but whose Islam is more liberal. It was members of this wing of the brotherhood who have called for reform of the brotherhood's authoritarian structure, have worked side-by-side with secular colleagues since their Kefaya days, are adept at using social media, and were at the forefront of the uprising.

This is not to say that the third current within the brotherhood will dominate in the future. It is important to remember that the brotherhood, like any other organization, not only shapes events but is shaped by them, and that brotherhood members are as motivated by political expediency as are members of any other organization. Thus, although the brotherhood declared in February 2011 that it would not field a candidate for president and would run candidates for only one-third of the seats in parliament in Egypt's first post-uprising elections, three months later two presidential candidates linked to the brotherhood threw their hats into the ring and the brotherhood revised the number of seats it would contest to one-half. In the meantime, members of the third current within the brotherhood abandoned the political party set up by members of the second current to found one of their own.

Why did the armies in Tunisia and Egypt refuse to put down the uprisings?

After the Tunisian protests reached Tunis, the chief of staff of the armed forces ordered the army not to fire on protesters, forcing Ben Ali to flee. The Egyptian military went further: having decided that the army would not fire on the protesters, the Supreme Council of the Armed Forces staged a coup d'état. It deposed Mubarak and took over the government while protesters chanted, "The army and the people are one!" Why did the militaries act as they did?

In Tunisia, the military has historically been relatively small compared to militaries in the rest of the Arab world—about 36,000 officers and men at the time of the uprising. This was no accident: Tunisia did not win its independence by force of arms, as did Algeria, nor did the regime come to power as a result of a military coup, as the regime in Egypt had. Habib Bourguiba, a politician (not a soldier), negotiated independence from France on behalf of Tunisians. The Tunisian army was thus the product of independence, not the progenitor of independence. Bourguiba, not wishing to risk a coup, deliberately kept the army small and out of politics. Since Tunisia faced no real external threats, Bourguiba could follow this policy without risking the country's security. Ben Ali maintained the policy of his predecessor in spite of the fact that he came from the army. Instead of depending on the army to ensure domestic peace, Ben Ali depended instead on security forces he controlled directly and indirectly. The fact that the military and the regime were separate entities, that conscripts reluctant to fire on their relatives and neighbors filled its ranks, and that there was in fact no love lost between the marginalized military and the regime made the chief of staff's decision that much easier.

The Egyptian military is the polar opposite of its Tunisian counterpart. It is huge: the army alone includes nine hundred thousand men (including reservists). Unlike the Tunisian military, it is battle-tested and even participated in the largest tank battle since World War II (the "Battle of the Chinese Farm" during the 1973 war with Israel). Furthermore, unlike the Tunisian military, it has been pampered financially, both by the Egyptian government and by the United States, which has given it $1.3 billion annually since 1979. Finally, unlike the Tunisian military, the Egyptian military has historically been involved in politics: all three presidents of Egypt came from its ranks.

Nevertheless, it would be a mistake to overestimate the military's political involvement. Although all three presidents of Egypt were military men, the process of demilitarizing the government began as early as the Nasser years. This process accelerated under Sadat, who felt threatened by the military's opposition to his policies, particularly the peace with Israel, which put in question the military's very reason for being. In place of preparing for another round against Israel, Sadat gave the military a different reason for being: it became a major player in the Egyptian economy.

No one knows for sure the size of the military's economic involvement (it is a state secret). Economists estimate that the military controls anywhere from 5 to 40 percent of the economy, and according to the IMF the military oversees about half of all Egyptian manufacturing. The reason is that the military can beat out all competition: (conscript) labor is cheap, the military can guarantee a steady supply of raw materials (some of which it produces itself, some of which it has priority claim to), it has access to the highest levels of government, and it is after all heavily subsidized. Thus over time the military has become involved in everything from construction and manufacture of consumer durables (like washing machines and refrigerators) to defense production and dairy and poultry farming. In addition, since many military bases are on Egypt's coasts and along the Nile, the military has had access to prime real estate ripe for development. And develop it it has.

The military's involvement in the economy, of course, violates the fundamental principles of neoliberalism, and some observers have noted the tension between the interests of military men and the crony capitalists around Gamal Mubarak who benefited from economic reform. As a matter of fact, this may have been one of the reasons the military was not particularly distressed to see the Mubaraks go, and why it immediately began rounding up the "whales" once they did. But there were other reasons as well for the military to push Mubarak out: it had a good thing going, and rather than see Mubarak take it all down, military leaders were more than willing to sacrifice the man at the top. And then there was the still-unknown, behind-the-scenes role played by the military's cash cow—the United States—in the waning days of the Mubarak presidency.

What changes did the uprising in Tunisia bring about?

After Ben Ali fled Tunisia, Mohamed Ghannouchi, his prime minister and political crony, announced he was taking the job of transitional president, in violation of the Tunisian constitution. Ghannouchi's reign lasted only a few hours, and he returned to his old position when the speaker of the parliament became transitional president, as the constitution mandated. Nevertheless, the real power still lay with Ghannouchi, who formed a national unity government made up of representatives of opposition parties, activists, and six members of the old ruling party. Protesters, fearing that their movement had been hijacked, went back out on the streets.

The "second Tunisian revolution"[7] lasted through March 2011, and by the six-month anniversary of the flight of Ben Ali, Ghannouchi was gone for good and the government had given in to a number of the protesters' demands. The government dissolved the former ruling party, dismissed scores of officials close to the old regime, lifted censorship, seized the assets of more than one hundred members of the Ben Ali–Trabelsi clan and their associates, established commissions to propose political reforms and investigate corruption and abuses under the old regime, and appointed one council to draft a new electoral law and scheduled elections for an assembly that would rewrite the constitution. And shortly after the six-month anniversary of Ben Ali's flight, the government sentenced the former president and his wife in absentia to prison terms of thirty-five years for theft.

That was the upside. On the downside, the economy remained in shambles, more than ten thousand Tunisians had fled aboard rickety boats to the Italian island of Lampedusa to escape unemployment and poverty, rumors of plots and counterrevolution circulated widely, protests continued, and protesters could still be seen at demonstrations carrying signs reading, "Rien n'a changé!" ("Nothing has changed!").

What changes did the uprising in Egypt bring about?

In Egypt, the military remained in control after Mubarak stepped down. As the civilian government did in Tunisia, Egypt's military acted swiftly to meet some of the high-profile demands of the protest movement. As in Tunisia, many of the actions taken by Egypt's rulers were relatively painless and even superficial. Thus they arrested former officials and high-ranking members of the NDP (including Ahmad Ezz) on corruption charges, forced out Mubarak's prime minister, dissolved the NDP and one of the leading security forces, appointed a commission to oversee amending the constitution, and, once the commission had done its work, organized a referendum on the amendments as the first step toward parliamentary elections. They also indicted Hosni Mubarak and his sons on charges of graft and the premeditated murder of protesters during the uprising.

It was not long, however, before those who participated in the uprising realized that they confronted two serious problems. The first was that the military much preferred stability to reform. Egypt's rulers dragged their feet on some of the uprising's central demands (including prosecution of the Mubaraks and lifting the state of emergency) and took a confrontational stance toward workers who continued their strike wave as well as protesters who continued their demonstrations. Thus, when baltagiya once again attacked protesters, the military stood by or fired into the air to disperse those under attack. And far from being democrats in uniform, the military continued to use torture against those who "disturbed the peace," attempted to intimidate women protesters by forcing them to undergo "virginity tests" while detained, and, in an obvious warning to others, sentenced a blogger to prison for three years for criticizing the military.

The second problem those who participated in the uprising faced was that the coalition that brought down Mubarak fragmented. This took place along a number of fault lines. For example, leaders of the April 6 Movement and their allies abandoned the "dialogue" about constitutional changes conducted between the government and the various groups involved in the uprising because of the presence of former NDP politicians. Many of the groups at the forefront of the uprising also called for a "no" vote in the referendum on the constitutional amendments, asserting that the amendments did not go far enough and that their passage would mean elections being held before they had time to organize themselves. The Muslim Brotherhood, on the other hand, was already organized and stood to benefit from early elections. It thus urged a "yes" vote. According to reports, the brotherhood also floated the rumor that those who opposed the amendments did so because they wanted to remove Article 2 of the constitution, which made Islam the "religion of the state." The amendments passed with 77 percent of the vote. Finally, and what was perhaps most ominous, sectarian violence pitting Muslims against Coptic Christians flared up within a month of the departure of Mubarak. Although those who incited the violence are known in some cases, in others they are not, and suspects have run the gamut from radical Islamists to former regime loyalists. (Anyone thinking that Mubarak might have been on to something when he claimed that only his heavy-handed repression prevented such incidents from taking place should remember that this "wave" of sectarian violence began with a bomb attack on a Coptic church in Alexandria on January 1, 2011—that is, on Mubarak's watch—and his interior minister's failure to deal with it fed popular anger at the regime.)

In sum, the Egyptian uprising, like the Tunisian uprising, brought down an autocrat. It is still too early to determine whether either uprising will bring down an autocracy.

What are the ten greatest myths about the Egyptian uprising?

1. It was a "Facebook Revolution."
2. It was a youth revolution.
3. It was all about Tahrir Square.
4. It demonstrates the power of nonviolent protest.
5. The Muslim Brotherhood played puppet master from behind the scenes.
6. The Muslim Brotherhood played no role.
7. Further "economic reform" (neoliberal policies) will bring stability to Egypt.
8. "The army and the people are one!"
9. The Egyptian revolution marks the standard by which other uprisings in the Arab world should be measured.
10. Mubarak left! The people won!

3

UPRISINGS IN WEAK STATES

YEMEN AND LIBYA

What did the political systems of Yemen and Libya have in common before the uprisings?

In both Yemen and Libya, corrupt, aging despots who stifled civic and economic life lorded it over states they treated as their personal fiefdoms. As a matter of fact, Ali Abdullah Saleh of Yemen and Muammar al-Qaddafi of Libya were two of the three longest-ruling heads of state in the Arab world at the time of the uprisings (the third being Sultan Qaboos of Oman), and both intended to keep their posts in the family after they were gone.

What was political life in Yemen like before the uprising there?

Ali Abdullah Saleh became president of the Yemen Arab Republic (YAR, or "North Yemen") in 1978, when Yemen was still divided into two independent states, the YAR and the People's Democratic Republic of Yemen ("South Yemen"). At the time, the presidency of the YAR was literally a dead-end job: both of Saleh's predecessors had been assassinated, the latter by a suitcase bomb brought by an envoy from the South. Rumor has it that other than Saleh, no one wanted the job at the time. Saleh was a military officer who had had little formal education before entering the army. But he did have ambition. Shortly after assuming control, parliament confirmed him as president. He ruled the YAR until the merger of the two Yemens in 1990, at which time he was elected the first president of the unified Republic of Yemen, a position he continued to hold for the next two decades.

Although Saleh was reelected president in 1999 with more than 91 percent of the vote (running against a weak candidate from his own party), observers considered the election to have been relatively free. It was thereafter that Saleh began to show his true colors. After announcing in 2005 that he would not contest the upcoming presidential elections to give a chance to a new generation, he changed his mind—bowing, as he claimed, to "popular will." Unsurprisingly, he won. In 2010, Yemen's parliament, which Saleh's party controlled, announced a plan to amend Yemen's constitution and eliminate presidential term limits, in effect making Saleh president-for-life. Only the uprising forced him to back down. And his plans went beyond the grave: he was grooming his son, Ali Ahmed Saleh, the commander of the Republican Guard and Special Forces, to succeed him. He had already begun shunting aside former allies and rivals—including prominent politicians, military officers, and tribal leaders—to make the transition smoother. This was one of the reasons many defected to the opposition when Saleh needed them most.

Ali Ahmed was not the only family member to benefit from his father's rule, nor were political and economic benefits restricted to family members alone. Corruption held the regime together and connected it to the broader society. Graft and bribery have been endemic to Yemen: auditors estimate that 30 percent of revenues do not make it into the government's coffers. Like other autocrats, Ali Abdullah Saleh peppered the security and military apparatus with relatives to ensure its loyalty. Such positions carry their own financial rewards in the form of kickbacks, access to government reserves of foreign exchange, smuggling and black marketeering of contraband, and the like. Other relatives held prominent positions in government ministries dealing with planning and insurance and real estate regulation, while still others served on the boards of public enterprises begging to be looted, such as the national airline and the national petroleum company. Then there were relatives who used their access to enrich themselves in more traditional ways, such as through acquiring a monopoly over trade in tobacco, real estate speculation, and investing in hotels.

Outside the immediate family circle, Saleh regarded loyalty as a commodity to be purchased. And he was not the only one: the government of Saudi Arabia has regularly paid off Yemeni tribal leaders to keep their restive followers quiet (about the nature of the tribal systems in Yemen and Libya, and why they are not throwbacks to some earlier time, see below).

All this provided the context in which Yemeni politics played itself out, and no one with political or economic aspirations, either regime loyalist or regime opponent, could exempt themselves from it. For instance, the Saudis have paid tens of millions of dollars to the Ahmars, the leading family of the Hashid tribal confederation (a tribal confederation is a group of affiliated tribes). Because it is the leading family of one of the two largest tribal confederations in Yemen, and because Saleh is himself a member of one of the confederation's smaller tribes, he has also been solicitous of its support. The relationship was so close that the former patriarch of the family was called Saleh's "co-president." Members of the Ahmar family served the regime in the positions of speaker of parliament, vice speaker of parliament, head of the ruling party, and even presidential bodyguard.

One member of the family who has been the recipient of millions from the Saudis is Hamid al-Ahmar, a billionaire (who calls himself "the sheikh of Hashid Tribes Conglomerate"[1]) and member of parliament. He thus had an insider's advantage when Yemen privatized its telecommunications industry. Acting in partnership with Orascom, an Egyptian communications firm, he built Yemen's largest cellular phone company. (The executive director of Orascom was a crony of Gamal Mubarak, the son of the former president. After the Egyptian uprising, he was indicted for corruption.) Hamid al-Ahmar is also the leader of Yemen's largest opposition party, the Islah Party. *Islah* is Arabic for "reform." Although led by a crony capitalist and associated with the Ahmar family, the quintessential political insiders, it has wrapped itself in the mantle of Islamic virtue and presented itself as the "clean" Islamic alternative to Saleh's ruling party. Thus, even though the party opposed the idea of amending the constitution so that Saleh might run for a third term, it played the role of "loyal opposition" in a system from which its leaders benefited. It was thus slow to endorse the overthrow of the "nizam" (regime), as those who led the uprising demanded.

Making corruption all the more grating is Yemen's status as the poorest state in the Arab world, its 35 percent unemployment rate and 50 percent illiteracy rate, and an infrastructure that barely exists outside the major cities.

What was political life in Libya like before the uprising there?

Like Saleh, Muammar al-Qaddafi was a military man. In 1969, he led a group of "Free Officers" in a coup d'état that overthrew a monarch. If this seems reminiscent of events in Egypt, it is because Qaddafi modeled himself on Gamal Abd al-Nasser (in spite of the fact that two years before the coup the Israelis had demonstrated the hollowness of Nasser's pretensions to glory by routing the Egyptian army and occupying the Sinai in a mere six days). But after a short period of experimentation with Nasser-style institutions, Qaddafi concluded that Libya was no Egypt. He shifted course and imposed a regime whose chief characteristics were megalomania, repression, and corruption.

At times, Qaddafi's megalomania appeared farcical, as when he ordered soccer players to wear only their numbers on their jerseys, not their names, to prevent them from rivaling Qaddafi in popularity. In his attempt to don the mantle of Nasser, Qaddafi pursued Nasser's pan-Arab vision, and once it became clear that no Arab state took the vision as seriously as he did, he became champion of pan-African unity with Libya at the forefront, in the process demanding recognition as the "king of kings" of Africa. And instead of taking the title "president of Libya," Qaddafi adopted titles such as "Guide of the First of September Great Revolution of the Socialist People's Libyan Arab Jamahiriya" and "Brotherly Leader and Guide of the Revolution," so that he might appear more a philosopher king than a politician and so remain above the fray.

But this is where Qaddafi's megalomania became deadly serious. In 1977, he made his "Third Universal Theory," as presented in his *Green Book*, the foundation for remodeling the Libyan state, society, and economy. For Qaddafi, representative institutions were fraudulent, since the wealthy were bound to dominate them. What was needed, Qaddafi argued, was direct democracy. He therefore ordered the establishment of nested "people's congresses," which, he declared, would make direct democracy possible, and the dismantling of representative institutions. That is why by the time of the uprising there were no trade unions, political parties, or independent media in Libya. Likewise, he ordered the dismantling of economic structures that, he argued, would have created inequalities. Hence, no privately owned enterprises (or even independent grocery stores) were permitted. Libya was to be a *"jamahiriya"*—a term he coined to mean "rule by the masses." Of course, since this system could not possibly work, government in Libya consisted of two layers: a formal layer of "people's" institutions, and an informal layer controlled by Qaddafi & Co. that actually did the governing. Rule by the masses was, in fact, an Orwellian nightmare. After the price of oil spiked in 1973, the influx of cash into Libya made it seem that the system was functional; the illusion was swept away with the collapse of oil prices in the 1980s.

Repression also kept the system going. Like many of his colleagues, Qaddafi employed multiple, overlapping security agencies, led by members of his extended family and close associates, many of whom he had known since childhood. But in addition to the usual agencies, Qaddafi took a page out of Mao's Cultural Revolution and established his own version of the Chinese Red Guards, the Revolutionary Committees Movement, which he entrusted to "safeguard the revolution." Members of the committees embedded themselves in every institution (even other security agencies) to ensure they maintained their commitment to the gospel of the *Green Book*, and, more important, that they not play host to anti-Qaddafi activity. The committees did more than just encourage right thinking, however; they also assassinated regime opponents wherever they might be found.

The security agencies established by Qaddafi won a well-deserved reputation for brutality. Examples of this brutality abound, but one incident in particular is significant for understanding the outbreak of the uprising. In 1996 the head of the Jamahiriya Security Organization, Abdullah al-Sanusi (who happened to be married to the sister of Qaddafi's wife), took charge of putting down a riot at the notorious Abu Salim prison in Tripoli. The rioters, many of whom had been jailed for belonging to the Islamist opposition to Qaddafi, took hostages, demanding better living conditions and the reinstatement of privileges that had been taken away. As negotiations between al-Sanusi and the prisoner representatives were taking place, guards herded the prisoners into courtyards. The guards then threw grenades and opened fire, and by the time the smoke had cleared about twelve hundred prisoners lay dead. The arrest of the lawyer representing the prisoners' families seeking information about their "disappeared" relatives was the event that touched off the Libyan uprising of 2011.

Although the level of repression engineered by Qaddafi far exceeded the level even imagined by Saleh (until the outbreak of the uprising, that is), one would be hard-pressed to determine in whose state corruption was worse. As in Yemen, corruption in Libya was built into the system, in large measure because so much of the system depended on personal contacts and informal structures. According to a U.S. state department cable released by WikiLeaks, "Libya is a kleptocracy in which the regime has a direct stake in anything worth buying, selling or owning."[2] Under the guise of "signing bonuses" or "consulting fees," Qaddafi, his family, and his associates shook down companies wishing to enter the Libyan market or expand their operations there; rumor had it that Qaddafi himself had to sign off on any contract worth more than $200 million. As in the case of Yemen, corruption was used to buy loyalty. Hence, Qaddafi set up foreign accounts for leaders of tribes loyal to the regime. And as in the case of Yemen, corruption simply flourished in an unregulated market in which members of the ruler's extended family could use their influence to ensure they got a cut of almost anything. It being Libya, competition among family members sometimes approached farce. In one instance, two of Qaddafi's sons engaged in an armed confrontation over control of a Coca-Cola bottling plant. It being Libya, however, the farce usually contained a strong dose of brutality.

Why do political scientists consider Yemen and Libya "weak states"?

The endurance of "strongmen" in Yemen and Libya seems to indicate that those states are strong. As a matter of fact, both Yemen and Libya have been poster children for a very different phenomenon: the weak-state syndrome.

According to political scientists, normal states exhibit three characteristics: a territory, a functioning government and bureaucracy that rules over the entirety of the territory, and a national identity. Weak states lack at least the second of those characteristics, and commonly the third as well. Government institutions are insubstantial in Yemen and Libya, and observers contest the extent of "national" identity in both states. Weak states survive only because of two factors. First, international law and international institutions guarantee their authority over a given territory, no matter how feeble that authority might be. Second, weak states adopt a common set of strategies to ensure their survival. Those strategies include winning the support of society's elites by granting them access to wealth and power, repressing the opposition, creating sham democratic institutions to act as a safety valve for political opponents, manipulating ethnic or geographic or religious divisions to prevent formation of a unified opposition, and outsourcing security functions to mercenaries or foreign governments to protect the regime without strengthening any groups or institutions. Ali Abdullah Saleh and Muammar al-Qaddafi used all of these strategies to maintain their power.

Four factors have contributed to state weakness in Yemen and Libya. The first is geography. Yemen's varied landscape, ranging from mountain to desert to canyon, makes it a difficult country to control, particularly since two-thirds of the population live in scattered and isolated villages beyond the reach of the state. Libya, on the other hand, is almost entirely desert, and although more than 85 percent of the population is urbanized and almost the entire population lives on a relatively small strip of land along the Mediterranean, that coast is long and huge stretches of desert separate the major population centers from one another.

The second factor contributing to state weakness is history. Unlike Tunisia and Egypt, which experienced two centuries of continuous institutional development over autonomous political communities, neither Yemen nor Libya had experienced either much institutional development or, until very recently, unity. The territory that is Yemen had been divided since the early nineteenth century into a "north" and a "south" (actually, a west and an east, but no one seemed to notice). Each political unit developed independently of the other. In the south, the British, who had taken the main port city, Aden, to use as a coaling station for ships en route to India during the nineteenth century, left behind a legacy typical of colonial outposts: a modern port, an active trade union movement, and politically savvy anti-imperialist schoolteachers, bureaucrats, journalists, and the like. After independence, some of their number would establish the only "people's democratic republic"—that is, a Marxist government—in the Arab world. Little of this sort of thing took place in the north, where a Zaydi imam—the leader of a local Shi'i sect to which about 35–40 percent of all Yemenis still belong—established a kingdom with tribal assistance. Unification between north and south did not take place until 1990 and was not smooth, as the civil war of 1994 demonstrated.

Similarly, there was no unified Libya until 1934, when the Italians, who had begun colonizing the territory that is now Libya two decades before, united their three separate colonies into one. When the Allies pushed the Italians out of Libya in World War II, they could not agree on what to do with the territory, so they turned the question over to the United Nations for resolution. The result was the "United Kingdom of Libya," more united in word than deed, ruled by a descendant of a legendary anti-Italian resistance fighter who showed neither inclination nor talent for state building. During his reign, regional identities trumped the national identity, and even though a raft of ministries multiplied as the years went on, they functioned more as centers for redistributing revenues from Libya's newly tapped oil reserves than for actual planning and development—a practice continued by Qaddafi after he overthrew the monarchy in 1969.

Which brings us to the third factor contributing to state weakness in Yemen and Libya: choices made by the leaders. We have already seen how this was done in both states. In the case of Yemen, what appears to be corruption to an unapprised observer is actually a deliberate attempt to incorporate family, friends, and potential rivals into the system to make them stakeholders. Formal institutions—whether a strong ruling party that exists for reasons other than to distribute patronage or a professional military that might become dangerous—would have diminished Saleh's flexibility to neutralize potential threats to his rule or absorb newcomers into the ranks of the elites. As a result, Saleh kept the role of formal institutions in governance to a minimum. Similarly, Qaddafi created a cult around the lack of formal institutions within his jamahiriya—so much so that even one of his sons, in a rare moment of honesty, criticized the system his father built, blurting out, "We want to have an administrative, legal, and constitutional system once and for all, rather than change…every year."[3] It has been said about Libya that the only ministry that worked was the Ministry of Oil, which played an essential role in ensuring the steady flow of revenue from the state to the state's clients.

Oil is the final factor that has enabled Yemen and Libya to survive as weak states. Before the uprising, Libya acquired about 95 percent of its revenues from oil, which Saif al-Islam al-Qaddafi (Muammar's second son and, until the uprising, heir apparent) disbursed directly to loyal clients. In the case of Yemen, the story is a bit more complex. At the time of the uprising, the Yemeni state was deriving about 75 percent of its revenues from oil, which it used in the same way Libya used its oil revenues. But Yemen's dependence on oil goes further: Yemen exports not only oil but labor to the oil-rich Gulf states as well. Yemeni guest workers then send home the bulk of their earnings to their families. These remittances, as they are called, are not negligible; from 2000 to 2007, Yemeni workers sent home about $10 billion, making Yemeni families the top recipients of remittances in the Middle East. Remittances take a financial burden off the Yemeni government by providing the population with an independent source of income, and they actually enrich the government as well: Yemenis buy foreign-produced goods with the money sent to them, and the government collects customs duties imposed on those goods.

Why is the fact that Yemen and Libya are weak states important for understanding the uprisings there?

Whatever the future might hold in Yemen and Libya, there was always one certainty about the outcome of the uprisings: they would not follow the same path as uprisings in Tunisia and Egypt. In the latter two countries, with their long history of state construction and institutional development, a functioning military stepped in to prevent complete elimination of the old regime by sending the most visible symbol of that regime—Ben Ali in the case of Tunisia, Mubarak in the case of Egypt—packing. This scenario was impossible in the cases of Yemen and Libya, because no unified and autonomous military, replete with a functioning chain of command and *esprit de corps*, existed in either. Indeed, because institutions in both Yemen and Libya were weak and unlikely to survive the overthrow of the ruling clique, it is in these two countries that the best possibility exists that the uprisings will lead to true revolutionary change. We have already witnessed the beginning of that change in Libya.

What role have tribes played in Yemen and Libya?

Tribes consist of groups of individuals who are bound together by real or fictitious ties of kinship. Western media have focused a great deal of attention on the tribal system in Yemen and Libya, but much of their coverage is ill-informed. The common view of tribes in the Arab world is that they are exotic and archaic institutions. They are not, in spite of the fact that both Saleh and Qaddafi portrayed tribes as the time-tested and fundamental building block of their societies in order to legitimate their method of rule. The structure and role of tribes have changed as times have changed, and the tribal units that exist in the Arab world today are as much a part of modern political and social life as parties and trade unions. As a matter of fact, it is because of the weakness or absence of other institutions in Yemen and Libya—from government ministries to parties and trade unions—that the state turned to tribes to perform functions it could not otherwise carry out. The tribes of Yemen and Libya kept their members in line, dispensed patronage, adjudicated disputes, and, in the case of Yemen, got out the vote. The tribal system enabled regimes to bind influential tribal leaders to them, and tribal divisions were useful to the regimes as a means of dividing their populations and preventing the emergence of a unified opposition.

Although it is important to acknowledge the role tribes and tribal affiliation have played in Yemen and Libya, it is important not to overstate that role. Tribal leaders do not speak for the entirety of their tribe, and tribal members retain multiple other identities, such as regional or national identities, which often take precedence over their tribal identities. During the uprisings in both Yemen and Libya, tribes and tribal confederations even divided along political lines, with some members taking the side of the government and others the side of the opposition.

How did the uprising in Yemen evolve?

At the time of the uprising in Yemen there were two protest movements. One fostered the uprising, the other had a checkered history with it.

At the end of January 2011, a coalition of opposition parties called the Joint Meeting Party (JMP) began a series of demonstrations in Yemen's capital, Sana, protesting the plan adopted by parliament to eliminate presidential term limits and Saleh's plan to have his son succeed him. This was the so-called Pink Revolution, named after the color they had chosen to identify their movement. It was led by political "outs" seeking "in," and their agenda was anything but the sort of regime change advocated by the protesters who had just brought down Ben Ali in Tunisia. Social networking youths similar to those who were leading protests in Egypt participated, but their role was peripheral—as was their call for Saleh to depart immediately. By the first week in February, Saleh had not only acceded to the political demands of the Pink Revolution, he made economic concessions as well, promising to create a fund to employ university graduates and to increase wages, among other initiatives. He also declared his willingness to resume the dialogue with the opposition that had collapsed months before. The Yemeni revolution appeared to be over before it had begun.

On February 11, the date of Egyptian president Mubarak's resignation, the JMP and the youths swapped roles. That night, students, youth activists, and others gathered outside Sana University. They marched to the city's main square, which, like its counterpart in Cairo, was named Tahrir Square, demanding the immediate resignation of Saleh. After a brief demonstration, security forces and "pro-regime demonstrators" (actually baltagiya—hoodlums employed by the government) forced them out and seized control of the square. The protesters returned to the university and set up camp in the square outside, renaming it "Taghrayr [Change] Square." This would remain the epicenter of the rebellion in Sana as larger and larger numbers of demonstrators, inspired by events in Egypt and repelled by the violence the regime inflicted on protesters, joined them.

As in the case of Egypt, the world focused its attention on the capital city. But as in the case of Egypt, the capital was not the only city in which protests broke out. University students and workers in the city of Taiz (pronounced Ta-*iz*), south of Sana, for example, also began their protests on February 11, and within a few days their numbers exceeded the numbers of those participating in marches in the capital. Likewise in the southern port city of Aden, where protesters advocating a restoration of south Yemeni independence joined others calling for the immediate departure of Saleh. And as in the case of Egypt, the level of violence outside the capital exceeded that within it—at least initially. During the first week of protests in Taiz, an unidentified government supporter threw a grenade into a crowd, killing two and injuring more than forty. In Aden, government snipers shot and killed eleven.

The regime in Yemen depended on the compliance, or at least the quiescence, of influential tribal, political, and military leaders whom it bought and balanced off against one another. As the protest movement broadened its base of support and spread throughout the country, and as the regime's resort to ever-increasing levels of violence provoked further resistance, those leaders smelled blood in the water and began to defect. First, members of the Ahmar family threw their support behind the protesters and flooded Sana with thousands of their followers. Then the JMP reversed itself and called for Saleh to leave immediately. After the massacre of forty-six protesters in Sana, a top military commander whom Saleh had given the thankless task of fighting a rebellion in the north followed suit and established a protective cordon around Taghrayr Square.

By the end of March 2011, Sana was a city divided between military units and armed supporters loyal to the regime and military units and armed supporters opposed to it. To break the stalemate, regime loyalists attacked the Sana compound of the Ahmar family. Although the attack failed, it sparked heavy fighting in the city. Soon thereafter, a bomb detonated in the presidential palace, killing eleven and severely wounding Ali Abdullah Saleh. He was evacuated to Saudi Arabia for medical treatment. It appeared that the protesters had achieved their main goal. Then, in September 2011, Saleh returned, further prolonging Yemen's agony. Saleh's resignation two months later (in exchange for immunity) came too late to relieve that agony.

How did the uprising in Libya begin?

In the aftermath of the Tunisian and Egyptian uprisings, a coalition of groups, including an umbrella group called the

National Conference for the Libyan Opposition, issued a call on social media for Libyans to participate in their own "Day of Rage" to protest political and economic conditions in Libya. The date they chose was February 17, 2011, the fifth anniversary of a demonstration held in front of the Italian consulate in the eastern city of Benghazi. That demonstration was held to protest an Italian minister who had printed the infamous Danish cartoons mocking the prophet Muhammad on a T-shirt. When demonstrators began shouting antigovernment slogans, however, security forces opened fire, killing eleven.

Events overtook the planned Day of Rage. On February 15, the Libyan government arrested Fathi Terbil, the lawyer representing the families of the "disappeared" prisoners of Abu Salim prison. Several hundred family members and their supporters gathered at the headquarters of a local Revolutionary Committee in Benghazi, then clashed with security forces. By the time the actual Day of Rage rolled around, six thousand protesters were in the streets of Benghazi calling for the overthrow of the regime, and protests and clashes had already spread to a number of towns surrounding Libya's second largest city, which protesters declared to be "liberated" from the regime.

It is not surprising that the uprising broke out in eastern Libya, where government control was less concentrated than in the west and where resentments about higher unemployment and lower government investment festered. But within days the uprising had spread west to Libya's capital, Tripoli, where protesters set fire to government buildings and engaged government forces in street battles, as well as to other cities and towns as far west as the Tunisian border. And as in Yemen, the lack of institutional development and formally established lines of authority resulted in a wave of defections from the regime, including ambassadors safely ensconced abroad, tribal leaders, and ranking military personnel who sometimes brought their units with them.

From the beginning, the regime met the uprising with an appalling level of violence. Security forces and the military treated the protesters as combatants: government forces forswore teargas for live fire, and the government deployed helicopter gunships to put down the uprising in Tripoli. Elite units under the command of four of Qaddafi's seven sons remained loyal, of course, as did the twenty-five-hundred-man Islamic Pan-African Brigade, made up of mercenaries from Chad, Sudan, and Niger. Most of the air force, whose leaders were affiliated with Qaddafi's tribe, and the security forces, which consisted of members of Qaddafi's family and tribe and members of allied tribes, also remained loyal. Qaddafi had lavished his special units with military hardware while starving the regular army of resources to prevent a coup. It is for this reason that even after foreign intervention, the uprising, which had already morphed into a civil war, settled into a protracted stalemate. It was only after six months of intense fighting, and the engagement of NATO jets providing close combat air support to the rebels, that the tide of battle turned. Tripoli fell to the rebels in August 2011, and two months later rebels found and killed Qaddafi in his home town of Surt.

Was Qaddafi crazy, or crazy like a fox?

Besides excelling in megalomania, Muammar Qaddafi was also the Arab leader most likely to be characterized as "bizarre." After Swiss police arrested one of his sons, Hannibal (yes, Hannibal!), and his wife for beating two of their servants, the elder Qaddafi called for the abolition of Switzerland at the United Nations. He slept in a tent on state visits, introduced Italian prime minister Silvio Berlusconi to something called "bunga-bunga parties" (apparently, variations on more prosaic orgies), and surrounded himself with a special unit of all-female bodyguards known as Amazons. More seriously, he sponsored terrorist activities such as the downing of Pan Am flight 103 over Lockerbie, Scotland, which killed all 259 aboard and 11 on the ground. For acts such as these, President Ronald Reagan referred to Qaddafi as "the mad dog of the Middle East."

Although none of this seems like the actions of a sane man, there might have been method to Qaddafi's madness. In a state in which few formal institutions existed (even before the *Green Book*), charismatic leadership trumps bureaucratic stability. And there is no question that charisma was Qaddafi's strong suit, at least in his younger days. Furthermore, it might be argued that earning international opprobrium and even sanctions and supporting anti-imperialist revolutionaries everywhere had a domestic upside, inasmuch as it might have bonded a fractious population with one another and with their leader. Dueling with a superpower *mano a mano* certainly put a rather inconsequential country of 6.5 million people on the map, which might have been as much a source of pride for Libyans as a source of embarrassment. Finally, Qaddafi's buffoonish behavior shifted attention away from his regime's horrific human rights record—that is, until the uprising put that record in stark relief.

Why did the uprisings in Yemen and Libya turn violent?

Saif al-Islam al-Qaddafi blamed the violent nature of Libya's uprising on Libya's "tribal character." The highly respected International Crisis Group cites infiltration of violent elements into the ranks of peaceful demonstrators in Benghazi. Still others have blamed the euphoria of the protesters after their initial successes and the looting of armories abandoned by government troops.[4] Yemen too is "tribal" (although this explanation rests on two dubious assumptions: that tribal affiliation and violence are necessarily linked, and that calling a society "tribal" actually tells you something meaningful about the society). Then there is the fact that Yemen has the most heavily armed population in the Arab world. It is, after all, a country in which carrying a ceremonial dagger is considered a fashion statement.

Lurking behind the question is the contrast between events as they purportedly unfolded in Tunisia and Egypt and events in Yemen and Libya. Although the nonviolence of the earlier uprisings has been overstated, there *is* an important contrast between Tunisia and Egypt on the one hand and Yemen and Libya on the other. The first two uprisings succeeded in dislodging autocrats because the army acted as a unit, declared *its* commitment to nonviolence, and in some cases even kept protesters and the thugs hired to attack them separated. Such was not the case in Yemen and Libya, where, rather than quashing the violence, militaries and a variety of other armed groups divided into loyalist and opposition camps. It was not that the protesters in Yemen and Libya weighed nonviolence against violence and found the former somehow lacking. Rather, the weakness of the two states and the fragmentation of the army—the very institution that had imposed order in Tunisia and Egypt—defined the tactics protesters had at their disposal.

Who were the "rebels" in Libya?

The identity of the so-called rebels in Libya (they preferred the Arabic term *thuwwar*—revolutionaries—when referring to themselves) has provoked considerable debate, much of it based on speculation. In testimony before the U.S. Senate, Admiral James Stavridis, the supreme commander of NATO for Europe, claimed that intelligence agencies had found "flickers" of an al-Qaeda presence among them,[5] a claim Republican presidential candidates took up as a stick with which to beat President Obama for ordering the American military to intervene on the rebels' behalf. Although it is entirely possible that former al-Qaedists joined the ranks of the rebels, their presence would demonstrate a fundamental shift in their ideology, since al-Qaeda works on a transnational level and views the division of the Islamic world into nation-states as a Western plot to keep Muslims weak. Those who fought for the liberation of Libya from Qaddafi obviously do not.

The Libyan Transitional National Council, originally based in Benghazi, is the government-of-Libya-in-the-process-of-formation. The rebels had to establish a government—the first such revolutionary body brought about by any of the uprisings—so that they might maintain order, organize rudimentary services and defense, gain international support, claim Qaddafi's overseas assets, and sell the national patrimony, oil. As constructed during the uprising, the council included the heads of local councils established in liberated towns. Its membership was diverse: there were Islamists and secular academics and lawyers (including Fathi Terbil), reformists and revolutionaries, all united in their opposition to Qaddafi but not particularly united programmatically. The executive branch of the government consisted of a crisis management committee and a president, vice president, and prime minister. Soon after the government's formation, a technocrat became president, a human rights lawyer became vice president, and a former judge and justice minister under Qaddafi became prime minister. During the combat phase of the uprising, the authority of the council was more moral than actual, and lines of authority among tribal leaders, military commanders, and civic leaders remained unclear so long as the rebels focused on winning the civil war.

Why did outside powers intervene directly in Libya and not in Yemen?

The day before the United States and its NATO allies began air strikes against Libyan targets, security forces killed almost fifty protesters in Yemen's capital, Sana. Yet no world leader publicly advocated intervention in Yemen. Why the different approach to Yemen as opposed to Libya?

The two main foreign players with interests in Yemen are Saudi Arabia and the United States. Saudi Arabia's policy toward Yemen has traditionally been to keep it stable but weak enough not to pose a threat to the kingdom—two goals that are not necessarily compatible. Hence, the payments to tribal leaders and hence the readmission of Yemeni workers to Saudi Arabia after they had been expelled in 1991 because of Yemen's pro-Iraq stance during the Gulf War. Once the uprising broke out, Saudi Arabia initially threw its backing behind Saleh, possibly because Saudi leaders feared contagion.

For its part, the United States has viewed Yemen as a vital partner in the battle against terrorism since 2000, when al-Qaedists bombed the U.S.S. *Cole* while the American destroyer was anchored in Aden's harbor. Al-Qaeda has a strong presence in Yemen, and the United States has been financing and training Yemen's counterterrorism forces (in 2010 alone the United States spent more than $150 million on training and equipping Yemen's armed forces). And, according to state department cables posted by WikiLeaks, Saleh's government even took responsibility for air strikes actually launched by American aircraft.[6] Thus the United States, like Saudi Arabia, was reluctant to see Saleh go.

When the protests did not abate and Saleh's behavior grew more erratic, however, the United States and Saudi Arabia shifted their position, urging dialogue and a compromise between Saleh and the opposition. The Gulf Cooperation Council, an association of six Persian Gulf nations (Bahrain, Kuwait, Oman, Qatar, Saudi Arabia, and the United Arab Emirates), even drew up a plan for a political compromise. The plan called for Saleh to step down and for a national unity government to run the country until elections. In return, Saleh was to receive immunity from prosecution. At first he dithered, promising to sign on to the plan but backing out at the last minute. Apparently, he viewed it more as a tool he could use to split the opposition between compromisers (the JMP) and hardliners than as an actual proposal. Only after months of rising tensions were the Saudis and Americans able to convince Saleh that the deal was the best he could hope for (hardliners were appalled).

One of the reasons the United States could participate in the international campaign in Libya was that it has no real interests in Libya. The United States had cut relations with Libya and imposed sanctions on the country in 1986 because of its sponsorship of terrorism. It removed sanctions in 2002 after Libya assumed legal and financial responsibility for its most outrageous terrorist acts and after Qaddafi renounced the pursuit of weapons of mass destruction. Although the United States once again began importing oil from Libya, Libyan oil accounted for only 0.6 percent of American oil imports—not a very impressive amount and one that could easily be made up elsewhere. And in addition to the fact that Qaddafi's departure or death had no strategic implications for the United States, American participation in a "no-fly zone" did not involve a serious military commitment. In fact, it was a tactic chosen more because it was relatively undemanding than because it was effective. And besides, it was endorsed by the Arab League and the United Nations.

Europe has greater interest in Libya for two reasons: oil and immigration. Before the uprising, the European Union imported about 10 percent of its oil from Libya (Italy was the largest market, importing about 25 percent of its oil from Libya). As for immigration, Europeans feared not only a massive wave from Libya if Qaddafi continued his violence but also a massive wave from sub-Saharan Africa if government control over Libya's ports broke down. With these issues in the background, there was another one that likely impelled the French to take the lead in pushing for international intervention: domestic politics. The government of French president Nicolas Sarkozy, the first to recognize the revolutionary government in Benghazi, was slow to support the uprising in Tunisia, a state in which France had a long-standing interest. Furthermore, in the run-up to the intervention, Sarkozy was entering an electoral campaign deeply unpopular. Before he began to play the role of Charles De Gaulle, fewer than 30 percent of voters thought he was doing a good job as president.

What is "R2P"?

In 2005, the UN Security Council adopted a resolution establishing as an international norm a doctrine known as R2P (sometimes rendered RtoP)—responsibility to protect. In the wake of the multiple failures of humanitarian intervention in the 1990s (Bosnia, Somalia, Rwanda), the international community formally recognized the principle that individual governments could not be allowed to abdicate the responsibility to protect their populations from atrocities, nor could they be permitted to commit those atrocities themselves. Furthermore, it agreed that ultimate responsibility to protect civilians rested with the international community, which has a number of options at its disposal to enforce compliance. These options run the gamut from sanctions and arms embargoes to military intervention. Security Council Resolution 1973, which authorized the air campaign against Qaddafi's forces, explicitly invoked the doctrine, citing "the responsibility of the Libyan authorities to protect the Libyan population." Although the Obama administration did not invoke the doctrine when it authorized American participation in the air campaign against Libya, Obama did use the phrase "responsibility to act" in his speech to the American people explaining his rationale for taking action. He specifically cited the brutality of the Qaddafi regime and its indiscriminate use of force against rebels and civilians alike.

Although the uprising in Libya amounted to the highest-profile test of R2P so far, it might also have provided the death knell for practical application of the doctrine. The Security Council passed Resolution 1973 to prevent, according to its backers, the impending massacre of innocents in Libya. Critics argue that the decision to take military action was made with undue speed, that the initial proposal to constitute a "no-fly zone" somehow expanded into a more open-ended military commitment, and that NATO intervention soon went beyond protecting civilians. It became, they argue, regime change hidden behind a humanitarian façade—the sort of precedent that permanent Security Council members Russia and China (both of which abstained during the vote on Resolution 1973) might just take to heart the next time the United States or one of its allies raises the issue of R2P.

Why is al-Qaeda in Yemen?

Estimates of the number of al-Qaeda members in Yemen range from several hundred fighters to several thousand. Some are Yemeni, others come from Saudi Arabia or further afield. Yemen is the ancestral home of the bin Laden family, but this, of course, does not explain the current presence of al-Qaedists there. They are there for other reasons. First, the pressure put on al-Qaeda in Saudi Arabia after 9/11 forced al-Qaedists out of the kingdom and over the border into Yemen. In 2009, they joined forces with Yemeni al-Qaedists to found a local franchise known as "al-Qaeda in the Arabian Peninsula." The organization gained a territorial foothold in Yemen's badlands soon thereafter, in part by playing the game of tribal politics, in part by bribing local tribal leaders who were not averse to selling their loyalties to the highest bidder.

In addition, the government itself had prepared the ground for al-Qaeda by encouraging the spread of "salafism." Salafism might be defined as a method some Muslims use to get at religious truth. The method is based on literal interpretation of the founding texts of Islam. For salafis, a close reading of those texts will reveal the activities Islam prescribes and the activities Islam proscribes. All Sunni Islamists are salafis, although not all salafis are politically inclined Islamists, and it is the rare salafi or even Islamist who agrees with al-Qaeda's idiosyncratic message and tactics. As a matter of fact, al-Qaeda represents a fringe of a fringe of salafis. Ali Abdullah Saleh encouraged the spread of salafi schools and organizations to check the power of his opponents, particularly the political left and Yemen's Zaydi population. That is, until they too represented a threat. By then, however, it was too late, and the spread of salafism and the empowerment of salafis created a supportive environment for al-Qaeda.

The final reason al-Qaeda has established a presence in Yemen is strategic. Although al-Qaeda distinguishes itself from other Islamist organizations by a lack of interest in taking over states per se, it does seek to implant itself in territories over which governments have little or no control so as to harass and thus exhaust the "Crusader-Zionist alliance" and its agents. Yemen, with a weak central government and rough terrain, thus provides an ideal location for the group (as do the outreaches of Libya).

Just how powerful al-Qaeda is in Yemen is debatable, though. It has been reported that al-Qaeda-type groups, if not al-Qaeda in the Arabian Peninsula itself, have taken over towns in the south as a first step toward establishing an "Islamic emirate" there; that is, a base from which al-Qaeda could continue its battle against the Crusader-Zionist alliance. These reports may or may not be accurate: events in the south reflect the al-Qaeda *modus operandi*, but no one knows for sure who is actually behind them. In the past, the Yemeni government has exaggerated al-Qaeda presence and activities to representatives of the United States, from which it has received generous support for its antiterrorism efforts. It is thus possible that the government blamed al-Qaeda for acts committed by others, including unaffiliated militants, tribes, and even government agents.

What are the fissures in Yemen and Libya that might divide them in the future?

Citizens feel loyal to a state in part because they participate in common activities and subscribe to a common national myth. States promote common activities and common national myths through state institutions. It therefore stands to reason that a state with weak institutions would be more prone to division than one with strong institutions. This is not to say that the uprisings in Yemen and Libya, which have destroyed the delicate political balance established by Saleh and Qaddafi, will lead to the division of either country. Rather, it is to say that in the wake of the uprisings such a division is possible, particularly as crises drag on and central authority remains absent or weak. What are the possible dividing lines in Yemen and Libya?

There are three fault lines in Yemen. At the time of the outbreak of the uprising, the Saleh regime was fighting a secessionist movement in the north called the Houthi Rebellion, after a leading Zaydi cleric and his family. The rebels had multiple complaints against the government, including underdevelopment of the north, heavy-handedness on the part of the Saleh regime there, and marginalization of Zaydis at the hands of the government and government-sponsored salafis. The second fault line is the one that separates what had been North Yemen from South Yemen. Many residents of the south believe that the unification of the two Yemens had been mishandled. The south did not achieve the representation in government promised it in 1990, and after the 1994 civil war southerners complained that carpetbaggers from the north "colonized" the south, taking positions of power and control over southern resources. And since the largest of Yemen's oil fields lies in the south, their complaints had wide resonance. Government intransigence transformed a protest movement into a movement promoting southern secession. The leaders of the Houthi Rebellion and of the "Southern Movement" joined the anti-Saleh uprising, putting their demands for independence on the back burner. The ambitions of a third group did not slow down, however. That group is al-Qaeda.

During the six-month Libyan uprising, when the rebels held eastern Libya and Qaddafi's forces the west, it appeared that the east-west split just might prove to be enduring. This was a logical assumption; east and west had not been effectively unified under the monarchy (the king rarely left the east), and regional loyalties remained after Qaddafi took power. To this day, westerners boast of their (relative) cosmopolitanism and complain of the tribalism of the east. Since the rebels entered Tripoli, however, the chances of such a division have diminished. Both halves of Libya are once again united under a single government (albeit one that has yet to prove its chops), and the final victory of the rebel forces came about as a result of a joint push from the east and far west on the capital, lessening the chances that westerners would equate the end of Qaddafi's rule with "foreign" occupation.

On the other hand, there remain a number of fault lines that might affect the future stability—and even the future integrity—of Libya. The final push came with the help of fighters from Libya's Berber community. Although only about 10 percent of the Libyan population, with the fall of Qaddafi the community immediately began asserting its right to teach and broadcast in Berber, an act that had been forbidden under the old regime and that may not sit well with a new one seeking to forge a post-Qaddafi national identity. Most important, the rebels organized themselves town by town, which further intensified already robust local identities—perhaps at the expense of a national one. Thus, soon after the occupation of Tripoli, the head of the "Misurata Brigade"—named after the western city in Libya from which it came—refused the order of the provisional government's interior minister that he remove his unit from the capital. "Mr. Darrad's declaration that we should leave touches the dignity of the revolutionaries," the brigade commander declared. "It shouldn't be done like this and it's not the way to talk to us."[7]

4

TWO SURPRISES

ALGERIA AND SYRIA

Why did events in Algeria and Syria surprise most experts?

After the uprising in Tunisia sent President Zine al-Abidine Ben Ali packing, and after mounting protests in Egypt demonstrated that events in Tunisia were no fluke, Middle East experts began to look around the Arab world to determine which other states appeared vulnerable to popular anger. At the top of nearly everyone's list was Tunisia's neighbor, Algeria (a Google search for the phrase "Is Algeria Next?" in the summer of 2011 came back with 26,600 hits). At the same time, experts argued that the contagion sweeping the Arab world would not affect Syria. They were wrong on both counts. Algeria turned out not to be next (if by next we mean facing the sort of maelstrom that has occurred in Tunisia, Egypt, Yemen, and Libya). Syria, on the other hand, was. The moral of the story is not that the experts got it wrong; rather, it is that they thought they could get it at all.

Why did observers believe that after Tunisia, Algeria would be next?

Algeria appeared vulnerable for a number of reasons. First, there was its historical role in the Arab world as a trendsetter.

There is a certain amount of truth to the saying that wherever the Middle East is going, Algeria will get there first (and probably with more violence). Algeria had fought a very bloody but successful war of national liberation against France from 1954 to 1962. It thus became an object of emulation for anti-imperialists throughout the region, and indeed throughout the world. During that war, Algerian revolutionaries not only committed acts of violence against soldiers and civilians alike, they fetishized those acts, claiming those acts provided the only route to national cleansing and national self-awareness. This "cult of armed struggle," as it came to be called, later became the central pillar of the revolutionary doctrines of the Palestine Liberation Organization and other national liberation movements. Algeria was the first state in the Arab world to nationalize its oil and natural gas industries in the 1960s, and it led the battle for Third World economic rights in the 1970s. The Algerians were also the first in the Arab world to experiment with free multiparty elections in 1989, and when Islamists won the first round of the balloting and the army stepped in to end the experiment in democracy, Algeria descended into the hell of "civil war" (the term is contested) during which as many as 150,000 Algerians may have died. Pundits predicted that the electoral victory of the Islamists and subsequent violence would be the hallmark of the Arab world's future—and events that followed in Palestine, Lebanon, and elsewhere seemed to prove them right. Finally, Algeria experienced popular protests beginning the first week in January 2011. Thus it appeared certain that it would live up to its reputation as a trendsetter once again.

And there were plenty of signs that it would be. Over the course of the two decades that preceded the uprisings in Tunisia and Egypt, and particularly in the immediate run-up to the uprisings, the same four factors that made other authoritarian regimes in the Arab world vulnerable made the Algerian regime vulnerable as well.

First, the Algerian state, like other states in the Arab world, abandoned the ruling bargain it had made with its population.

Algeria was one of the pioneers of "Arab socialism," and the period 1963–1987 was the golden age of Algerian economic nationalism and the "benefits for compliance" compact between the regime and the population. Algeria was able to carry out these policies because of its huge reserves of oil and natural gas (it is currently the world's fourteenth-largest producer of oil and third-largest producer of liquefied natural gas), which tied the fate of the Algerian economy to the price and demand for the two hydrocarbons. In 1986, however, the price of hydrocarbons collapsed and Algeria, which had borrowed heavily during flush times, had to go hat-in-hand to the International Monetary Fund (IMF) for relief. The result was a 1988 commitment by the Algerian government to neoliberal economic policies, which began in earnest in 1991. The Algerian public then faced the twin provocations of neoliberalism in tandem: first, cuts to subsidies, then privatization, with all its attendant problems, including corruption and a spike in unemployment that left four hundred thousand public sector employees without jobs between 1994 and 2000 alone.

Then there were the shocks precipitated by demography and food prices. A U.S. State Department cable posted by WikiLeaks in 2010[1] puts a human face on the problems faced by the cohort of young Algerians caught in the "youth bulge." According to the cable, in one year alone, 2007, about fifty thousand Algerian youths, called *harraga* (Arabic for "those who burn"—meaning, in this case, those who burn their identity papers), embarked from Algeria on small boats seeking a better life in Europe. They did this knowing the chances of ever reaching Europe were slim (the cable put them at 10 percent). When asked why they risked drowning and imprisonment, most responded by describing life in Algeria in three words: *hogra* (humiliation), poverty, and corruption—the very complaint Muhammad Bouazizi might have made about life in Tunisia.

The last of the four factors making Algeria and other Arab autocracies vulnerable has to do with the nature of the regime and its resulting brittleness. Since Algeria won independence in 1962, the state apparatus has been in the hands of the victorious National Liberation Front (FLN). Trying to explain the FLN to non-Algerians is a lot like trying to explain the mystery of the Trinity to a non-Christian. The state apparatus of Algeria is both *of* and coextensive *with* the FLN, while the FLN itself consists of three parts: the army (which has been kingmaker), the president and the political leadership (those anointed by the military), and the party (the FLN's link to the public).

This odd setup came about as a result of Algeria's peculiar history. Before 1962, there had never been an Algeria. Before 1830, the territory that is now Algeria was part of the Ottoman Empire, and after 1830 it became French. And not a French colony either: Algeria was integrated into France and before independence was as much a part of France as Paris. During the Algerian war of independence, the FLN constructed an army, a trade union apparatus, a state apparatus that included various ministries, and legislative, executive, and judicial branches. Once the FLN proved victorious, it established the first independent Algerian state in history, and this apparatus became the regime. All presidents of Algeria have come from the ranks of the FLN. All but the first (who was overthrown in a military coup) have come from the ranks of the army. Although there have been elections, presidents in fact govern at the sufferance of the army. A reminder of this came in 1992: after Islamists won the first round of multiparty elections, the army, dismayed by the results, removed the president and ruled directly for a year, after which it handpicked a new president.

In addition to the four factors Algeria shared with other states that had experienced uprisings (or were about to), Algeria appeared to many to be "on the brink" because of its recent history of rebellion. Here it is important to differentiate between the so-called civil war of 1992–1999 and subsequent events. What is called a civil war was, in fact, a battle between an Islamic insurgency whose level of bloodletting repelled even al-Qaeda and an equally bloodthirsty counterinsurgency campaign led by a group within the military known as "eradicators." Most Algerians affected by the war were victims, not participants—which is why the cable cited just above contended that "Algerian society is still suffering from 'cultural post traumatic stress syndrome' after the violence of the 1990s." More to the point is the fact that since 2001 Algeria has been the site of almost constant strikes, demonstrations, and riots in which Algerians acted less as victims than as citizens committed to resisting what they perceived to be economic injustice and arbitrary rule. Although the figure of 9,700 incidents of unrest in 2010 cited by an opposition leader seems exaggerated,[2] it is difficult to dispute that such activities have become woven into the Algerian political fabric because *"Le Pouvoir"* (equivalent to "The Man") has eliminated other means for people to air their grievances and because protesters have been known to get their way. Little wonder, then, that most observers saw this as an environment ripe for a Tunisian- or Egyptian-style uprising.

What were the Algerian protests of early 2011 like?

In January 2011 Algerians responded to price hikes in basic staples by taking to the streets throughout the country. The government responded by ordering prices lowered, by offering other economic and political concessions, and, perhaps most important, by displaying a considerable show of force. Although the trigger for the riots was initially economic grievances, Algerians were not unmoved by what was going on in neighboring Tunisia—as was demonstrated by a wave of Bouazizi-style self-immolations. By the third week in January, the political opposition, student and women's groups, and representatives from unofficial trade unions had organized the National Coordination for Change and Democracy (CNCD), which called for a massive demonstration on February 12 in the capital, Algiers. The largest component of the CNCD was the Rally for Culture and Democracy, a political party whose main base of support was in the Berber areas of Algeria. The demonstration turned out to be less than massive: about three thousand protesters squared off against about ten times that many riot police, who blocked the demonstration's route of march. A second demonstration, called for a week later, met the same fate. Protesters outside Algiers fared no better.

The sorts of demonstrations that brought down autocrats in Tunisia and Egypt fizzled in Algeria during the high season for Arab uprisings, but this did not mean protests had ended. In the months following the ill-fated February 12 demonstration, a strike wave spread throughout the country, as did sporadic rioting, which reflected continued dissatisfaction with high prices, housing, and unemployment. The strikes and protests were, however, local and triggered by specific grievances. Furthermore, the fact that the February protests fizzled did not mean that nothing changed in Algeria. The government restored subsidies on consumer products, promised limited political reform, and lifted the emergency law banning demonstrations that had been in effect since 1992 (the ban continued in Algiers, however). Nevertheless, Algerians did not have their Tahrir Square, and they did not have the pleasure of hearing a somber announcement over the radio that their president had resigned, as had Egyptians.

Why did the results of the uprising in Algeria differ from those in Tunisia and Egypt?

Observers have suggested a number of reasons for the "failure" of the January/February uprising in Algeria (although if another uprising occurs one can be sure the same observers will trace its roots to the "failed" uprising of early 2011). Among them are effective repression; the inseparability of the military from the regime; the reluctance on the part of Algerians to revisit the horrors of civil war; Algeria's two-decade-long hemorrhaging of young professionals, the very people who played a leading role in the Tunisian and Egyptian uprisings; divisions within the protest movement on everything from tactics to goals; the leading role in the CNCD played by a political party identified with an ethnic minority; the lack of support from labor on nonbread-and-butter demands; and the key role in the initial riots played by slum dwellers.

Confronted with explanations like these, we must keep two things in mind: first, since uprisings are extraordinary events, the lack of one is commonplace and therefore does not call for explanation. Second, no explanation would be adequate anyway because, as we have seen, explanations do not take into account the role of the human factor or happenstance in setting off an uprising.

Did Algeria ever experience a pro-democracy uprising?

In the wake of the collapse of oil prices in 1986, the Algerian government began to apply economic measures suggested by the IMF, such as cutting subsidies on basic goods and reducing public sector employment. What began as a labor strike in Algiers soon became the "Black October riots," as protests spread throughout Algeria. The uprising was eerily similar to those taking place throughout the Arab world a quarter century later. Although strikers and protesters initially focused on economic demands, they soon expanded their focus to include broad political ones. Indeed, one of the popular slogans chanted on the street was, "We don't want butter or pepper, we want a leader we can respect."[3] Like the contemporary uprisings, the uprising of 1988 targeted regime corruption, torture and other forms of repression, and the lack of democratic institutions and rights. Like the contemporary uprisings, youth and labor played a key role in the 1988 uprising. And like the contemporary uprisings, the regime responded with both carrots, in the form of political and economic concessions, and sticks, which resulted in the deaths of about five hundred protesters. The regime even played the same game of "dialogue" with the protesters in the hope of splitting the opposition, as contemporary regimes have done. The group it chose to parley with, however, was the Islamists, perhaps because the government believed them to be more easily containable than other groups participating in the uprising. In the wake of the uprising, the regime authorized new elections (the first truly free elections in the Arab world), and when the Islamists won, the military stepped in to cancel the results—not the sort of lesson one would necessarily like to learn from history.

It would be wrong to think the events of 1988 are important because, when it comes to a pro-democracy uprising, each country gets one bite of the apple and Algeria got its then. Rather, they are important because recounting the story of such uprisings lends historical depth to the current fight against autocracy in the Arab world.

Why was the Syrian uprising a surprise?

On January 31, 2011, a little over two weeks after Ben Ali fled Tunisia and three days after the reoccupation of Cairo's Tahrir Square, Syrian president Bashar al-Assad gave an interview to *The Wall Street Journal* in which he said:

> I am not talking here on behalf of the Tunisians or the Egyptians. I am talking on behalf of the Syrians. We have more difficult circumstances than most of the Arab countries but in spite of that Syria is stable. Why? Because you have to be very closely linked to the beliefs of the people. This is the core issue. When there is divergence between your policy and the people's beliefs and interests, you will have this vacuum that creates disturbance. So people do not only live on interests; they also live on beliefs, especially in very ideological areas. Unless you

understand the ideological aspect of the region, you cannot understand what is happening.[4]

Assad might be forgiven for not seeing what was about to take place. Few experts did either. There are five reasons experts thought Syria would be immune from the uprisings spreading throughout the region.

First, as difficult as it is to believe now, before the uprising Bashar al-Assad enjoyed a reputation as a reformer. His father, Hafez al-Assad, who governed Syria from 1970 until his death in 2000, groomed Bashar's much despised elder brother to succeed him. When the brother died in an automobile accident, Hafez recalled Bashar from London, where he had been studying ophthalmology, and gave him a crash course on politics. After the elder Assad died, parliament amended the constitution, reducing the minimum age for president from forty to thirty-seven—which was, not coincidentally, Bashar's exact age. Soon after acceding to power, Bashar oversaw the brief "Damascus Spring," a period of time when the government took a rather benign view of unsupervised political organizing and free expression. And when the Damascus Spring turned into the Damascus Winter, it was Hafez al-Assad's old cronies who took most of the blame.

Bashar alluded to the second reason few saw the uprising in Syria coming: as leader of the anti-imperialist "resistance camp" in the region, he had reserves of goodwill both domestically and regionwide from which his deposed counterpart, Hosni Mubarak—who was widely seen as an American puppet and whose government continued to abide by a peace treaty with Israel—could not draw. Syria's capital, Damascus, was home to the leader of the Palestinian Islamist group Hamas, and Syria had close alliances with both the Lebanese Islamist group Hizbullah and the group's primary sponsor, Iran. Syria never signed a peace treaty with Israel, and indeed it is still in a state of war with Israel. In the eyes of many, therefore, Syria stood at the forefront of resistance to the imperialist designs of the United States and Israel.

The third reason the Syrian uprising was surprising was that the Syrian government had demonstrated in the past that it was not to be messed with. Besides deploying a legion of security forces not averse to using torture, there was the example of Hama. In 1982, the Syrian Muslim Brotherhood, which was engaged in a war against the Syrian government, attempted to take over that city. The Syrian government struck back viciously, shelling the city and leaving an estimated ten to twenty thousand dead.

In addition, Syria is a religiously heterogeneous country, and the Syrian government has enjoyed the support of religious minorities that constitute almost a quarter of the population. As a matter of fact, Assad and the inner circle of the government belong to a religious minority, the Alawite sect, which is closer to Shi'i Islam than to Sunni Islam (to which approximately 75 percent of Syrians belong). Alawites make up about 11 percent of the population of Syria; Christians and other religious minorities compose the remainder of non-Sunni Syrians. The government maintains the support of many who belong to minority communities because of the widespread belief, promoted by the government itself, that it is the only barrier standing between minorities and a sectarian bloodbath or rule by the Syrian Muslim Brotherhood.

Finally, events in Syria themselves seemed to bear out Assad's prediction that the country would remain stable. Demonstrations of social-networking youths, similar to those who participated in the Egyptian protests, did not capture the public's imagination. The first such demonstrations, held in Damascus in January 2011, were quickly broken up by security forces. Other sporadic demonstrations continued, but they met with the same fate. One such demonstration, held in Damascus on March 15, was organized by a group called "Syrian Revolution 2011 against Bashar al-Assad." Protesters demanded, among other things, that the government rescind the emergency law and release political prisoners. It attracted only an estimated 200 to 350 protesters.

How did the uprising in Syria begin?

The beginning of the uprising in Syria bears a closer resemblance to the beginning of the uprising in Libya than to that in Egypt. Whereas protesters in Egypt made the capital city, Cairo, the symbolic center of the uprising, in Syria, as in Libya, the uprising broke out in the provinces. This was not simply because regimes in the latter two countries concentrated the repressive apparatus in their capitals. After all, such was the case in Egypt as well. More to the point, unlike the uprising in Egypt, the uprising in Syria, like the one in Libya, did not take place in the wake of meticulous preparation. It was spontaneous.

Three days after the anemic March 15 demonstration in Damascus, all hell broke loose in Syria. In the first week of March, security forces had arrested ten schoolchildren aged fifteen or younger in the dusty provincial city of Daraa (population seventy-seven thousand). Their crime? Borrowing a slogan from the Egyptian revolution, they had written, "Down with the regime (nizam)" on a wall. They were imprisoned and, while in prison, tortured. For about two weeks their families attempted to gain their release. Then they took to the streets. Security forces opened fire, killing several. The next day, their funeral procession brought out twenty thousand demonstrators who chanted antigovernment slogans and attacked government buildings.

Coincidentally, protests erupted the same day far to the north in the coastal city of Banias. As in the case of the Daraa protests, the protests in Banias initially reflected local concerns (the secular regime had cracked down on female schoolteachers there who wore the *niqab*, the Syrian variant of the veil), then expanded their focus to national issues, such as the brutality of the regime, the absence of democratic institutions, and corruption. Protests soon spread to other cities, including Latakia, Homs, Hasaka, and Qamishli, as well as to the small towns surrounding Damascus. By summer, the uprising had reached the ghost-ridden city of Hama, which security forces hastily abandoned (to the astonishment of the protesters), only to retake again, repeating the devastation of 1982. Although some cities—including Damascus and Syria's second largest city, Aleppo—remained relatively quiet, six months after it broke out the Syrian uprising showed no signs of subsiding.

How has the Syrian regime responded to the uprising?

Like other regimes, the Syrian regime has taken a carrot-and-stick approach to the uprising. However, the carrots offered have been too little, too late. The stick has been applied with a brutality that rivals the Libyan regime's war against *its* people.

Throughout the uprising, the regime has attempted to mollify the protesters with piecemeal and cosmetic reforms. For example, the government repealed the hated emergency law that had been in effect since 1963, when the Baath Party, of which Hafez al-Assad was a member, assumed power in a coup d'état. The law allowed the government to override the constitution and criminal code and to suspend habeas corpus (that is, to detain those accused of crimes indefinitely). It was thus used as the legal basis to clamp down on the protests, and its repeal had been one of the principal demands of the uprising. Although the government rescinded the law, however, it did not rescind presidential decrees that were equally onerous. One such decree put members of the security forces beyond prosecution; another made membership in the Syrian Muslim Brotherhood a crime punishable by death. Furthermore, the government replaced the emergency law with another designed (to borrow from the government's Orwellian explanation) "to protect national security, uphold the dignity of the citizenry, and combat terror." In the end, annulment of the emergency law did little to curb the government's bloodlust.

The state also offered concessions to various constituencies, probably with the aim of ensuring their quiescence or of splitting the opposition. For the government, the two most important (or easily suborned) constituencies to be mollified were the Kurdish population and moderate Islamists. Kurds constitute approximately 10 percent of the Syrian population. They had rebelled against the regime in 1982 and in 2004, and although they had remained relatively quiet during the recent uprising the government wanted to keep it that way. As a result, the government granted citizenship to 250,000 Kurds who, it maintained, had crossed into Syria from Turkey illegally in the early sixties. It also established the Kurdish New Year, *Nawrooz*, as a national holiday. To appease moderate Islamists, the government authorized formation of a (pro-government) Islamist party, closed down Syria's only legal casino, and promised to rehire twelve hundred women schoolteachers fired for wearing the *niqab* at work.

Throughout the uprising, the government blamed the troubles on salafis, ex-convicts, smugglers, armed gangs, and an odd conspiracy made up, at various times, of the United States, Israel, Palestinians, Saudi Arabia, and the supporters of Lebanese prime minister Saad Hariri (it is widely believed that Syria played a role in the assassination of Hariri's father, former Lebanese president Rafiq Hariri, in 2005). Blaming the uprising on Islamists, criminals, and foreigners justified for the regime and its loyalists the stomach-churning brutality that the government applied to quell it. Take, as an example, the way the government dealt with Daraa, the city at the heart of the uprising. The government surrounded the rebellious city with tanks, cut off water and electricity, and prevented anyone from entering or leaving. Security personnel and the army deployed snipers, shelled parts of the city with artillery and tanks, used live fire against unarmed protesters, and engaged in mass arrests. Throughout Syria, the government refused to hand over the bodies of those killed during protests or forced families to bury their dead in private to prevent protesters from gathering at funeral processions. It even warned those so inclined against attending Friday prayers to ensure that services would not erupt into demonstrations. And as if to demonstrate Lenin's maxim that "the purpose of terrorism is to terrorize," the government committed seemingly purposeless acts of violence, frequently against children and even infants, in an attempt to cow the population. Here is how CNN reported one such act, the murder of thirteen-year-old Hamza al-Khatib:

> On April 29, demonstrators from villages surrounding Daraa, Syria, marched on the city in an attempt to break the Syrian military siege there.... On that day, eyewitnesses say, security forces fired indiscriminately on them, killing and wounding dozens. Countless others were detained in a mass roundup. Among them, says his family, was Hamza. He got separated from his father in the chaos. A month later, the family received his body. The video was taken at that time by a relative, the family says. Much of the video of the child's corpse is too graphic to broadcast. His face is bloated and purple. His body is covered in bruises. There are gunshot wounds to his torso, and his genitals are mutilated.[5]

Al-Khatib's death had an effect that defied the government's expectations when it launched its campaign of terror. About two weeks after the government turned over the child's body, residents of the Damascus suburb of Douma went out on the streets shouting a slogan reminiscent of the Egyptian uprising: "We are all Hamza al-Khatib!"

What made the Syrian regime vulnerable?

The same four factors that have made other regimes in the Arab world vulnerable (reneging on the ruling bargain, demography, a food crisis, regime brittleness) made the Syrian regime vulnerable as well. As with other regimes, however, there have been local variations on regional themes.

First, over the course of the past decade Syria has combined the worst aspects of a state-dominated economy with the worst aspects of a market economy. The state-dominated economy took root during the late 1950s, when Egypt and Syria united to form the United Arab Republic (UAR). The UAR lasted only three years (1958–1961), but during that time the Egyptians exported their brand of Arab socialism to their northern neighbor. When the Baath party—to which Hafez al-Assad belonged—came to power in 1963, it maintained, and in some cases expanded, Egyptian-style programs and institutions. The economic efficiency of the programs was much the same in Syria as in Egypt, so when Assad took power in 1970 he launched the "corrective movement" that rolled back many of the most radical programs, such as the Baath's draconian land reform policies. Besides economics, Assad had another motive for his corrective revolution: he sought to win over the important Syrian merchant community, which the Baathists had alienated in their earlier incarnation. Nevertheless, under Assad *père* the state remained the engine of the economy.

When Bashar inherited the presidency in 2000, he promised reform. What he meant by this was the economic reform that, he claimed, would have to precede political reform. Thus in 2005 he introduced what he called a "social market economy" to shift from an economy run by the state to a more liberal one. In large measure, the IMF drew up the blueprint for the social market economy. As elsewhere, Syrians found two aspects of the social market economy particularly repellent: first, the fraying of the social safety net and replacement of middle-class entitlements, such as across-the-board subsidies for food and fuel, with targeted subsidies; second, privatization of government assets. The public sector in Syria remains more bloated than elsewhere. Nevertheless, as in other states in the region, privatization led not to capitalism but rather to crony capitalism. The worst of the crony capitalists became symbols of corruption and targets of popular anger. Egypt had its Ahmad Ezz; Syria, its Rami Makhlouf, Bashar al-Assad's first cousin. Makhlouf is not only principal owner of the mobile communications giant Syriatel; his empire also includes holdings in real estate, transport, banking, insurance, construction, and tourism. (Then there is Firas Tlas, the son of a former defense minister, who is known as the "sugar king.")

Overall, the social market economy failed, and the IMF estimates that in 2010 Syria's GDP grew by a mere 3 percent. Syria's own State Planning Commission has estimated that the GDP would have to grow at an annual rate of 7 percent merely to absorb new job seekers.[6]

In terms of demography, the Syrian experience differs little from that of its neighbors. As in other states in the region, a huge part of the population is under the age of thirty. In Syria, youths under twenty-five constitute 59 percent of population. And as in the rest of the Arab world, youths in Syria make up the bulk of the unemployed: 67 percent of young males and 53 percent of young females in the labor pool are unemployed. On the average, 81 percent of college graduates spend at least four years looking for work before landing their first job. We can say, therefore, that young people make up more than their share of the disaffected.

The Syrian experience does differ a bit from that of other Arab states when it comes to the third factor underlying recent events: shocks to the international food supply chain. Unlike its neighbors, Syria was self-sufficient in wheat production until 2006, after which there were four consecutive years of drought before the uprising. As a result, 30 percent of Syrians currently live below the poverty line, 11 percent below the subsistence level. This is because in Syria about 48 percent of household income is spent on food. And economists have added an entirely new statistical category to Syria's country profile: the "new poor," which includes the 1.3–1.4 million Syrians who have left the countryside for nearby cities because of the drought. This exodus might offer a partial explanation why the epicenters of the uprising have been cities and towns in agricultural areas, such as Daraa and the towns in the Hawran region surrounding the capital, rather than Damascus or Aleppo.

The government had planned for several years to establish a National Social Aid Fund, but the first payments to the 420,000 most vulnerable families were not delivered until February 13, 2011. This was a targeted subsidy, which the government did not extend more generally until after the uprising had begun.

Finally, the Syrian regime is among the most entrenched and brittle in the region. As a result, it was logical that protests beginning with calls for reform quickly gave way to protests calling for the end of the nizam.

What made the Syrian regime so resilient?

Two features have marked the uprising in Syria since it began: The first has been the extraordinary bravery of those Syrians who chose to join it in the face of a government that has shown them no mercy. The second has been the resilience of a regime that always seemed one or two steps behind the protesters. How can we account for this?

Unlike in Egypt and Tunisia, the ruling clique and the repressive apparatus (the security forces and the military) are tightly interwoven in Syria. Unlike in Yemen and Libya, where what there was of a state apparatus depended on tribes and similar groups to maintain control and extend patronage, in Syria the state apparatus and key nonstate actors are also tightly interwoven.

Between 1946, when Syria got its independence, and 1970, when Hafez al-Assad took over, Syria experienced ten coups d'état—a record in the Arab world. Since 1970, there have been none. Hafez al-Assad, in effect, "coup-proofed" Syria.[7] Coup-proofing involves a series of steps a leader might take in order to protect himself. In Syria (and in Saddam Hussein's Iraq and elsewhere) it centered on three processes: distribution of "coup-critical positions" to trusted members of family and religious sect, community outreach to build alliances, and creation of armed forces parallel to the regular military along with multiple security agencies having overlapping jurisdiction. In Egypt, the army had an institutional identity separate from Mubarak, from the most important security forces, and from the crony capitalists linked to the regime. Thus they could turn on Mubarak when he became a liability. In Syria, members of Assad's extended family and sect are distributed in high places throughout the military. Hafez appointed Bashar's brother, Maher, to be head of the presidential guard, and Bashar appointed General Assef Shawkat, his brother-in-law, deputy chief of staff. Neither can turn on the regime; if the regime goes, they go.

The regime believes that it can manipulate sectarianism, along with kinship, to lock minorities and the regime in a mutually supportive embrace. This is a risky gamble that had mixed effects during the uprising. On the one hand, Sunni conscripts, repelled by the level of violence their Alawite officers were willing to inflict on protesters, began to defect from the army in increasing numbers as the government showed no signs of backing down and the uprising showed no signs of abating. Joined by Sunni civilians, mainly from cities and towns with religiously mixed populations, they targeted Alawites along with other minorities they associate with the regime. Bashar al-Assad's assertion, made early on, that his opponents were sectarian and violent thus proved to be akin to a self-fulfilling prophecy. On the other hand, there were no mass defections from the ranks of political and military elites, as happened in Yemen and Libya. Those associated with the regime in Syria understood that they would all have to hang together or they would all hang separately. It is this regime cohesion that sets Syria (and Algeria) apart from Egypt and Tunisia, where in the face of popular anger the military felt compelled to align with the opposition against the president. It also sets Syria (and Algeria) apart from Yemen and Libya, where regimes under pressure from uprisings splintered.

The second process necessary for effective coup-proofing is to offer outreach to key layers of society to make them complicit with the regime. For the ruling clique in Damascus, this involved nurturing what some have called a "military-mercantile complex."[8] Under the elder Assad, the mostly Alawite political and military elite established connections with the Sunni business class of Damascus. Political elites channeled state contracts to the businessmen. By doing so, they enriched themselves through kickbacks and black marketeering. The businessmen got access not only to government contracts but also to tightly controlled foreign exchange and political protection. The connection between the regime and the Sunni business class was critical during the 1982 Muslim Brotherhood uprising in Hama. Rather than siding with their co-religionists, the Damascus business community chose the regime, providing it with crucial support during its worst crisis (and again demonstrating that political loyalty and sectarian identity do not necessarily coincide).

Finally, the Syrian regime has created military units outside the regular chain of command—such as Maher al-Assad's presidential guard—on which, when push comes to shove, the regime can count. In addition, the regime has relied on multiple security forces to do its dirty work. An example is the dreaded "*ashbah*" (Arabic for "ghosts"). These are black-clad security goons who hail from Assad's hometown. They too are fiercely loyal. Like members of the inner circle, they cannot turn on the regime, because if the regime goes, so will they.

The effectiveness of coup-proofing in Syria was one of the reasons most analysts were blindsided by the outbreak of the uprising, even as uprisings broke out in state after state in the region.

Who is the opposition in Syria?

Two of the major strengths of the Syrian opposition have been its diversity and loose structure, which have enabled it to draw from multiple layers of the population and be adaptive. Two of the major weaknesses of the Syrian opposition have been its diversity and loose structure, which have impeded consensus on a range of issues, including a vision for a Syria of the future and a strategy for achieving that vision.

The opposition in Syria consists of five main components. The most important so far is the spontaneous, mostly peaceful crowds that have come together in city after city, town after town to protest some local provocation or in solidarity with those in neighboring communities. At the beginning of the uprising, the crowds commonly formed after Friday prayers or funeral processions. They continued to do so later, but as the uprising progressed crowds would form routinely, commonly at night, when the snipers deployed by security forces were less effective. Although these crowds appear to have been leaderless, their members have been able to step into the breach when authorities absent themselves from their posts, as happened in Hama, where city dwellers themselves maintained a basic level of order and subsistence before the government returned.

The second group that has participated in the uprising is familiar from the Tunisian and Egyptian uprisings. It consists of a variety of pro-democracy, pro-human-rights, and social-media groups (such as Syrian Revolution 2011, Sham News Network, Insan, Sawasiah, Syrian Observatory for Human Rights). A number of these groups trace their roots back to the Damascus Spring of 2000, when Bashar al-Assad temporarily released some pressure from the Syrian pressure cooker after the death of his father. Others sprang up in the aftermath of the 2005 crisis when, after the assassination of President Rafiq Hariri, Lebanese launched their Cedar Revolution. The example of the Cedar Revolution and the ganging up of Western powers against Syria in international forums put the regime on the defensive, presenting opponents with an opening. Taking advantage of that opening, a broad coalition of groups, including the banned Syrian Muslim Brotherhood, signed on to the "Damascus Declaration" calling for a transition to democracy and pledging themselves to nonviolence and unity. Unfortunately for the opposition, Syria's defensive international posture did not last, and although the regime "tolerated" human-rights-type groups, their leaders could regularly expect to be jailed. The monitoring activities of these groups during the recent uprising have broken the news blackout imposed by the government and alerted the world to the atrocities being committed, but these groups have not been particularly successful at mobilizing substantial numbers of Syrians. Nevertheless, the government has taken them seriously enough to enter into a dialogue with some of the best known of their number.

The most intriguing group to participate in the uprising is something called the "Local Coordination Committees," whose communiqués began appearing in various places on April 22, 2011. The first communiqué made twelve demands, from ending the torture and imprisonment of peaceful demonstrators to amending the constitution to allow a democratic transition. It was signed by Local Coordination Committees in twelve towns and cities and two regions. It is likely that the committees have been behind the attempts to direct protests on specified days ("Day of Rage," "Day of Steadfastness," "Week of Raising the Siege of Daraa"), monitoring regime abuses, and sending out marching orders.

The "traditional opposition"—a category comprising a number of Kurdish and tribal leaders, dissident politicians, and the Syrian Muslim Brotherhood—has also aligned itself with the uprising. The brotherhood has been present only at opposition conferences outside Syria because it is illegal in Syria and its members are subjected to repression inside the country. And over the years, the brotherhood's opposition credentials among Syrians became tarnished. After 1982, the brotherhood redirected its focus away from overthrowing the regime to making peace with it. The justification was the regime's support for the Palestinian Islamist group Hamas and Palestinians in general—not a particularly convincing rationale. Once the uprising broke out, however, the brotherhood had its own Damascus road conversion (so to speak), declared its support for pro-democracy protesters, and called for a multiparty democracy.

The final group that has participated in the uprising is deserters from the army and their support networks. Included among the latter are merchants and smugglers, who have armed those who abandoned the military without weapons; local villagers, who have sheltered them; and the Turkish government, which has allowed deserters to establish a cross-border presence in Turkey. The activities of this group sparked a debate among other opposition groups about the efficacy of continued nonviolent protest. As the uprising spun out of control, that debate increasingly became moot.

There have been a number of attempts to bring the various elements of the opposition together around a common program and strategy, starting with a meeting held in May 2011 in Antalya, Turkey. Although the meeting established a set of committees to continue its work, issued a common declaration at the final session, and began a process that would culminate in the establishment of a permanent Syrian national council five months later, the acrimonious debate over just how secular Syria should be in the future, along with a fistfight between a Syrian-Kurdish and a Syrian-Arab delegate, does not bode well for future unity. In the meantime, the government initiated its own "national dialogue sessions" throughout Syria, which most of the opposition has boycotted.

It is worth mentioning one group that played an essential role in both the Tunisian and Egyptian uprisings but is missing in action in Syria: labor. As of this writing, there have been no wildcat strikes in support of the uprising; nor, to the best of anyone's knowledge, have there been serious attempts to organize trade unions independent of Syria's official trade union federation (as happened in Egypt).

Why have foreign powers treated Bashar al-Assad with kid gloves?

The international community responded to the Syrian regime's crackdown on the uprising with far less resolution than it showed in the case of Libya. Whereas the UN Security Council first imposed sanctions and then authorized military action against Libya, it has done no such thing against Syria. The United States and the European Union both imposed their own escalating sets of sanctions on Syria, but it took until July 2011 for Secretary of State Hillary Clinton to abandon the phrase "Bashar al-Assad is losing legitimacy" for the phrase "Bashar al-Assad has lost legitimacy" (President Obama went back to the previous phrase two days later, although he has since adopted Clinton's stronger language as his own). Whereas Washington repeatedly demanded that Qaddafi leave before and during the NATO bombardment, it repeatedly warned Bashar al-Assad, a bit meekly, to lead Syrian reform or get out of the way. Why the difference?

No international actor really wants to face the risk of an unstable or fragmented Syria such as might follow the collapse of the regime. For their part, American officials have believed that a collapse of the Syrian regime would be followed by one of two likely scenarios. On the one hand, there is the possibility of expanded sectarian violence, ethnic violence, or both, as Sunnis seek revenge against their former Alawi overlords (and those allied with the regime), or as Kurds square off against Arabs. On the other hand, there is the fear of a takeover by the Syrian Muslim Brotherhood.

Syria's immediate neighbors include Lebanon, Israel, Iraq, and Turkey. Policy makers believe sectarian violence would spill over into Lebanon, while ethnic divisions would have ramifications for Iraq and Turkey, which have their own sizable Kurdish communities. Further muddying the waters with American policy makers is the belief that only a strong autocrat at the helm in Syria can make the highly unpopular decision to sign a peace treaty with Israel. That is one of the reasons Obama attempted to reengage with Assad after his predecessor had severed relations with Syria in 2005.

Regional players also have a stake in a stable, if autocratic, Syria. Although Bashar al-Assad has not only maintained the state of war with Israel but presented Syria as a leader of the "resistance camp" against it, the border between the two states has remained quiet since 1973. The only time a problem did occur was in May 2011, during the uprising, when Palestinians in Syria staged a march to the Israeli border. Israeli border guards killed several, although one Palestinian made it as far as the Israeli coast before being arrested. One can assume that the Syrian government either knew about or orchestrated the march, perhaps to demonstrate what might happen if the heavy hand of the government were removed. Whatever the case, Israel's wariness of regime change in Syria gave rise to the improbable scene of Michael Oren, Israel's ambassador to the United States, making the rounds in Washington, D.C., to deny he had been organizing support for Assad.

Saudi Arabian leaders despise Assad and have been suspicious of his relationship with Iran. Nevertheless, they fear any shift in the status quo, particularly if it means the victory of a democratic movement. The traditionally timid Saudis recalled their ambassador to Damascus and denounced Assad's "killing machine" only after it became apparent that the uprising was not going away and that a change in Syria might actually benefit the kingdom by dealing a blow to Iranian influence in the Arab world.

Finally, in the case of Iran, Syria has proved to be a reliable partner, and its alliance with Syria provides Iran with a number of strategic benefits in the region. Syria has supported the Lebanese Shi'i group, Hizbullah (which has returned the favor), and opened its ports to Iranian warships, allowing Iran to project power into the Mediterranean. If the Iranians have been supplying Syria with assistance to put down the uprising—as American and European Union observers have asserted—this is surely the reason. (The Americans and Europeans accuse the Iranians of supplying the Syrians with the know-how to block the internet and social media, techniques pioneered by Iran during its own "Green Revolution" of 2009.)

What would happen to the Syrian alliance with Iran should Bashar al-Assad's regime fall?

Syrian opposition leaders say that, should they remove Bashar al-Assad from power, they will reorient Syria toward the United States and the West and away from Iran. Whether or not this is true or merely an attempt to curry favor, and whether or not anyone can speak for the current opposition (and, in the event of the opposition's victory, the future government of Syria), is of course a matter for conjecture. It seems logical that a pro-democracy movement would orient toward the West, particularly one fighting a regime allied with (and possibly aided by) Iran. However, among those who expect a dramatic shift in Syria's orientation should the opposition take power are some who base this expectation on their belief that the alliance between "Shi'i Iran" and "Alawite-dominated Syria" is rooted in religious affinities uniting two closely related minority sects of Islam. If there is majority (that is, Sunni) rule in Syria, they believe, Syria's natural inclination will be to tilt away from Iran and toward the predominantly Sunni Arab world.

Such reasoning is specious. The alliance between Syria and Iran, which began during the Iran-Iraq War (1980–1988), has not been based on religion; it is based on smart geostrategic reasoning. Syria was the only Arab country to align with Iran during that war. Syria derived economic benefits from this alliance in terms of discounted Iranian oil and inducements from Gulf Arab countries anxious to bring Syria back into the fold. Syria, a medium-sized state with a weak economy, also became an important regional player as both Iraq's allies and Iran offered political inducements to buy its favor. The current alliance with Iran continues to bolster Syria's anti-imperialist reputation and increases the price it can demand from the West in exchange for making peace with Israel or ensuring quiet in Lebanon. And with the Syria connection, Iran earns the cachet of a regional power whose field of operations stretches from the Mediterranean to the Gulf. Why tinker with that?

5

THE MONARCHIES

Why are there so many monarchies in the Arab world?

There are more monarchies in the Arab world (eight) than in any other region, save Europe (in which there are twelve, if one includes the Vatican): Morocco, Jordan, Saudi Arabia, Kuwait, Bahrain, Oman, Qatar, and the United Arab Emirates (the UAE). If one counts the number of monarchies in which kings or queens rule as well as reign, no other region of the world even comes close. Why is this the case?

In the past, scholars attributed the large number of monarchies in the Arab world to three factors: tradition, religion, and tribalism.[1] None of these factors holds up under scrutiny. In terms of tradition, there is little of it in the region to appeal to. Not only did all of the kingdoms in the region receive their independence in the mid-to-late twentieth century, it might be argued that none but Morocco was a distinct territorial unit until recently. Furthermore, the ancestors of contemporary rulers could not even begin to imagine the power wielded by their descendants or by the states those descendants ruled. This power is a product of the modern world—and, in the case of the Persian Gulf kingdoms, it is financed by revenues from oil, which was not exploited there until the 1930s. In other words, there is nothing traditional about modern kingdoms and kingship.

Scholars cited religion as a basis for monarchy because rulers need some reason to lord it over their subjects, and a special religious dispensation is as good a reason as any. And indeed, some rulers have played the religion card: among the titles of the king of Morocco is "commander of the faithful," a title that goes back to the early days of Islam. Both he and the king of Jordan claim descent from the prophet Muhammad, which puts them into a special category among Muslims. The king of Saudi Arabia, on the other hand, is not only the imam (leader) of the Wahhabi school of Islam (Wahhabism is a type of salafism promoted as the state ideology of Saudi Arabia) but also the "protector of the two holy cities" of Mecca and Medina. Apart from those three monarchs, however, one would be hard pressed to identify a fourth who uses religion to legitimate his rule.

Finally, some scholars argue that the rule of kings over states is similar to the rule of a tribal leader over his tribe, and this is why kingship is such a good fit for the "tribal" Arab world. Putting aside, for the moment, the question of whether designating the Arab world as "tribal" is accurate or, indeed, meaningful in any way, there are several problems with attributing the large number of kingdoms in the region to tribalism. First, the near-absolute power of the contemporary Arab king bears no resemblance to the "first among equals" role of most tribal leaders in the past, whose status was rarely formalized. In addition, tribes and modern states work at cross-purposes. Modern states can function only if they break the power of groups such as tribes that impose themselves between the state and the population the state seeks to rule directly. The few anomalies that fail to do so, such as pre-uprising Yemen and Libya, remain weak and vulnerable (and, it should be remembered, that even though one might associate Yemen and Libya with tribes, neither state retained its monarchy). Then there is Jordan, a monarchy in which tribes exist, but in which a majority of the population remains unaffiliated. The argument that the Arab world has monarchies because it is tribal is clearly wanting.

So if it is inaccurate to attribute the large number of monarchies in the Arab world to tradition, religion, or tribalism, then what does explain it? The only feasible explanation has to do with the historical circumstances that influenced formation of individual kingdoms in the region and are responsible for the endurance of those kingdoms.

Why did Morocco retain its king?

Although the king of Morocco bases his right to rule on his descent from a dynasty reaching back as far as the seventeenth century, the fact that Morocco is today a kingdom has more to do with the legacy of Morocco's nationalist struggle than with the legacy of tradition. Until the early twentieth century, the territory we associate with contemporary Morocco was an independent state ruled by a sultan (he became "king" after independence, but the two titles are equivalent). However, the sultan's power did not extend far beyond urban areas. In 1912, the Spanish and French, intent on resolving this part of the "scramble for Africa" amicably, split Morocco in two. The Spanish established a protectorate over the north, the territory closest to Spain, and the French established a protectorate over the remainder of the country. During the 1920s, a nationalist rebellion broke out in the Spanish protectorate. The rebellion's leader advocated not only an independent Morocco, but an independent Moroccan republic. The French and the Spanish, who depended on the sultan to provide a fig leaf of legitimacy for their presence, together put down the rebellion, thus preserving the sultan's rule. It was only in the 1930s that a nationalist party emerged that sought to benefit from the symbolic and religious stature of the sultan, and it was not until immediately after World War II that a sultan returned the favor and endorsed the nationalists' goal of independence for Morocco, which was won in 1956. Although at independence the nationalists controlled whatever rudimentary political structures that were in place, the palace controlled the army and police, which had pledged their allegiance to the sultan during the liberation struggle. The consequences were as one might expect, and power shifted from the nationalist politicians to the king. Hence, the extraordinary (but not particularly traditional) power of the monarchy against which protesters mobilized in 2011.

How did the Hashemite Kingdom of Jordan come to be?

Winston Churchill bragged that he had created Jordan "with the stroke of a pen one Sunday afternoon." This is only a bit of an exaggeration. The British invented Jordan in 1921 to provide a throne for one of the sons of Sharif Hussein of Mecca, an Arabian warlord who had pledged his support for the British cause during World War I (*sharif* is the title of a descendant of Muhammad). The British originally called the territory "Trans-Jordan"—that is, the territory across the Jordan (River), if one's point of reference is Britain. The British ran Trans-Jordan through an emir (prince) until 1946, at which time it received independence. Trans-Jordan/Jordan had never existed before as a territorial unit, much less a sovereign state, nor had there ever been an emir of Trans-Jordan. After independence "Trans-Jordan" became "Jordan"—actually, the "Hashemite Kingdom of Jordan," named after the ruling family—and the emir took the title of king.

What was the origin of the Kingdom of Saudi Arabia?

Like the Hashemite Kingdom of Jordan, the Kingdom of Saudi Arabia takes its name from the ruling dynasty because, as in the case of Jordan, the invention of the state and the enthronement of the ruling family took place simultaneously. The history of the "House of Saud" is linked historically with Wahhabism. The association between the family and the doctrine began in the mid-eighteenth century, when a local chieftain by the name of Muhammad ibn Saud met up with an itinerant preacher, Muhammad ibn Abd al-Wahhab. As the official story has it, the combination of sword and message proved unbeatable in Arabia. Actually, it was beatable, and after the suppression of the first Saudi state in 1818 and the collapse of a much smaller second Saudi state in 1891, it took until 1932 for the creation of a third. The House of Saud has ruled it ever since.

What was the British role in creating Gulf monarchies?

Beginning with their conquest of India in the eighteenth century, and continuing through the discovery of oil in the early twentieth century, the British took a strong interest in ensuring stability—and British dominance—in the Gulf. The Gulf was important to the British because of its proximity to India and, later, British oil facilities in southern Iran. Because it was situated at the frontier of the Ottoman Empire, where imperial control was weak, and because it was close to the expansive eastern coast of Africa, the Gulf was also a focal point for the British campaign to suppress piracy and the slave trade during the nineteenth century. The British thus played a key role in establishing monarchies there that would later become the State of Kuwait, the Sultanate of Oman, the Kingdom of Bahrain, the State of Qatar, and the United Arab Emirates.

Kuwait was the first state that the British carved from the Persian Gulf coastline to receive its independence. Members of the ruling house of Kuwait, the Sabah family, had emigrated to Kuwait with other clans from north/central Arabia during the eighteenth century and established themselves as the first-among-equals in what was to become a small city state. The Sabah family became a ruling dynasty in 1899 when the British, eager to suppress piracy and the slave trade, protect the route to India, and control trade, offered one of its members the position of emir in exchange for accepting a British protectorate. Like the House of Saud, the Sabah family has ruled ever since.

The Sultanate of Oman—the last remaining sultanate in a region awash with kingdoms—is the successor to a state known until 1970 as Muscat and Oman, a name that reflected the state's two large geographical divisions: northern Muscat, hugging the Persian Gulf coast, whose maritime economy was already in eclipse in the nineteenth century, and Oman, a far less cosmopolitan area oriented toward the Arabian Sea. Although never a British protectorate or colony, the state might as well have been; the British meddled in the affairs of Muscat and Oman throughout the nineteenth and twentieth centuries, defending the coast from the depredations of inland tribes, mediating royal disputes, and even arranging the coup d'état that the latest of the sultans, Qaboos, staged against his father to come to power.

The histories of Bahrain and Qatar are interwoven. During the eighteenth century, members of the Khalifa family, along with other families and tribes caught up in that century's great tribal migrations, conquered the island of Bahrain, ending two centuries of Persian rule. The conquest severed Bahrain from Persia, but it connected the island with the conquest's launch site, the peninsula that would become Qatar. During the nineteenth century, the inhabitants of the mainland rebelled, and even though the Bahrainis put down the rebellion the British used the Bahraini reinvasion of the peninsula as a justification to intervene, in the process recognizing Qatar as a distinct entity. The British even created a ruling dynasty for that entity: the Thani family, one of whose members had negotiated with the British during the crisis. The British established both Bahrain and Qatar as protectorates, a status they held until 1971. This was the year Britain implemented its "East of Suez" policy, so named because the British, responding to economic pressures, withdrew from their bases in the Middle East and Asia—that is, their bases east of Suez. Upon the British withdrawal, Bahrain, Qatar, and the principalities that would form the United Arab Emirates (UAE) became independent and attempted unification, but to no avail. The result was an independent Bahrain, under the Khalifa dynasty, and an independent Qatar, under the Thani dynasty.

Finally, the UAE. Before 1971, the seven emirates (principalities) that would become the UAE were known as the Trucial States because each had signed a treaty with the British pledging a "perpetual maritime truce" in the Gulf—that is, an end to piracy. In return, the British recognized the signatories—the heads of the leading families—as dynastic rulers. When the British withdrew from the Gulf, the emirates entered into a federation. Although the "president" and "prime minister" of the federation are, in theory, elected by the emirs of the seven states, the former position went to the emir of Abu Dhabi, the richest of the emirates, both times it was up for grabs. Similarly, the emir of Dubai, which is the most populous emirate, became the prime minister on the two occasions that job was open.

Why have so many monarchies in the Arab world endured?

The fact that all eight Arab monarchies have endured in spite of the fact that they exist in a world in which popular sovereignty constitutes the norm is a testament to the peculiar circumstances under which the state system in the Arab world has evolved. The contemporary Arab state system might be traced back only as far as the end of World War I, when Great Britain and France dismantled the Ottoman Empire and oversaw the transformation of Ottoman domains and frontier areas, along with their own protectorates and zones of occupation, into nation-states. The Arab state system thus evolved in the shadow of European, and then American, dominance in an age in which the acquisition of territory by force violates international norms. As a result, even the weakest states in the region found outside patrons whenever their existence was at stake. The British intervened in Jordan in 1958 when supporters of Gamal Abd al-Nasser threatened to overthrow the monarchy, deployed forces when Iraq threatened Kuwait in

1961, and assisted the government of Oman when that country confronted a separatist rebellion in the 1970s. Then, of course, there was the central role played by the United States in the Gulf War of 1991, when Iraq did more than just threaten Kuwait and when it appeared that Saudi Arabia might be at risk as well. Bahrain hosts the American Fifth Fleet to this very day, which is stationed in the Gulf to prevent a threat to Gulf (and American) security.

How has oil affected the stability of Arab monarchies?

Some Arab monarchies are hydrocarbon-rich, others are hydrocarbon-poor. All the Persian Gulf monarchies—that is, all the monarchies but Morocco and Jordan—are hydrocarbon-rich. As of 2010, oil exports accounted for 70 percent of Qatar's revenues, 90 percent of Saudi Arabia's, 94 percent of Kuwait's, and 95 percent of Abu Dhabi's. Even Bahrain, which is considered relatively oil-poor, currently derives 60 percent of its revenues from oil. Dependency on revenues from hydrocarbons has made the Gulf monarchies vulnerable to price fluctuations. This was bad news during the 1980s when the price of oil declined. However, before the recession of 2008 the price of oil rose consistently for six years, affording some monarchs a slush fund available for distribution after the outbreak of the uprisings in Tunisia and Egypt so that they might prevent or quell their own protest movements. True, the governments of both Jordan and Morocco have also made economic concessions to protesters. At the first sign of trouble, both governments restored subsidies they had eliminated or reduced as part of their economic restructuring, and both have lowered prices in their kingdoms. The difference, however, is that their pockets are not as deep as those of the governments in the Gulf. The Saudis have been particularly generous, announcing an estimated $130 billion worth of new expenditures to create sixty thousand new government jobs, raise the public sector minimum wage, grant bonuses to state employees, construct half a million new housing units, and relieve the personal debt of citizens. Of course, the effectiveness of such expenditures is hardly guaranteed: on the eve of the most turbulent protests that have broken out in a monarchy to date—the uprising in Bahrain—the king announced an unprecedented lump-sum payment of $2,650 to every Bahraini family. The protests continued anyway.

Some experts argue that a petroleum-based economy may also contribute to stability in another way. Throughout the Gulf, much of the population consists of noncitizen guest workers who have little stake in (and therefore little concern with) the political process of the states in which they work and whose involvement in protest would lead to deportation. Their presence enables the oil-rich monarchies to channel economic benefits—better jobs, housing, subsidies, and the like—to citizens. As of 2004, noncitizen guest workers made up between one-quarter and one-third of the inhabitants of Saudi Arabia, two-thirds of the inhabitants of Kuwait and Qatar, and four-fifths of the inhabitants of the UAE. Like economic concessions, the presence of noncitizen guest workers in and of itself has not been a guarantee of stability, however; in Bahrain, noncitizen guest workers make up about half the population. For that matter, they make up between one-quarter and one-third of the population of Libya.

As a matter of fact, a strong case might be made that in some states oil revenues actually contribute to disaffection with governments. They do this by triggering disputes over the fair distribution of the national wealth. For example, in the immediate aftermath of the Egyptian uprising, the bidoon population of Kuwait began holding antigovernment demonstrations. The word *bidoon* is Arabic for "without." Bidoons are Arab residents of Kuwait, often descendants of stateless bedouin, who are without citizenship and therefore without economic and political rights. Living in shanty towns while surrounded by opulence, they were undoubtedly unimpressed by the announcement made by the emir of Kuwait that his government would distribute $4 billion and free food for more than a year to Kuwait's citizens. In the UAE, disputes over the fair distribution of oil revenues pit oil-rich emirates against oil-poor ones. Oil revenues have made Abu Dhabi by far the wealthiest emirate, and three of the seven member emirates possess no oil at all, breeding discontent. In other places, such as Saudi Arabia and Bahrain, disputes over the distribution of oil revenues have taken a sectarian coloration: Saudi and Bahraini Shi'is complain that they suffer from a higher rate of unemployment and have access to fewer housing and educational opportunities than their Sunni compatriots.

How have ethnic and sectarian divisions affected the stability of Arab monarchies?

With the exception of the sultan of Oman, all the monarchs in the Arab world are Sunni Muslim (the sultan is, like a majority of Omanis, a member of an Islamic sect called Ibadi). In the Gulf, monarchs rule over societies that contain a significant number of Shi'is. In Bahrain, Shi'is are actually the majority, making up 70 percent of the population; in other places, they are a (sometimes substantial) minority. The division between Sunni and Shi'i matters only inasmuch as governments, activists, or both make it matter. And in this season of discontent, they have. In early 2011, protesters in the predominantly Shi'i Eastern Province of Saudi Arabia demanded an end to the systematic discrimination that Saudi Shi'is face. The government responded by painting the entire protest movement as an Iranian plot to destabilize the country (Iran is predominantly Shi'i and has played the role of "big brother" when it comes to Shi'i populations elsewhere). The Bahraini government followed a similar course: in March 2011, Bahrain requested military assistance from the Gulf Cooperation Council to put down the protest movement there, accusing its neighbor across the Gulf of "jeopardizing Bahrain's security and stability and sowing dissension among its citizens."[2]

In Morocco and Jordan, divisions also exist, but they do not follow sectarian lines. In Morocco, the main division is ethnic: anywhere from 40 to 70 percent of Moroccans are Berbers who have felt themselves economically, politically, and linguistically marginalized by the better educated, more urbanized Arab population. Berbers were active in the protest movement that broke out in Morocco in February 2011, calling it, in fact, the *Printemps Amazigh* ("Berber Spring"). Seizing on their demands for linguistic rights (and ignoring pretty much all their other demands, including those they shared with non-Berber protesters), the king endorsed a constitutional amendment recognizing the standardized Berber language as one of Morocco's official languages. Doing this was a ploy to co-opt one of the more symbolic planks of the opposition's platform and divert attention from the fact that the king had no intention of giving in to their main demand, which was to curb the powers of the monarchy.

The main division in Jordanian society separates those whose families originally came from the territory east of the Jordan River from those whose families came from the territory west of the Jordan River—that is, "East Bankers" and Palestinians ("West Bankers"). Palestinians began moving into Jordan during the creation of the State of Israel in 1948. They currently make up approximately 70 percent of the Jordanian population. Although Palestinians are accorded full rights of citizenship and have generally prospered in the private sector, East Bankers dominate the government and the public sector. In addition, the tribes of the East Bank are the main source of manpower for Jordan's military. As a result, East Bankers have been disproportionately affected by the wave of privatizations and government cutbacks that the Jordanian government began in earnest in 2003.

In January 2011 their dissatisfaction boiled over. Tellingly, a petition submitted to the king by thirty-six tribal leaders specifically cited excessive spending by the king's Palestinian wife as a primary example of regime corruption. The target of the petition was no accident but is indicative of the difficulty of organizing a protest movement in Jordan that encompasses both the East Bank and the Palestinian communities. Six months before the tribal leaders' petition, the National Veterans Committee, an organization to which tens of thousands of retired military men belong, circulated their own petition condemning the regime's corruption and its neoliberal economic policies—the sort of complaints that have sustained broad coalitions throughout the region. At the same time, however, the petition called for the disenfranchisement of Jordan's Palestinian population and guarantees that Jordan will never include the West Bank, with its nearly 2.5 million Palestinians.

Understanding the divisions among the populations of the Arab monarchies is not only important for understanding the vulnerabilities of the protest movements there; it is also important for understanding the coercive capabilities of the various states. According to political scientist F. Gregory Gause III:

> In divided societies, where the regime represents an ethnic, sectarian, or regional minority and has built an officer corps dominated by that overrepresented minority, the armies have thus far backed their regimes. The Sunni-led security forces in Bahrain, a Shi'ite-majority country, stood their ground against demonstrators to preserve the Sunni monarchy. The Jordanian army remains loyal to the monarchy despite unrest among the country's Palestinian majority. Saudi Arabia's National Guard, heavily recruited from central and western Arabian tribes, is standing by the central Arabian al-Saud dynasty. In each country, the logic is simple: if the regime falls and the majority takes over, the army leadership will likely be replaced as well.[3]

Only time will reveal the accuracy of this forecast, which comes from an article whose very title ("Why Middle East Studies Missed the Arab Spring") does little to inspire confidence.

Does monarchical rule inhibit development of political institutions?

A revealing difference among the monarchies has to do with the role extended monarchical families play in day-to-day governance and whether that role stifles the development of autonomous institutions. Another way of putting it is, "To what extent is a monarchy a wholly owned subsidiary of a royal family?" We might visualize the answer to this question in the form of a continuum, with Bahrain, Abu Dhabi, and in particular Saudi Arabia at the high end. In all three states, the royal family has operated in the same manner as the NDP did in Egypt before the uprising there: hundreds and even thousands of family members have occupied key positions in government and the business establishment, both of which are interconnected and function as cash cows for the connected (in the case of Saudi Arabia there is also the important link between royals and the influential religious community through marriage). On the other end of the spectrum are Jordan, Morocco, and even Kuwait with its raucous parliament. In these states power is centered in the monarchy, but monarchs maintain the appearance of being above the fray by delegating legislative authority. This is why during the initial Jordanian protests of January 2011 the protesters demanded the dismissal of the prime minister and cabinet and did not direct chants of *"Irhal!"* (Go!) in the direction of the king (protesters did the same in Kuwait in early June). Similarly, protesters demonstrating in February 2011 throughout Morocco demanded constitutional changes that would limit the powers of the monarchy; they did not demand the establishment of a republic.

There is an apocryphal story that in the 1980s the Jordanian government forbade the publishing of the American comic strip "The Wizard of Id" in the kingdom because it featured a character who wrote "The king is a fink" on the walls of buildings. The government, it seems, need not have been so touchy.

What were the demands of protesters in the Arab monarchies?

During the winter and early spring of 2011, protests broke out in every Arab monarchy but Qatar, whose day of rage was postponed several times before it was forgotten. Although some of the demands protesters made reflected local concerns, others were consistent from one monarchy to another. Days before the March 11 protests scheduled for Riyadh, Saudi Arabia's capital, protest organizers issued a fourteen-point manifesto entitled "Demands of the Saudi Youth for the Future of the Nation." As in most other monarchies, protesters in Saudi Arabia demanded expanded economic opportunities, an end to poverty (yes, there is poverty in Saudi Arabia), democratic reform, an end to corruption, transformation of the system of government to a constitutional monarchy, greater transparency in governance, equal rights for all citizens regardless of race or sect, release of "prisoners of conscience," and the like.

It being Saudi Arabia, protest leaders also focused on two concerns of local importance. First, since women's rights are more restricted in the kingdom than anyplace else in the Arab world except Yemen,[4] protesters demanded equal rights for women. "We demand an end to all forms of discrimination against women," the manifesto stated, "and giving women all their political, economic, social, and cultural rights... [including] their right to represent themselves without their guardian...."[5] In addition, Saudi protesters demanded disbandment of the "Committee for the Propagation of Virtue and the Prevention of Vice"—the religious police—which functions as a roving morals squad in the kingdom. According to the manifesto, the presence of the committee prevents citizens from developing their own sense of responsibility and self-censorship. Neither the Saudi protest movement nor most other protest movements among the Arab monarchies called for the abolition of the monarchy or for deposing the king. Protesters made such demands only in Bahrain, whose protest movement proved exceptional in a number of ways.

Who were the protesters in the Arab monarchies?

All the protest movements that emerged in the first months of 2011 have included a core of social networking youths whose ability to mobilize street demonstrations ranged from impressive to nonexistent. In many places, there was not a protest movement per se, but rather a number of individual protest movements made up of different groups with their own sets of grievances or demands acting simultaneously or in tandem. Shi'i protesters in the Saudi city of Qatif in the Eastern Province, who focused on anti-Shi'i discrimination and economic demands, acted independently from the more privileged social networkers in Riyadh, whose agenda concentrated on political demands. In Jordan, tribal leaders, the Islamic Action Front (the political arm of Jordan's Muslim Brotherhood), leftists and youths, and workers led or engaged in the protests, which were sometimes coordinated, sometimes not, that began in January and continued into the summer. As with the Saudi protests and others, the Jordanian protests took place both in the capital and beyond. Wherever they took place, the protests took on a local coloration in terms of their demands and the profile of the participants.

How did Arab monarchs react to protests?

Overall, the protests have evoked similar responses from monarchy to monarchy. All monarchies, to a greater or lesser extent, have attempted to relieve economic pressures that contributed to popular anger by distributing benefits in the form of cash bonuses, jobs, lower food prices, and higher subsidies for consumer goods. They have also promised further benefits in the future. At the same time, the monarchies are not shy about displaying shows of force or engaging in acts of repression that have been so heavy-handed that they would appear comical if they were not so tragic. Qatar's lone raging blogger, whose quest to mobilize protesters for that kingdom's day of rage was in vain, found himself in jail, and even though a heavy presence of security agents have been able to swat aside small groups of protesters in Riyadh, they did not hesitate to use lethal force against Shi'is in the Eastern Province. And when it comes to repression, Bahrain once again is in a category of its own.

Finally, a number of monarchies have attempted to co-opt the demands of the opposition. As a matter of fact, one sociologist/political scientist argues that when it comes to co-optation, monarchies are better suited than republics, since their political structures are more flexible. Monarchs, he argues, can mollify crowds by ceding day-to-day governance to a legislature or prime minister, yet still keep executive power within the dynasty.[6] This flexibility also creates an environment in which monarchs themselves can push for (limited) political reforms, painting those in the government who oppose them as "reactionary" while gathering accolades for themselves as reformers (with the possible exception of the ruler of the UAE, all current rulers in the Arab world, even the kings of Bahrain and Saudi Arabia, have donned the mantle of "reformer" at one time or another). Hence, after sacking his prime minister in the wake of protests, King Abdullah of Jordan wrote a public letter to his prime minister–designate, asserting that Jordan's progress to democracy "has been marred by gaps and imbalances resulting from fear of change by some who resisted it to protect their own interests."[7]

The most successful case of co-optation during recent protests may be the one in Morocco, where a group calling itself the February 20 Movement (the Moroccan equivalent of Egypt's April 6 Movement) called for demonstrations throughout the kingdom on that day and issued a list of demands. The first two items on the list were the transformation of the constitutional monarchy into a parliamentary monarchy where "the king only reigns but does not rule," and the promulgation of a new constitution to be approved by the population.[8] The king agreed to a new constitution, but rather than preparing for the election of a constitutional assembly as the movement leaders expected, he appointed a committee to revise the document. Once their work was done, he put the new constitution to a vote. The new one was hardly what protest leaders had gone out on the street for; it does not explicitly lay out the chain of command linking the king to the elected prime minister, gives the king the power to declare a state of emergency and rule by decree, and gives the king, not the prime minister, the ultimate power to dissolve parliament and declare new elections. Furthermore, the king chairs every important council of state, from the Supreme Council of the Judiciary to the Supreme Security Council. And, for good measure, the constitution makes the king the commander-in-chief of the Royal Armed Forces. The new constitution won 98.5 percent of the vote in a referendum. Game. Set. Match?

How did the uprising in Bahrain differ from uprisings in other monarchies?

With the exception of Bahrain, Morocco, and perhaps Jordan, the protests of winter/spring 2011 in the Arab monarchies were limited, transient affairs, particularly when put in the context of uprisings elsewhere. Only time will tell if future historians continue to see them this way or categorize one or more of them as opening acts to further dramas. Whatever the case, the uprising in Bahrain stands out from all the others for two reasons. First, after the government met the protesters' initial demand for reform with violence, the uprising took a decidedly antimonarchical turn. Second, the manner of its suppression marked a new strategy for mounting counterrevolution in the region.

In the wake of events in Tunisia and Egypt, Bahraini activists, taking advantage of the anonymity of social media, called for their own Day of Rage protests to be held in the capital,

Manama, and elsewhere. Protests were not new to the country; they had been ongoing for upward of two decades. Sometimes protests had focused primarily on political issues, such as the king's on-again, off-again promises of political reform, and violations of human rights so widespread that a 2010 report of Human Rights Watch warned of "a return to full blown authoritarianism."[9] Social issues, such as unemployment and poor housing, had sparked other protests. Organizers of the February 14 protests demanded constitutional reform, free elections, release of prisoners of conscience, and an end to torture. They also made two other demands that the regime seized on to characterize the movement as sectarian: they demanded a truly representative consultative council (which, if truly representative, would have meant a majority Shi'i consultative council), and an end to "political naturalization"—that is, an end to the practice of naturalizing Sunni Arabs as citizens to raise the proportion of Sunnis in the population and to expand the predominantly Sunni military and security forces. (Readers can draw their own conclusions as to why soldiers in Qaddafi's Islamic Pan-African Brigade, drawn from sub-Saharan Africa, have commonly been called "mercenaries" in the media while Bahrain's equally bought-and-paid-for Arab soldiers have not.) As a result of this policy, there was little chance of the military and the security forces going over to the opposition, splintering, or even remaining neutral. Security forces thus broke up the February 14 protests throughout the country, drawing the first blood in a village in the north, then again at the victim's funeral procession the next day.

In Manama, organizers attempted to make the "Pearl Square" roundabout their Tahrir Square (pearl diving was Bahrain's most important industry before the invention of artificial pearls in the early twentieth century and the discovery of oil, and a huge monument with a pearl on top marked the roundabout). The security forces dispersed the protesters the first day, but when news of the killings spread the crowds grew. As members of legal and illegal political associations and Bahrainis from nearby villagers descended on the roundabout, Pearl Square came to resemble as much a street fair as the site of a political protest, just as Tahrir Square had in the waning days of the Egyptian protests. And as in the case of their Egyptian counterparts, Bahrainis occupying the square stuck as much as possible to a tactic of nonviolence, even in the face of provocation by baltagiya (thugs hired by the government). Nevertheless, the government also learned a lesson from the Egyptian protests. In the early morning of the fourth day, security forces stormed the roundabout, killing four, some reportedly as they slept.

The storming of Pearl Square was the first of two events that transformed the nature of the Bahraini uprising. Its effects were seen in a number of ways. Over the course of the next month, the number of protesters in downtown Manama swelled as associations of engineers, lawyers, and teachers, along with politicians and trade unionists, joined the protests. More significantly, the momentum of the protests shifted from those willing to engage in a dialogue with the regime (such as the largest of the legal political associations) to those calling for the downfall of the regime (such as the largest of the illegal political associations and many of the original protest organizers). In addition, although the slogans chanted by the protesters remained intersectarian, Shi'i religious leaders and grassroots organizers increasingly took the public stage.

The second event that transformed the nature of the uprising came in the wake of a planned march from the square to Manama's financial district. After the storming of the square, the confrontation between the government and the protesters had settled into a stalemate, with hardliners inside and outside the government pressing to finish the job and others inside and outside the government pressing for compromise. The government of Saudi Arabia was in the first grouping, that of the United States in the latter. The former grouping took the day. Exactly one month after the protests began, a thousand troops from Saudi Arabia and five hundred policemen from the UAE crossed the causeway linking Bahrain with the mainland and took up positions around government buildings, freeing up Bahrain's own military and security forces to partake in a binge of repression. For the first time, an Arab uprising was put down by the military intervention of foreign powers.

How have the uprisings transformed the Gulf Cooperation Council?

The Gulf Cooperation Council (GCC) is an organization made up of Gulf kingdoms that was formed in 1981 to promote cooperation in cultural, economic, and political affairs. Three years after its founding, the council took on a military dimension as well with the formation of a joint military force known as Peninsula Shield to deter and respond to aggression against any member state. Even though all the kingdoms are theoretically equal within the council framework, Saudi Arabia, the largest and wealthiest one, has played the dominant role. Since the uprisings began in the winter of 2011, the GCC has become what one political scientist pointedly called "the institutional home of the counterrevolution."[10] Under the guise of protecting Bahrain from Iranian subversion, Peninsula Shield forces assisted the government there in putting down the uprising, and the GCC offered Bahrain and Oman $20 billion in post-uprising economic assistance. The GCC also put forward its own compromise plan to quell the uprising in Yemen. Just as indicative of the transformation of the GCC's mission is its offer of membership to Jordan and Morocco, two non-Gulf monarchies whose only connection with the Gulf kingdoms is that they are also run by Sunni monarchs who have faced uprisings. (On the other hand, Iraq, which abuts the Gulf, received no such offer, perhaps because it would threaten Saudi Arabia's dominance of the organization, perhaps because of the role played by Shi'is in Iraqi governance since the American invasion in 2003.) Some experts link the GCC's new sense of purpose with Saudi Arabia's dissatisfaction with America's handling of the uprisings—particularly America's last-minute decision to abandon Hosni Mubarak, a staunch ally—and its fear that the United States might not be up to the task of preventing the expansion of Iranian influence in the region.

What might Bahrain's experience with a "national dialogue" tell us about future national dialogues in the Arab world?

The idea of resolving the issues that led to the uprisings in the Arab world through a "national dialogue" was first broached in Tunisia soon after the outbreak of the uprising there. It was taken up in a number of other cases, including Egypt and Yemen, and embraced by the Obama administration as a way to square its foreign policy circle by balancing America's desire to shore up autocratic allies while at the same time living up to its pro-human rights, pro-democracy rhetoric. Skeptics have looked at the call for a national dialogue as a cynical ploy on the part of rulers to play for time, split the opposition, make promises that will never be kept, and paint regime opponents as radical by presenting themselves as moderate "voices of reason."

Unlike the ill-fated call for national dialogue in Egypt and Yemen, the Bahraini government held a full-blown national dialogue, albeit while GCC troops were on the streets. What can the Bahraini national dialogue tell us about this tactic?

Although the king called for the national dialogue, he did not take part. Instead, the prime minister delegated the job of chairing the dialogue to one of his cronies, who heard presentations from three hundred participants about their visions for Bahrain's future. Of the three hundred, only thirty-five came from the legal opposition, and none of those who initiated the Pearl Square uprising participated, mostly because so many were in jail. In the end, the testimony was recorded, edited, and presented to the king in print form. It is up to the king to choose which, if any, recommendations to implement. Even the official government account found it difficult to spin Bahrain's national dialogue as a step in the direction of democracy:

> The National Dialogue completed its political discussions with consensus to further enhance the powers of the elected parliament.... Delegates agreed to grant the elected parliament greater legislative and monitoring powers. In particular, the presence of ministers will be required when MPs debate issues related to their respective ministries. MPs will be able to question ministers during the parliamentary sessions rather than in specific committees. The Parliament will be entitled to initiate discussions on any theme in addition to the agenda. Overall, these decisions reinforce the parliament's powers of scrutiny over the activities of the government, strengthening the accountability of ministers to the elected representatives of the people. Delegates did not reach consensus on a number of further suggestions, including whether the [appointed] Shura [consultative] Council should be granted the same powers as the Parliament, and whether the responsibility for law-making and oversight should be restricted to the elected chamber....[11]

6

STEPPING BACK

Was George W. Bush right?

The first time the phrase "Arab Spring" appeared in print was in 2005 in the wake of a series of events—including elections in Iraq and the Cedar Revolution in Lebanon—that some commentators believed were inspired by George W. Bush's "freedom agenda." Bush had announced his freedom agenda in a speech delivered in November 2003. "Sixty years of Western nations excusing and accommodating the lack of freedom in the Middle East did nothing to make us safe—because in the long run, stability cannot be purchased at the expense of liberty," Bush declared. "As long as the Middle East remains a place where freedom does not flourish, it will remain a place of stagnation, resentment and violence ready for export."[1] The Bush administration thus announced its public commitment to "democracy promotion" in the region. Two years after Bush's speech, Secretary of State Condoleeza Rice reiterated Bush's theme, declaring, "Throughout the Middle East, the fear of free choices can no longer justify the denial of liberty. It is time to abandon the excuses that are made to avoid the hard work of democracy." In the wake of the uprisings in Tunisia and Egypt, former Bush associates and their supporters in the press made what seemed to them the logical connection between then and now: the freedom agenda worked.

Others, however, have not found the connection so logical. Some assert that the connection the Bush administration made between "democracy promotion" and the American invasion of Iraq so linked "democracy" with "American imperialism" that pro-democracy activists in the Arab world were put on the defensive rather than empowered. They also assert that after a brief flirtation with the freedom agenda, the Bush administration pretty much returned to business as usual (rhetoric aside). Thus, when Rice returned to Cairo a year and a half after her 2005 speech there, she dropped all talk of democratic reform. Instead of pressuring Hosni Mubarak on human rights and democracy, she appealed to him for his assistance in restarting the stalled negotiations between Israelis and Palestinians.

Finally, there was the difference between the broad strategy the freedom agenda called for to bring about change and the broad strategy the uprisings have applied. The freedom agenda took a top-down approach, assuming concessions by autocrats would, over time, lead to true reform. Hence, the attempts to get them to undertake electoral reform and hold free elections. Populations in the region, on the other hand, knew that no autocrat would make any concession liable to put him out of business. Thus they took matters into their own hands. Indeed, a cynic might argue that elections held in Egypt, Jordan, and Bahrain in 2010 at American urging *are*, in fact, connected to the current pro-democracy movements because the governments so manipulated electoral results that the only option for those who truly wanted change was to ignore electoral politics altogether and take to the streets.

Perhaps the most telling argument against associating the uprisings with the freedom agenda comes from looking at the history of movements for democratic and human rights in the Arab world, a history that predates the Bush administration's concern with the issue. Algeria experienced its pro-democracy uprising in 1988, strikes for workers' rights in Tunisia and Egypt go back decades, Syrian human rights groups emerged during the "Damascus Spring" of 2000, and protest movements advocating one man, one vote in Bahrain date back to the mid-1990s. In addition, during the very month that Bush announced his freedom agenda, the king of Morocco, bowing to popular pressure, established the Equity and Reconciliation Commission to investigate human rights abuses in the country between 1960 and 1999—the so-called years of lead—when his father ruled. It is unlikely that any of the commentators who attribute the uprisings to the freedom agenda know any of this.

How did the United States come up with its policy toward the uprisings?

According to inside accounts, when Barack Obama became president in 2009 the prevailing view among his foreign policy staff was that the United States had expended far too much time and effort on Middle East issues during the administration of George W. Bush and far too little time and effort on Chinese and Pacific Rim issues—a policy that had contributed to American decline. This was one of the reasons Obama ordered the continued drawdown of American troops from Iraq and the eventual drawdown of American troops from Afghanistan. This was also in part why he used so much political capital in the early days of his administration trying to bring about a quick resolution to the interminable Israeli-Palestinian conflict. Once the conflict was resolved, Obama believed, other pieces of the Middle East puzzle would simply fall into place and the United States could turn its attention to more pressing matters.

Events in the Arab world overtook the refocus of American policy, and although Obama and top policy makers may not have foreseen the Tunisian uprising and those that followed, they were not totally unprepared either. Like some political scientists studying the Arab world, they saw, in general terms, the problems that might arise in the area as a result of aging autocrats and a series of succession crises. In August 2010, four months before the outbreak of the first uprising, Obama circulated a memorandum entitled "Political Reform in the Middle East and North Africa" to his top civilian and military advisors.[2] It noted a recent uptick in both unrest and repression in the region, which could imperil American interests there: "Our regional and international credibility will be undermined if we are seen or perceived to be backing repressive regimes and ignoring the rights and aspirations of citizens." Obama ordered a response that would maintain American interests while taking into account the on-the-ground situation in each country.

Although making the United States appear sometimes indecisive, sometimes hypocritical, the Obama administration consciously moved away from any all-encompassing doctrine such as the "freedom agenda" or the "you're either with us or with the terrorists" policy of the previous administration. Those policies, the Obama administration believed, had tied the hands of American policy makers and made them bend themselves out of shape in an attempt to justify any actions that deviated from the doctrine. Hence, the approach taken by Obama was based on a country-by-country assessment of policy needs: Egypt and Jordan, the administration believed, are key to resolving the Israel-Palestine conflict and Egypt carries a great deal of weight in the Arab world simply because of its size; Yemen plays a critical role in America's counterterrorism campaign; Bahrain is the home port to the U.S. Navy's Fifth Fleet; Saudi Arabia is the world's largest oil producer; the unraveling of Syria would have widespread implications for regional stability.

Guided by independent assessments of American objectives in each country and by events as they unfolded, the administration first supported Mubarak, then called for a transitional government in which Mubarak would play an ambiguous role. The administration spoke with a single, unambiguous voice only a few days before Mubarak resigned, telling the Egyptian president that he had to go. On the other hand, the administration hedged its bets in Yemen, Bahrain, and Syria, supporting "national dialogues" between rulers and the opposition. In the case of Yemen, the administration eventually decided the game was up for Saleh (although he initially ignored the message); in the case of Bahrain, the administration turned a blind eye to both the Saudi-UAE invasion and the horrific human rights abuses that took place thereafter; and in the case of Syria, the administration maintained in public that Assad could become part of the solution rather than part of the problem long after he had demonstrated he could not. As for Saudi Arabia, the administration had to demonstrate two things: it would not abandon its friends in the region, and it would provide a shield for the Gulf states from any threat from Iran. In the end, it demonstrated neither. If the United States needed a place to demonstrate it was still a power to be reckoned with, that place would have to be Libya.

It is far too early to determine the effects of the American response to the uprisings on future American influence in the region; too much depends on how the uprisings play themselves out, the actions and reactions of regional players, and the perception in the region about whether or not America is truly in a state of decline. For an administration that has touted the importance of tempering "hard power" with "soft power" in foreign affairs—that is, tempering the use of force with diplomacy and cultural interchange—there is, however, cause for concern. Six months after Zine al-Abidine Ben Ali fled Tunisia, a poll taken in Morocco, Egypt, Lebanon, Jordan, Saudi Arabia, and the United Arab Emirates indicated that Obama's approval ratings were even lower than those for Bush at the end of his term.[3]

Whatever happened to Iraq?

The Bush administration argued that after "liberation" from Saddam Hussein, Iraq would become a beacon of democracy in the Middle East. However, things did not go as planned. Although Operation Iraqi Freedom proved successful in toppling the Iraqi government, the postwar occupation floundered. By the spring of 2004 coalition forces found themselves first confronting a reinvigorated insurgency, then sectarian violence. Violence subsided—not ended, but subsided—only in 2007. In 2005, Iraq held its first post-Saddam election for parliament. In line with the adage that democracy does not begin with holding a first election but with holding a second, Iraqis went to the polls again to elect representatives in 2010. One would expect, then, that Iraq would remain quiet at a time pro-democracy uprisings swept the region. This was, however, not the case.

Iraq hosted its own Day of Rage on February 25, 2011 (an event overshadowed in the international media by the deepening crisis in Libya). From Mosul in the north to Basra in the south, tens of thousands of Iraqis went out on the streets protesting shortages of electricity and water, high unemployment, and the government corruption and gridlock that they held responsible for their plight. Rather than being a beacon, Iraq's democracy was virtually dysfunctional. After the March 2010 elections, it took eight months before the United States was able to broker a power-sharing agreement between the leaders of the two largest parliamentary blocs so that a government might be formed. Not that it mattered all that much; the central government was so weak that most powers had devolved from the national to provincial governments, which bickered incessantly with the central government and with each other over provincial boundaries, power sharing, and the control of resources. It was probably for this reason that many of the protesters vented their rage by attacking the headquarters of those governments. It was probably also for this reason that the protests were disjointed, bearing a closer resemblance to protests in Algeria than to those in Egypt.

Fifteen Iraqis died on February 25, and the Iraqi prime minister's promise to hold his ministers accountable for the functioning of their ministries had the effect of quieting the protests only because it was accompanied by a show of force put on by the American-trained security forces. In all, it appears that whatever the future holds in store for Egypt, the legacy of Tahrir Square, not the legacy of Operation Iraqi Freedom, will provide the beacon of democracy in the region.

Have the uprisings strengthened or weakened al-Qaeda?

The year 2011 was not a good one for al-Qaeda. In early May, U.S. Navy Seals stormed a compound in Abbottabad, Pakistan, and shot dead Osama bin Laden, al-Qaeda's mastermind. Although this event grabbed the headlines, it is debatable just how important bin Laden remained to an organization that had become one in name only. For years, a number of al-Qaeda franchises—al-Qaeda in Mesopotamia, al-Qaeda in the Arabian Peninsula, al-Qaeda in Islamic North Africa—had operated autonomously and not always without friction. When al-Qaeda in Mesopotamia adopted the strategy of provoking sectarian conflict between Iraqi Sunnis and Shi'is to radicalize the former, for example, it received a strong rebuke from "al-Qaeda central." Thus it is entirely possible that historians of the future will mark the Arab uprisings, not the assassination of bin Laden, as the milestone event for al-Qaeda in 2011.

At first glance, it might seem that the uprisings afforded both ideological and tactical openings for al-Qaeda. They removed or threatened autocrats who had warred on their Islamist opposition and on al-Qaeda, autocrats who had supported American policies such as a two-state solution for the Israel-Palestine conflict and the global war on terrorism. Not only might it be argued that the uprisings have weakened the American position in the region by eliminating American proxies, they have weakened the control of some Arab governments over their territories, thus providing al-Qaeda affiliates with sanctuaries from which they might "vex and exhaust" their enemies.[4] By fostering an environment in which repression was lifted and people could more freely debate a wide spectrum of ideas, they created an environment in which al-Qaeda could more openly compete for hearts and minds.

Finally, the uprisings in Libya, Yemen, Syria, and Bahrain seemingly confirmed al-Qaeda's core belief that victory against oppression could be won only through violence.

On the other hand, there were aspects of the uprisings that al-Qaedists found difficult to deal with. For years they argued that removing local autocrats—the "near enemy"—did not matter so long as the "Crusader-Zionist" alliance—the "far enemy"—still controlled the world and warred against Islam. Protesters in the Arab world clearly did not listen and even scored successes by taking on the near enemy. Al-Qaedists believe that the boundaries separating Muslim states from each other were engineered by the Crusader-Zionist alliance to divide Muslims and keep them weak. Thus the boundaries and the divisions they foster had to go. Although protesters in various countries found inspiration and learned from protests elsewhere in the Arab world, each uprising was a *national* uprising, targeting a specific government against which protesters held specific grievances. Al-Qaedists believe that the Crusader-Zionist conspiracy against Islam obligates every Muslim to engage in "defensive jihad," which, for them, means armed struggle. Yet from Tunisia to Egypt to Bahrain, protesters embraced the tactic of nonviolent resistance. Finally, al-Qaedists believe that Muslims should obey the rule of God, not the rule of man, and that true freedom lies in obedience to Islamic law and freedom from the materialism and oppression of the West. Yet the central demands of the protesters include democratic governance—rule by the majority, not by the word of God—and respect for internationally accepted norms of human rights. These are certainly not al-Qaeda's ideals.

Clearly, the uprisings put al-Qaeda on the defensive, which is evident in the strained efforts its adherents have made to put a positive spin on everything from the tactics used by the protesters to the goals of the uprisings. "We didn't mean that non-violence is not a useful tactic, only that non-violence must be accompanied by violent jihad to be effective," they write on their web pages and announce in their videos. "We didn't mean you should focus only on the far enemy—sometimes it is necessary to focus first on the near enemy." "We didn't mean that democracy might not be a possible way station on the path to God's rule, only that it is not the final destination." Al-Qaedists are quick to remind Tunisians and Egyptians that nothing in their countries has really changed because the Crusader-Zionist conspiracy will just replace two of its puppets with others, Libyans that their fight demonstrates the futility of nonviolence, and Syrians that their problem is rule by disbelievers (Alawites). Then there are the open letters to opposition movements, all of which follow the same format, that are posted on the Internet:

> We salute our brothers in X for rising up against the bloody regime of Y. Understand, however, that simply replacing Y will not end your oppression. That will only come about by destroying the Crusader-Zionist conspiracy that keeps us subjugated. We cannot be free unless we replace the rule of man—which is tyrannical whether it be in the form of autocracy or democracy—with the rule of God everywhere there are Muslims.[5]

It is important to point out, however, that if the uprisings indeed have the effect of turning people away from al-Qaeda in the Arab and Muslim worlds, they only accelerate an ongoing trend. Surveys conducted by the Pew Global Attitudes Project found that starting from an initial high in 2003, there has been an overall erosion of support for bin Laden and al Qaeda in every state surveyed, except, for some reason, Nigeria.[6] For example, in answer to the question "How much confidence do you have in Osama bin Laden to do the right thing regarding world affairs?" the percentage of those answering "a lot" or "some" fell by at least a half—and sometimes quite a bit more, depending on the country—from 2003 to the months leading up to his assassination. How can this decline be explained? One reading of the polls is that the first findings were made on the heels of 9/11 and the American invasion of Iraq and reflected what Germans call *Schadenfreude* (delight in another's—in this case, America's—misfortune). The last surveys, conducted in the wake of far too much al-Qaeda-induced savagery with far too little to show for it, reflected something akin to "buyer's remorse." This is the good news. The bad news is that it is possible the trend might change should the uprisings fail to induce substantial reforms anywhere in the region.

What was the state of the Israel-Palestine conflict at the time of the first uprisings?

By the time the uprisings began in December 2010, the Israel-Palestine conflict had been stalemated for years. On the one hand, the Palestinian national movement could not negotiate effectively with Israel because it was split between Fatah, the largest grouping within the Palestine Liberation Organization (PLO), which controlled the West Bank, and the Islamist group Hamas, which was not part of the PLO and which seized control over Gaza in 2007. For their part, the last three Israeli prime ministers had not been ideologically disposed to making compromises on such critical issues as the future status of Jerusalem and the growth of Israeli settlements in the West Bank. Even were this not the case, the prime minister who governed when the uprisings first broke out, Benjamin Netanyahu, was incapable of making compromises lest his shaky coalition government collapse. Both George W. Bush and Barack Obama attempted to broker a settlement, but to no avail. The stalemate continued.

What effects have the uprisings had on the Israel-Palestine conflict so far?

The Arab uprisings have had two effects on the Israel-Palestine dispute. First, with the overthrow of Hosni Mubarak, the

United States and Israel lost a reliable collaborator on Israel-Palestine issues. The Egyptian population has always enjoyed the benefits of peace with Israel but for the most part never *embraced* peace with Israel. Since taking power, Egypt's Supreme Council of the Armed Forces has sought to garner support for itself by bowing to popular sentiment on this issue. It is, after all, secondary to the council's main concern, which is to maintain control of Egypt. The council pledged that it will uphold obligations under the peace treaty Egypt signed with Israel in 1979, but it has also sent the United States and Israel clear signals that it has no intention of following Mubarak's compliant course.

The council broadcast its intentions early on. Soon after assuming power it announced that it would no longer cooperate with Israel's policy of blockading Gaza—a policy Israel claimed was necessary to prevent the smuggling of weapons into the territory, but one that most Egyptians did not support. Mubarak had cooperated with the blockade because the United States and Israel asked him to and because there was no love lost between him and Hamas, a group with close relations to the Egyptian Muslim Brotherhood. He certainly did not wish to grant Palestinian Islamists access to Egypt, which they would have had if Egypt opened the border crossing with Gaza, nor did he wish to ease the economic plight of Gazans who might have credited Hamas for their better fortunes. With Mubarak gone and the Egyptian Muslim Brotherhood entering into the political process, there was no need for an Egyptian government to maintain the policy, and so the supreme council opened the crossing, albeit with restrictions.

In addition, the council brokered a new round of reconciliation talks between Fatah and Hamas. Talks between the two factions had dragged on for years, in part because of bad blood between them, in part because Mubarak put Omar Suleiman, his intelligence chief and future vice president, in charge of them. Rather than facilitating reconciliation, Suleiman strung out the talks with the blessings of the United States and Israel, both of which considered Hamas a terrorist group to be suppressed rather than a political group to be brought into the fold. As of this writing, reconciliation is still to be worked out, but the Egyptians did what they could.

The Egyptian initiative was not the only reason reconciliation talks began in earnest. Besides toppling a regime that was more than willing to work hand-in-glove with the United States and Israel, the uprisings gave both Fatah and Hamas an incentive to pursue reconciliation, while at the same time putting them on notice if they failed to do so.

With the overthrow of Mubarak, Fatah lost its chief patron in the Arab world, and once the Syrian uprising broke out it appeared entirely possible that Hamas would lose *its* patron as well. More important, the uprisings shook the leadership of both factions. Both Fatah and Hamas are dinosaurs. Fatah was founded in the 1950s, during the glory days of national liberation movements. Hamas was founded in the 1980s, when violent Islamic movements seemed the wave of the future. Most of the population of the Palestinian territories is too young to remember the excitement and hope that each group aroused when it first burst on the scenes. And most of the population of the territories has been closely watching developments in the rest of the Arab world, where new forms of political activism are replacing stale models. Indeed, at the very moment the Tunisian uprising was gathering steam, a group calling itself Gaza Youth Breaks Out posted a manifesto on Facebook entitled "Gaza's Youth Manifesto for Change." The manifesto begins "F— Hamas. F— Israel. F— Fatah," and goes on to declare, "There is a revolution growing inside of us, an immense dissatisfaction and frustration that will destroy us unless we find a way of canalizing this energy into something that can challenge the status quo and give us some kind of hope."[7] That energy was "canalized" through the March 15 youth movement, a loose association of social-media-savvy young people, similar to Egypt's April 6 Movement, that began holding demonstrations in both the West Bank and Gaza demanding reconciliation.

And there was a further reason for reconciliation: Since the peace process with Israel was hopelessly deadlocked, Palestinian leaders decided to take their case to the United Nations to seek recognition for statehood there. Reconciliation would be the first step in that process, since the international community would be more inclined to recognize a state in which the major political players agreed to play nice than one rife with violent divisions.

Thus it was that in short order the Egyptians defied the United States and Israel with respect to the blockade of Gaza, the Egyptians and the Palestinians defied the United States with respect to the reconciliation of Hamas and Fatah, and the Palestinians defied the United States by circumventing American-sponsored bilateral talks with Israel. In the 1970s, Egyptian president Anwar al-Sadat remarked that he had renounced Egypt's alliance with the Soviet Union in favor of an alliance with the United States because the United States "held 99 percent of the cards in the region." Such a statement could not be made today. There are multiple reasons for declining American influence in the Arab world—its Iraq policy, the economic meltdown of 2008, China's emergence as a major economic and political power, Turkey and Iran's claim to regional leadership, etc. When it comes to the Israel-Palestine front, at least, the Arab uprisings must also be given their due.

How has Iran greeted the uprisings?

The first "Twitter Revolution" (again, the media's term, not mine) in the Middle East took place in Iran in 2009 after widespread electoral irregularities made many Iranians suspect that their presidential election had been stolen. The army and the reigning *faqih* (the supreme religious and political figure in the country) both sided with the declared winner, and together they unleashed a wave of repression that snuffed out the uprising. A year and a half later, the Iranian regime found itself in the ironic position of heaping praise on participants in all but one of the uprisings—Syria's. To the extent that the uprisings weaken America's position in the region, the Iranian leadership views them as strengthening Iran's.

Iran and the United States have had a hostile relationship since the Iranian Revolution in 1979, although there were periods of thaw. Iranian policy makers viewed the American invasion of Iraq in 2003 as both an opportunity and a wake-up call. It was an opportunity not only because it got the United States bogged down in a bloody and expensive land war that was widely unpopular in the region but also because Iraq was a powerful and hostile neighbor and, with the exception of the United States, the only power capable of blocking the expansion of Iranian influence in the Persian Gulf. Post-invasion Iraq was far less powerful and far more open to Iranian meddling, both of which strengthened Iran's strategic position.

The American invasion of Iraq acted as a wake up call because more than ever Iranian policy makers viewed the world in defensive terms. After all, with troops in Iraq, Afghanistan, the Gulf, and elsewhere in the region, the United States had Iran virtually surrounded. This is one reason Iran has chosen not to give up its quest for nuclear weapons, and this is why Iran increasingly saw the Middle East as a zero-sum game against the United States, with a loss for one being a gain for the other. Iran has thus strengthened its alliances with Hizbullah, Hamas, and Syria, and reached out to the Supreme Council of the Armed Forces of Egypt, which returned the favor.

Then there is the ambiguous case of Bahrain. On the one hand, the GCC justified occupation of the island as necessary to counter Iranian subversion, demonstrating a willingness on the part of the Gulf monarchies in general and Saudi Arabia in particular to take whatever steps they deem necessary to suppress threats to the status quo. On the other hand, the occupation may have benefited Iran by opening up a rift between the United States and its most important Gulf ally and by exposing to all the raw violence that was necessary to sustain monarchic rule.

There is also a downside to the Arab uprisings for Iran. The uprising in Syria imperils Iran's most important Arab ally, and even if a new government replaces the old there and finds it advantageous to maintain the Syrian-Iranian alliance, it would be difficult for that government to be as close to Iran as the present government has been. In addition, an uprising-induced Hamas-Fatah reconciliation would bring Hamas in from the cold and, quite possibly, away from the nurturing arms of Iran.

What can history tell us about "revolutionary waves"?

Ever since the Egyptian uprising, when events in one country (Tunisia) found a receptive audience in another (Egypt), historians and other social scientists have looked to the past to explore other "revolutionary waves" that might help explain current events and instruct us about the course those events might take. In chronological order, the most common historical analogies are: 1789, the kick-off date for the French Revolution, which spread notions of "liberty, equality, fraternity" among subjugated populations throughout Europe; 1848, the "Springtime of Nations"; 1968, when a wave of "youth revolutions" demanding an end to social and political hierarchies (to oversimplify a bit) engulfed France, Mexico, the United States, and Japan, among others; and 1989, when the Berlin Wall fell and Soviet domination of central and eastern Europe ended. So far, 1989 seems to be the most popular touchstone, although Thomas Carothers of the Carnegie Endowment for International Peace makes the intriguing suggestion that the current series of uprisings in the Arab world most closely approximates "the wave of authoritarian collapse and democratic transition" that took place in sub-Saharan Africa during the 1990s: "After more than two decades of stultifying strongman rule in sub-Saharan Africa following decolonization, broad-based but loosely organized popular protests spread across the continent, demanding economic and political reforms."[8]

For his part, President Obama has been studying the close to sixty "people power" uprisings of the 1980s, the most famous of which occurred in the Philippines, South Korea, and Indonesia. And while we are at it, what about the wave of constitutional revolutions that broke out around the turn of the twentieth century, when rebels in the Ottoman Empire, Persia, Egypt, Russia, Mexico, Japan, and China demanded a written contract with their rulers specifying their rights?

The list of possible analogies seems endless, depending on what particular characteristics and outcomes one wishes to highlight and what particular characteristics and outcomes one wishes to forget. It is doubtful, for example, that Obama is looking for lessons from the first of the so-called people power revolutions—the 1978–79 Islamic revolution in Iran—or from what is arguably the last—the Palestinian *intifada*, which broke out in 1987. Instead, he has chosen his revolutions on the basis of their demands (an end to authoritarian rule and a more open system) rather than their tactics (which is, after all, what people power is all about). Optimists are likely to find assurance by comparing the current uprisings in the Arab world with 1989; pessimists, with 1848. The moral of the story is that historical analogies do not explain and do not instruct, although for historians and history geeks their entertainment value cannot be overestimated.

When will we be able to judge the significance of the Arab uprisings?

As anyone who has studied European history can tell you, the French Revolution began in 1789 with the storming of the Bastille and ended in 1799 with the coronation of Napoleon as emperor. At least, that is the most common narrative. Other narratives are, of course, possible. What about beginning the story of the French Revolution in the early eighteenth century, with the spread of Enlightenment ideas, or during the reign of the centralizing Bourbon monarchs? After all, "liberty, equality, fraternity" was a product of the Enlightenment, and arguably the greatest accomplishment of the French Revolution was the centralization of France, which the Bourbons did so much to further. And what about ending the story of the French Revolution in 1945, when French women voted for the first time, thus fulfilling the revolution's promise of equality and political rights for all? If one focuses on battles and treaties, the American Revolution lasted from 1776 to 1783, which is the way the story is commonly told. On the other hand, the eminent scholar of American history Gordon S. Wood focused on the radical social transformation the American Revolution brought about. His American Revolution began in 1760 or so and ended in the early nineteenth century.[9]

Historians invent narratives to tell a story. Like all stories, they must have a beginning, a climax, and an end. So the answer to the question "When will we be able to judge the significance of the Arab uprisings?" is: it depends what you are looking for.

What conclusions might we draw from the uprisings so far?

Assuming we adopt the common narrative of the French Revolution and date it from the storming of the Bastille to the coronation of Napoleon as emperor, we are dealing with events that unfolded over the course of an entire decade. Only a fraction of that time has passed since the Tunisian street vendor Muhammad Bouazizi set himself on fire, and, as of this writing, events in the Arab world are still unfolding at a remarkable speed. Although it is still too early to gain the distance from events that historians need to render judgments, here is my top ten list of what we have learned from the uprisings so far:

1. Uprisings are extraordinary events, and being extraordinary they defy prediction.
2. Although the site of political action in the Arab world is the nation-state, the "imagined community" Arabs share with one another is remarkably robust.

3. There is no evidence to demonstrate that social media have played any more of a role in the current uprisings than the printing press and telegraph played in earlier uprisings.
4. The internal strength or weakness of a state and the relative independence of state institutions play a critical role in determining the course an uprising will take.
5. The Arab world has not been impervious to norms of human rights that have emerged since the 1970s.
6. Neither culture nor religion has prevented the emergence of democratic aspirations in the Arab world.
7. The spontaneity, leaderlessness, diversity, and loose organization that have marked the uprisings have been both their greatest strength and their greatest liability.
8. When staging an uprising, having the army on your side may prove to be a mixed blessing.
9. Since neoliberal policies sparked widespread anger throughout the region, further neoliberal policies are unlikely to defuse it.
10. Whatever the rhetoric, the default position of American foreign policy remains expediency.

NOTES

Chapter 1

1 The full text of the reports can be found at http://hdr.undp.org/xmlsearch/reportSearch?y=*&c=r:Arab+States&t=*&lang=en&k=&orderby=year (accessed June 6, 2011).

2 http://www.imf.org/external/np/g8/052611.htm. The phrase "Middle East and North Africa" is not equivalent to the phrase "Arab world" because it includes non-Arab majority states such as Turkey, Israel, and Iran. Although the report does not define what is meant by the phrase, it appears to be concerned with the Arab world (accessed June 6, 2011).

3 Clement M. Henry, *The Mediterranean Debt Crescent: Money and Power in Algeria, Egypt, Morocco, Tunisia, and Turkey* (Gainesville: University of Florida Press, 1996).

4 http://www.cato.org/event.php?eventid=3729 (accessed June 11, 2011)

5 The United Nations has chosen the ages fifteen to twenty-nine to define *youth* because most countries divide their data into five-year increments.

6 http://www.shababinclusion.org/content/document/detail/559/ (accessed June 12, 2011).

7 http://www.businessinsider.com/governments-food-price-inflation-2011–1#25 (accessed June 12, 2011).

8 The statistics come from the 2010 *Egypt Human Development Report*, http://www.undp.org.eg/Default.aspx?tabid=227 (accessed June 15, 2011).

9 http://www.jadaliyya.com/pages/index/1606/neoliberalisms-forked-tongue (accessed June 15, 2011).

10 Samuel P. Huntington, *The Third Wave: Democratization in the Late Twentieth Century* (Norman: University of Oklahoma Press, 1993).

11 http://www.defense.gov/news/newsarticle.aspx?id=4486 (accessed June 15, 2011).

Chapter 2

1 Cited in Kenneth J. Perkins, *A History of Modern Tunisia* (Cambridge: Cambridge University Press, 2004), 197.

2 http://www.economist.com/node/12202321?Story_ID=E1_TNNDNPNT (accessed June 26, 2011).

3 See John Sfakianakis, "The Whales of the Nile: Networks, Businessmen, and Bureaucrats During the Era of Privatization in Egypt," in *Networks of Privilege in the Middle East: The Politics of Economic Reform Revisited*, ed. Steven Heydemann (New York: Palgrave Macmillan, 2004), 77–100.

4 http://middleeast.about.com/od/tunisia/a/tunisia-corruption-wikileaks.htm (accessed June 28, 2011).

5 http://www.stratfor.com/analysis/20110203-breakdown-egyptian-opposition-groups (accessed June 28, 2011).

6 http://www.foreignaffairs.com/articles/67348/carrie-rosefsky-wickham/the-muslim-brotherhood-after-mubarak (accessed June 28, 2011).

7 See http://www.merip.org/mero/mero043011 (accessed June 30, 2011).

Chapter 3

1 http://alsalamest.com/Ahmar_profile.pdf (accessed July 11, 2011).

2 http://www.telegraph.co.uk/news/wikileaks-files/libya-wikileaks/8294920/AL-QADHAFI-THE-PHILOSOPHER-KING-KEEPS-HIS-HAND-IN.html (accessed July 9, 2011).

3 http://nymag.com/news/politics/saif-qaddafi-2011–5/index2.html (accessed July 11, 2011).

4 http://www.crisisgroup.org/~/media/Files/Middle%20East%20North%20Africa/North%20Africa/107%20-%20Popular%20Protest%20in%20North%20Africa%20and%20the%20Middle%20East%20V%20-%20Making%20Sense%20of%20Libya.pdf; http://www.jadaliyya.com/pages/index/1001/is-the-2011-libyan-revolution-an-exception; http://www.lebanonwire.com/1103MLN/110341612MER.asp (accessed July 15, 2011).

5 http://online.wsj.com/article/SB10001424052748704559904576231172563565048.html (accessed July 14, 2011).

6 http://www.telegraph.co.uk/news/worldnews/middleeast/yemen/8166610/WikiLeaks-Yemen-covered-up-US-drone-strikes.html (accessed July 15, 2011).

7 http://www.telegraph.co.uk/news/worldnews/africaandindianocean/libya/8739845/Can-the-NTC-unite-a-divided-Libya.html (accessed August 4, 2011).

Chapter 4

1 http://www.fpif.org/blog/wikileaks_xxxiii_algerias_youth_too_dazed_and_confused_to_even_become_terrorists (accessed July 18, 2011).

2 http://af.reuters.com/article/topNews/idAFJOE70K02X20110121?sp=true (accessed July 18, 2011).

3 Hugh Roberts, *The Battlefield Algeria, 1988–2002: Studies in a Broken Polity* (London: Verso, 2003), 107.

4 http://online.wsj.com/article/SB10001424052748703833204576114712441122894.html (accessed July 19, 2011).

5 http://articles.cnn.com/2011-05-31/world/syria.tortured.child_1_security-forces-damascus-body?_s=PM:WORLD (accessed July 20, 2011).

6 http://www.merip.org/mer/mer236/syrias-curious-dilemma (accessed September 12, 2011).

7 To the best of my knowledge, the term *coup-proofing* was invented by RAND Corporation analyst James T. Quinlivan in 1999. See his "Coup-Proofing: Its Practice and Consequences in the Middle East," *International Security* 24 (Autumn 1999), 131–165.

8 Patrick Seale, *Asad: The Struggle for the Middle East* (Berkeley: University of California Press, 1988), 456.

Chapter 5

1 F. Gregory Gause III, "The Persistance of Monarchy in the Arabian Peninsula: A Comparative Analysis," in *Middle East Monarchies: The Challenge of Modernity*, ed. Joseph Kostiner (Boulder, CO: Lynne Rienner, 2000), 171-180.

2 http://bna.bh/portal/en/news/449972 (accessed July 29, 2011).

3 http://www.foreignaffairs.com/articles/67932/f-gregory-gause-iii/why-middle-east-studies-missed-the-arab-spring (accessed July 29, 2011).

4 http://www3.weforum.org/docs/WEF_GenderGap_Report_2010.pdf (accessed September 13, 2011).

5 http://www.jadaliyya.com/pages/index/818/demands-of-saudi-youth-for-the-future-of-the-nation (accessed July 30, 2011).

6 http://www.foreignaffairs.com/articles/67694/jack-a-goldstone/understanding-the-revolutions-of-2011 (accessed July 30, 2011).

7 http://www.jordanembassyus.org/new/newsarchive/2011/02012011001.htm (accessed July 30, 2011).

8 http://www.jadaliyya.com/pages/index/676/morocco-on-the-eve-of-the-demonstrations (accessed July 30, 2011).

9 http://www.hrw.org/en/news/2010/10/20/bahrain-elections-take-place-amid-crackdown (accessed July 30, 2011).

10 http://lynch.foreignpolicy.com/posts/2011/05/11/the_what_cooperation_council (accessed July 30, 2011).

11 http://mideast.foreignpolicy.com/posts/2011/07/18/after_bahrain_s_dialogue; http://www.nd.bh/en/index.php/the-dialogue/news/item/96-national-dialogue-agrees-additional-powers-for-parliament (accessed July 30, 2011).

Chapter 6

1 http://www.ned.org/george-w-bush/remarks-by-president-george-w-bush-at-the-20th-anniversary (accessed August 2, 2011).

2 http://www.newyorker.com/reporting/2011/05/02/110502fa_fact_lizza (accessed August 3, 2011).

3 http://blogs.telegraph.co.uk/news/nilegard/100096840 (accessed August 3, 2011).

4 See Abu Bakr Naji, *The Management of Savagery: The Most Critical Stage Through Which the Umma Will Pass*, trans. William McCants (Cambridge, MA: John M. Olin Institute for Strategic Studies, 2006), 28.

5 See, for example, http://www.tawhed.net/; http://publicintelligence.net/inspire-al-qaeda-in-the-arabian-peninsula-magazine-issue-5-march-2011 (accessed August 3, 2011).

6 http://pewglobal.org/2011/05/02/osama-bin-laden-largely-discredited-among-muslim-publics-in-recent-years/ (accessed August 3, 2011).

7 http://www.intifada-palestine.com/2011/01/gazas-youth-manifesto-for-change (accessed August 3, 2011).

8 http://www.foreignpolicy.com/articles/2011/03/10/think_again_arab_democracy? (accessed August 6, 2011).

9 Gordon S. Wood, *The Radicalism of the American Revolution* (New York: Vintage, 1993).

FURTHER READING

General Works on the Middle East

Beinin, Joel. *Workers and Peasants in the Modern Middle East.* Cambridge, UK: Cambridge University Press, 2001.

Gelvin, James L. *The Modern Middle East: A History* (3rd ed.). New York: Oxford University Press, 2011.

Henry, Clement M., and Robert Springborg. *Globalization and the Politics of Development in the Middle East.* Cambridge, UK: Cambridge University Press, 2001.

Algeria

Le Sueur, James D. *Between Terror and Democracy: Algeria Since 1989.* London: Zed, 2010.

Roberts, Hugh. *The Battlefield Algeria 1988–2002: Studies in a Broken Polity.* London: Verso, 2003.

Egypt

Osman, Tarek. *Egypt on the Brink: From Nasser to Mubarak.* New Haven, CT: Yale University Press, 2010.

El-Mahdi, Rabab, and Philip Marfleet. *Egypt: The Moment of Change.* London: Zed, 2009.

Libya

El-Kikhia, Mansour O. *Libya's Qaddafi: The Politics of Contradiction.* Gainesville: University of Florida Press, 1997.

Vandewalle, Dirk. *A History of Modern Libya*. Cambridge, UK: Cambridge University Press, 2006.

The Monarchies

Gause III, F. Gregory. *Oil Monarchies: Domestic and Security Challenges in the Arab Gulf States*. New York: Council on Foreign Relations Press, 1994.

Hertog, Steffen. *Princes, Brokers, and Bureaucrats: Oil and the State in Saudi Arabia*. Ithaca, NY: Cornell University Press, 2010.

Nakhleh, Emile. *Bahrain: Political Development in a Modernizing Society*. Lanham, MD: Lexington Books, 2011.

Kostiner, Joseph. *Middle East Monarchies: The Challenge of Modernity*. Boulder, CO: Lynne Rienner, 2000.

Robins, Philip. *A History of Jordan*. Cambridge, UK: Cambridge University Press, 2004.

Sater, James N. *Morocco: Challenges to Tradition and Modernity*. Oxon, UK: Routledge, 2010.

Syria

Lawson, Fred H. *Demystifying Syria*. London: Saqi, 2010.

Lesch, David W. *The New Lion of Damascus: Bashar al-Asad and Modern Syria*. New Haven, CT: Yale University Press, 2005.

Tunisia

Alexander, Christopher. *Tunisia: Stability and Reform in the Modern Maghreb*. Oxon, UK: Routledge, 2010.

Perkins, Kenneth J. *A History of Modern Tunisia*. Cambridge, UK: Cambridge University Press, 2004.

Yemen

Boucek, Christopher, and Marina Ottaway. *Yemen on the Brink*. Washington, DC: Carnegie Endowment for International Peace, 2010.

Dresch, Paul. *A History of Modern Yemen*. Cambridge, UK: Cambridge University Press, 2000.

WEBSITES

Foreign Policy
www.foreignpolicy.com
International affairs periodical with contributions from top experts

International Crisis Group
www.crisisgroup.org
Independent analysis of conflicts and potential conflicts in Middle East and beyond

Jadaliyya
www.jadaliyya.com
Ezine of the Arab Studies Institute, covering culture, politics, economics of the Arab world

al-Jazeera (English)
http://english.aljazeera.net
English language site of the widely read Arabic language newspaper

Middle East Research and Information Project (*MERIP*)
http://www.merip.org
Online edition of alternative news source on the Middle East

INDEX

SOME NIGERIAN FERTILITY CULTS

Omone, son of Chief Benebo of Buguma, in the costume of the Peri play

SOME NIGERIAN FERTILITY CULTS

P. AMAURY TALBOT

NEW YORK

BARNES & NOBLE, INC.

Publishers · Booksellers · Since 1873

Published by
FRANK CASS AND COMPANY LIMITED
67 Great Russell Street, London WC1
by arrangement with Oxford University Press.

Published in the United States
in 1967
by Barnes & Noble, Inc.
105 Fifth Avenue, New York, N.Y. 10003.

First edition	1927
New impression	1967

Printed in Holland by
N. V. Grafische Industrie Haarlem

PREFACE

THE facts collected here are almost exclusively such as came to my notice in the course of the ordinary administrative work in Degama Division, to which I was posted in June, 1914.

The region is mainly inhabited by sections of the two great tribes of Ibo and Ijaw. A full description of these will be given later, but it appeared best to issue without further delay this little monograph, dealing with a certain aspect of their religion, the publication of which has already been long postponed owing in the first place to the war and then to pressure of other work.

As regards the remaining tribes, the subject will be found discussed in other books, especially the *Ethnological Sketch*, comprising the second and third volumes of *The Peoples of Southern Nigeria*, published by the Clarendon Press. The descriptive parts in the following pages were written by my first wife.

P. A. T.

June, 1925.

CONTENTS

LIST OF ILLUSTRATIONS

I

THE GREAT DRUM

The outbreak of war seemed a favourable opportunity for discontented natives to throw off the restraints imposed by Government and return to old customs, and disturbances occurred in various parts of Nigeria. One of these took place in Aba District to the north-east of Degama. We have since learned that the native name for this region is Aba-Ala, *i.e.* Aba of the Earth Goddess Ale or Ala. Here two messengers employed by the Native Courts were seized and dragged before the great drum, described as from 18 to 20 feet in length, which stood in one of the Juju houses. Later, reliable testimony declared this to have been one of the principal shrines of the Earth Mother herself.

According to the account given us, the unfortunate victims were forced to kneel at the end of the long, trough-like base, from the centre of which the rounded portion of the drum was carved, and their heads struck off so that they fell forward into the cavity. The drum was then splashed with blood and the heads, still bearing the uniform caps, were placed thereon amid the skulls of former victims as a defiance to British rule, which, the insurgents hoped, was no longer powerful enough to protect its servants.

Shortly afterwards, a policeman passing through the region with a prisoner, whom he was bringing down to Degama, was also seized and done to death. Vengeance, swift and sure, followed these crimes. By order of the Resident, the blood-stained drum was burnt to ashes and justice meted out to the guilty persons. The destruction of this fetish was an act of necessity, since no other measures would have produced the same effect upon its worshippers; yet the step was taken with great regret, for the drum was of an interesting type and most elaborately carved.

Some weeks later our road led us through the town of Ihie, where we came upon a similar drum, of a kind then new to us. Cleft from an even larger trunk than the Ibibio big drum at Jamestown, to which it showed some points of resemblance, the giant bole extended at both ends in a Noah's Ark-like base, on which were seated, at either extremity, a male and female figure—the latter holding a babe in her extended arms. (See Fig. 1.)

We were informed that the name of the drum, and of the cult, was Ikoro (or Ikuru). One of the chief towns devoted to its worship was Ohambele nearby. 'This town,' in the words of Mr. B. M. Pepple,

> has a big Ikoro drum which is highly respected. Before Government came, they gave it human sacrifices, but now only goats and fowls. They beat this drum during war time. Any human head cut off in war is brought and placed on the drum with blood. No man can see the big Ikoro drum unless he has cut off a human head and presented it to this. It does not matter whether the head was got by war or not. The Ikoro play falls twice a year. The first is called Mkpukpu-Chi (thanksgiving) and falls at harvest time. The second is carried out in the farming season, and is called

FIG. 1. Ikuru drum at Ihie

Omehie Ogugu (remembrance of the Juju Ogugu). Any man in the town has the right to dance the Ikoro. The big Ikoro is beaten in the house, while the dancers keep outside. Those men, who had cut off a human head, would come to the front of the big Ikoro house and play their motion by raising the sword and telling of the brave deeds they have done; then they would begin to dance again. The Ikoro drum was never carried to another town. Before the time of Government small towns did not make an Ikoro drum. If any small town ventured to do so, the big towns fought them and seized the drum.

Detailed examination of the drum at Ihie showed that the ornamentation carved in relief was of exceptional interest. In the middle, between the figures of a man and woman rudely enough represented and probably depicting the carver and his wife, who were usually sacrificed on the completion of the work, was the carefully chiselled shape of a great serpent folded round on round. On either side of this, various symbols were to be seen, several of which were easily enough recognised as the crescent moon, the sacred crocodile, a Juju horn, and, what seemed to our eager imagination, a fresh example of the double-headed axe, but which was explained by the natives as a musical instrument called, in Ibo, Igilla. The reason why, on closer investigation, our interpretation rather than theirs seemed to be the right one, will be stated later. For the moment our attention was caught by an object quite new to us, the meaning of which we could not even conjecture. On asking its significance we were told simultaneously and with like positiveness from two different sides, one that it was a representation of the familiar tortoise, while the other volunteered the unexpected statement that it pictured the labia majora, with the clitoris showing between.

Those who voiced the opinion first given asked contemptuously whether it was not a matter of common knowledge that tortoise played an important part in the greater number of Jujus. On this, the second party subsided for the moment as if abashed by their opponents, but later one came in private to point out that tortoise is depicted with the crossed lines which indicate the cracks in her shell, whereas in this case the small vertical dashes are the conventional representation of hair. He further explained that the opposition party was right to a certain extent, in that tortoise herself symbolises the feminine generative organs, just as the serpent is well known to typify the phallus.

Till then, the presence of the impaled tortoise before most Jujus, even remotely concerned with the granting of fertility, had been more or less of a puzzle; for, although the snake is recognised by anthropologists as the phallic emblem, no widespread feminine symbol of like significance appears to have been known here hitherto.

The supremacy of tortoise in most tales of African origin has often proved puzzling to folklorists. The subject is mentioned in *The Times Literary Supplement* of 10th December, 1914:

> There is one very curious point which these and other stories of the kind have in common—that though these professional jokers, so to call them, have the better of all

the animals with whom they ordinarily enter into a contest of wits, there is one . . . who always has the better of them all, even of the jokers themselves—the tortoise. He appears under that name in the translation of the bushman's tales; he is, of course, Uncle Remus's Brer Tarrypin and he has no less credit in South American stories. Why is the tortoise credited with such wisdom? One wonders. . . . Is it just this—that the bright little up-looking head and eyes, when put forth, suggested the idea of intelligence? It is something of a serpentine head and we have read a piece of folklore which tells us that the serpent was the most subtle of all the beasts of the field.

Surely the meaning of the tortoise symbol, stumbled upon thus unexpectedly, goes far to explain the difficulty. To the native mind the 'serpentine head,' appearing between the walls of shell, as naturally pictures the clitoris as does the serpent its male counterpart. By a train of thought not difficult to follow, this particular part of the body has grown to symbolise femininity in general. For Africans, therefore, tortoise stands for the feminine qualities of persuasion—sometimes, perhaps, not untinged by guile—as opposed to the more forceful male attributes. It may be remembered that, in Pliny's day, a powder made of a whole tortoise shell was thought to be an aphrodisiac.

A few days later, in an Mbari house close to Okpala market-place, the two emblems, snake and tortoise, were found modelled side by side in the very centre of the first row of symbolic figures. Further on at Obogwe, where the Mbari house is built in two separate sections—the first, dedicated to the Thunder

God Amade Onhia, usually contracted into Amad-ongha, and the second to his spouse, the Earth Goddess Ale or Ala—the phallic serpent was found in a position of great prominence in the shrine of the male deity, while tortoise was seen, modelled alone, in that of the goddess. Another example in which the two symbols were found, this time again in juxtaposition, was upon the main post of the shrine of the Juju Ogboloma at

Fig. 2. Phallic serpent (Eke) and tortoise (Naba), Okpala.

Fig. 3. Chief juju at Tema.

Tema near Degama—one of the principal Kalabari Jujus. Here, as so often, the two are combined with the figure of the sacred crocodile.[1]

With the new suggestion in mind, the detailed drawing of the sacred drum was examined, with the result that the emblems carved thereon seemed to take upon themselves a deeper significance. As already mentioned, at either end of the trough-like base, sits a male or female figure carved from the solid wood and distinct from the drum. To the left, the male, bearing

[1] See also figures on the ancestral tablet described on p. 121.

the symbols of manly strength, the sword in the one hand and the horn, typifying plenty and masculine virility, in the other. To the right the Mother—her head adorned with the high coiffure which, among Ibo, designates pride in offspring—a babe in her outstretched arms. In the centre of the drum itself, in the place of honour, carved in bold relief, is shown the phallic serpent. To the left of its pointed head rises the crescent moon—the world-wide symbol of growth—especially connected with childbirth, since expectant mothers count their time by its waxing and waning.

On either side, in the one case above and on the other below, are seen, twice repeated, the disputed signs, in both cases in conjunction with the old Cretan symbol of the union of the sexes—the double-headed axe. That the native explanation of the last-named figure was given in good faith, there is no reason to doubt. It is only another case of the way in which a symbol has survived long after the loss of its meaning. Indeed, a certain similarity exists; but, to those acquainted with native ways, I venture to think that the sharpness of angle marked in the joining of haft to head, instead of the easy curves called for by a representation of the musical instrument, is clear enough indication that the carver was following faithfully, though blindly, in the footsteps of long dead craftsmen whose work once bore another significance. A considerable number of examples of the old Minoan double-headed axe cult were found in other parts of West and Central Africa.

Besides those already discussed, only three other symbols are shown on the front of the great drum: viz. (1) the sacred crocodile—the terrible emblem of West Coast cults such as the Human Alligator Society and the great Ekoi women's secret cult of the Nature Goddess Nimm. Possibly the crocodile sometimes symbolises another plane of being or the future life; it is a common belief here that many souls live in crocodile form both during the life, and after the death, of the human body. There may also be some connection with the Egyptian worship of this creature. (2) The horn placed beneath the double-headed axe, as the so-called tortoise symbol is above—considered so powerful an emblem of virility that even its representation in bronze is supposed to excite desire, and, held in the hand of a pregnant woman, to assist delivery; and (3) the figure of a dog—regarded among Ibo and Kalabari as the means of first bringing fire to earth—possibly typifying the brute creation in general, or at least that part of it which is friendly to man.

Among some tribes, especially the Ekkett Ibibio, the tortoise shell is looked upon as the symbol of the Earth Deity, the goddess of fertility. The snake is the chief phallic symbol, not only on account of its shape but also because many species live underground and are therefore taken to represent the dead, to whose influence the fruitfulness of the crops is in many places considered mainly due.

II

MBARI HOUSES

From Aba, we passed through Omo Dim, in Owerri District, to visit the Mbari house there.

According to Ababua, priest of Amade Onhia at Ibo near Okomoko, the meaning of the word Mbari is 'fine' or 'decorated.'

The central part of the strange structure at Omo Dim proved to be a rectangular building with steeply pointed roof and overhanging eaves, the latter so wide as to make a broad verandah. The walls, forming the central chamber, were painted with elaborate frescoes, mostly in red and white upon yellow, or red and yellow upon white. On either side of the main entrance to the inner, sacred apartment were here, and in most Mbari houses subsequently visited, figures so strikingly like those of Omogwa and Otammelli, the two strangely elongated guardians of the Thunderer's shrine at Ibodo,[1] as to make it probable that all had a common origin and were set there for the same purpose, namely to warn trespassers from approaching the shrine.

To others the people had only answered vaguely in reply to questions as to the purpose of the building: 'We make it for nothing, only to please ourselves.' The identity of the white figure at the top of the ladder

[1] See p. 45.

Fig. 4. Outside the Mbari house, Omo Dim

was explained, as a portrait of the District Commissioner!

We were more fortunate, mostly on account of the energy displayed by the interpreter, Chief G. A. Yellow, a man of unusual intelligence, to whom the reason of our enquiries had been explained and who was far-sighted enough to wish to aid them by every means in his power. By his persuasion an old chief was induced to come forward and give somewhat more information. According to his account the name of the structure was Njokku Mbari, and it was erected in honour of a great ancestor, long dead, named Njokku and his wife Mbafor. The white figure at the top of the ladder on the right of the building represented Njokku himself and, as the chief artlessly pointed out, the birds upon the rungs of the ladder showed that this was the road by which the spirit of the dead man had climbed to his place in the sky, whence he now ruled as a great chief. The fact that he was painted white signified that he was no longer an earth child but had passed to the ghost realm, from whence he watched over his descendants who brought offerings at certain times of the year in order that he might be gently disposed towards them and grant plentiful harvests. As mentioned elsewhere, there is little doubt that the word Njokku is the same as that in use on the Nile, where Jok is the Dinka appellation for ancestral spirits and the Lango name for God.

On the testimony of a considerable number of Ibo we learned that no Mbari house is built save at the orders of, and in honour of, one of the great deities worshipped throughout the Etche country and Owerri District, namely Ala, Amade Onhia, Otaminni (the genius of the Otaminni River) called, by the priest of his principal shrine at the Etche town of Opioro, 'The Lover of Ale,' and Oloba, a spirit living in the Owerri bush. So far as we could hear, the cult of the latter is quite local.

The more than life-sized figure, facing the principal entrance to the enclosure, was explained by the same chief as that of the ancestress Mbafor, with her small girl-piccan on her knee. It was, he said, the head priest of Ale, the Earth Goddess, whose shrine is close to the Mbari house, who ordered the erection of the building, chose out those who were to raise it and himself directed every detail of decoration. There seemed, however, reason to believe that the figures of the so-called ancestors Mbafor and Njokku really represented Ale and Amade Onhia, regarded, in many parts, as consorts and jointly responsible for the crops. The resemblance between the figures of the deities, as here shown, and those admittedly meant to depict the Earth Goddess and Thunder God in other Mbari houses, is so striking as surely to be more than a mere matter of coincidence.

It is indicative of the position of Ale that only the head chief of a town can aspire to become her priest. This is the case with all dominant Jujus; for instance, Otaminni at Opioro and Amade Onhia at Ozozo, the parent shrine of the Thunder God's worship, from which all other centres of the cult derive their power

FIG. 5. Clay figure of Ale in an Ibo Mbari house

The following was the account given by the Omo Dim chief as to the erection of the Mbari house:

'At the time of the new yam harvest the building is begun and, throughout the first part of the dry season, men and women, chosen for the purpose by the priest of Ale, work hard at beautifying and adorning it.' Only those specially designated for this purpose may take part. Should anyone not called thereto by the priest attempt to share in the work, death would fall upon such unauthorised intruders as surely as that which overtook him who, of old, stretched forth a presumptuous hand to the Ark.

Before the making of new farms the house must be finished and ready for the celebration of its strange rites. Later, when the germs of the new season's crop—corn-grains, sections of yam-tubers and seeds of pumpkins, great and small—have been confided to the dark bosom of Mother Earth, men and maids of the region gather together bringing gifts, 'rack upon rack of dried fish, goats, sheep and fowls without stint, palm-wine in plenty and all else needed for a great feast.' Of the maids, who have undergone initiatory ceremonies, a certain number are chosen by the Ezale (head priest of Ale) to act as priestesses for the rites about to be held in and around the Mbari shrine.

As to the nature of the ceremonies, the natives were naturally reluctant to speak; but Mr. Whitehouse, a former District Commissioner, in a short account published in the *Journal of the African Society*,[1] declares

[1] 1904, pp. 134, 135.

them to have been of licentious character. Subsequent enquiries confirmed this, and the nature of the rites is borne out by the groups of clay figures set both round the central shrine and beneath the roof depending from the inner side of the wall, which encircles the whole erection cloister-wise. These images represent, with remarkable fidelity, the life-cycle of bird, beast and human being, from the act of procreation—depicted with astounding naïveté—to the lying down, when life is done, for a last long rest in the arms of the Earth Mother.

It is noticeable that, though beasts of prey play a great part in the series, as is only natural under the conditions here prevalent—such, for instance, as leopard or hippopotamus devouring human beings—these fierce beasts are shown either as destroyers or as falling beneath the weapons of the hunters, never in the propagation of their kind. Harmless or useful creatures, on the other hand, such as fowls, both wild and domesticated, dogs, sheep,[1] etc., together with human beings, are depicted first in the act of procreation, secondly that of giving birth, thirdly suckling their young and later in every conceivable scene of life. Men are modelled as engaged in hunting, fishing, canoeing—as police, court messengers, clerks or musicians. Women are shown grinding cam-wood, arranging elaborate coiffures, undergoing operations of extreme delicacy from native doctors—every act

[1] In the Mbari houses of the neighbourhood of Omo Akani, Owerri District, where the Juju Ogugu holds sway, monkeys also are shown in the act of procreation.

of life indeed from cradle to grave, and even beyond, here finds itself reproduced.

The following account of the raising of an Mbari shrine was given by Amuneke of Umo Yekki quarter, Owerri:

There are many such houses in our part, and they are starting to make a new one, in honour of Ala, this month (October 1915) in my own quarter. First of all, when she, Amad'ongha or Otaminni, wish for a new house, they send a messenger called Abara.[1] This is a sort of devil, very dreadful to see! In his hand he carries a sword, because he is not only the messenger but also the executioner of Ala. The image at Omo Dim is made with birds perched upon the four horns on his head to show that he is of the Sky People and is often sent by Amad'ongha. The grasses in his hand show that he is also a servant of Ala.

He goes straight to the compound of the head chief (who is always priest of one of the four great cults already mentioned). Ordinary people are not able to see him; only Juju people can do this, but all hear the place shake as he enters. So soon as the chief knows, from this shaking, that the messenger has come, he sends to a native doctor who goes into the little shrine, where he talks to the spirits, and starts to beat drum. This is a sign to Abara that he is ready to hear the message. When the devil appears, the Juju man sees him clearly, listens to the commands he brings and reports them to the people, saying: 'The Juju asks for an Mbari house to be begun on such and such a day.' Then the head chief chooses out those who are to do the work, four men and three women from each compound. These go out secretly at night time so that no man may see them. If a strong Juju orders an Mbari house to be built and the people

[1] A different word to Abara 'Juju.'

do not obey at once, then at least twenty men from that quarter will die.

Before beginning to build, they make a high fence round the place so as to hide up the work they are going to do.

FIG. 6. Abara, the Messenger of Ale and Amad'ongha or Otaminni

Then they start to make a long house, called Eki-Wari,[1] in which to sleep. Across the middle of this a line is drawn.

[1] Our informant did not know of any link, yet it seems not without significance that the phallic pillars, raised by maidens before marriage to ensure plentiful offspring, also bear the name of Eki. See chapter vii.

Men sleep on the one side and women on the other. It would be regarded as a very bad thing should a woman permit a man to approach her at this time.

From the moment of starting the work till it is quite finished, even if it lasts for a year, no one may go home again, save the one man chosen from each compound to fetch food every day. That is why four men are always chosen to every three women ; because one is needed to go backwards and forwards on 'chop palaver.'

During all the time that the workers live inside the fence, they are forbidden to eat coconut, palm-nuts or cassava. Only cooked yams and soup may be eaten. Also, they may never sleep at night time, only by day. This rule is made because no one must see them when they go out to get the clay from which the figures are formed. This must be taken from the centre of a white ant hill, softened with water and carefully kneaded. No other clay is permitted to be used. So soon as darkness falls, they must begin to work and keep on till just after sunrise.

When the building is finished, on a day appointed by the Juju, all people, whose sons or daughters have been working, make ready for a great feast. After nightfall, they go to the Mbari house bearing a new-made pot. This must be one never before used, filled to the brim with clear water. Also they carry a cock for every son and a hen for each daughter. All their kinsfolk follow them up to the fence which hides the workers. Only the fathers and mothers may go inside, while the rest of the people wait without. Each couple steps, one after the other, in order of rank, together with the priest, before the big Juju set in front of the main doors. There the Juju priest kills a fowl and mixes its blood with water in the new bowl. Then, with a small wooden spoon, he throws some upon the head of son or daughter and pours the rest upon the great image to whom manillas are also offered.

At this point the father says :

'Ubu anyi abiala. Bia ikpe ogu. Anyi
'Now we are coming. Come judge matter. We (*i.e.* between us)

agi oku awsaw ade pa. Anyi emena nhie icheri.
you words again are no(t). We have done things thought your.

Ubu anyi abiala bia ekpaw nwa anyi. Oku
Now we are coming come to take son our. Words

awsaw adr pa.'
again are no(t) (*i.e.* all is finished).'

After this the mother says (for a son):

'Ubu-laka nhie oma ka ega enyi anyi na nwam
'Now things good you are going to give us and son my

makana ihie oma onu oma onu nagi. Nam na
because (he has done) things good work good work for you. I and

dim na ji unwenne na omu umonu na ewu
husband (my) and yam I have and children I born and goats

mwenne nhie oma ka anyi ega anhu afor anhua.'
I have things good make (for) us go see year this coming.'

For a daughter the mother says :

'Aborolam nwam obi oma. Mejiea na mejieadia
'I am taking my child (with) mind good. Give gifts to her and gifts to her husband (for)

onu-ma ka. Aronona ge anyi. Mfu ga ezi ubu-laka
work good your. Have worked for you we. If (I) go out now

afu na nam nhie ojo.'
finished for me things bad.'

So soon as the last word 'ojo' has been spoken, the priest seizes son or daughter and pushes him, or her, towards the parents who at once catch hold on either hand. All three *walk backwards* towards the gate. As the first foot strikes the threshold, they face round and the relatives waiting outside catch up the worker without an instant's delay and bear him back to his home. No foot of any such may be set to ground, lest Ala should be vexed.

When they reach the house all join in a great feast, with fish of every kind, plenty beef and tombo too much! That night the people tear down the fences, which were put up to hide the work, and burn them in a very great fire.

Those years, in which a new house is built, the yams grow bigger in our farms, goats and sheep have more piccans, while nearly always the girls chosen by the Juju for her work bear babes fine past those of other mothers. Usually they conceive soon after the work is finished—often within one or two moons of the play.

About every five or six years a new Mbari house is raised to Ala. She has more than any other god. Next in number come those built for Amade Onhia and still less for Otaminni and Oloba. I have never heard of any such house being made for the ancestors, as was said to be the case at Omo Dim. This may be true for that part; only I know nothing of it.

It is in the little inner room that the god lives. In each of these a tall stone, shaped like an Ibudu, is set. After making its face smooth and clean all about, they cover it with a piece of white cloth. It is into this stone that the spirit enters.

Suppose one man charges another with doing bad things. Then they bring the accused for night time and lock him up alone in the small inner room. Next morning, if he be innocent, he walks forth unharmed; suppose he be guilty, then Juju kills him and his dead body is carried out at dawn. Perhaps Juju beat him to death, perhaps kill him other way; but always he die. No help for such man.

When a big pointed stone is found in our bush, an Mbari house is always built for it. In places where such things are, the knives, with which the old people made them, may be dug up out of the earth. I myself found one such knife at Baro. It was of very strong stone, hard past iron and curved over in a sharp point.

At Olakwaw near Owerri one very big stone was found. They carved it into an Ala figure and built a house for it. This they put in the place of honour, facing the big door. Also at Ne-Ewu and Ihuara in Owerri District there are stone

Fig. 7. Girl ꞌMgbe, Otaminni house, Opioro

Fig. 8. Humorous figures

figures of Ala, Amad'ongha, Okpara Ala (the first born son of the Earth Goddess) and Eke, the great snake. This is the kind of big snake which lives for bush and always has a shining stone in its head, such as white people call diamond. It is because of these serpents that Eke day is said to take its name.

Images of Ale and Amad'ongha may be carved out of stone or moulded in clay, but must never be cut from wood like the Agu Isi (*i.e.* wooden images consulted by native doctors): for so the Juju orders. Ala has other sons beside Okpara Ala.[1] Among Etche Ibos and those of Owerri the younger sons are worshipped every month, four days after the coming of the new moon. They are represented under the shape of small cut stones such as were taken from the bad Onye Dibia (medicine man) at Awka. These stones are always kept in one of the round box stools, rubbed with cam-wood. The medicine man sits upon the box, then rises and shows the stones to the people who throw themselves upon the ground before these, praying for piccans, kids, lambs and yams. These sons are never represented in any other shape. No figures of them are to be found in Mbari houses.

Sometimes we call these buildings Mbari, sometimes 'Mgbe. This last word means a small boy or girl orphan. There are two kinds of 'Mgbe—those who have relatives to look after them and those who have none. We call the latter Osu 'Mgbe, *i.e.* the worst 'Mgbe. He is so very poor he can only get food by searching round the bush for palm nuts. For this reason his image is nearly always made with palm nuts in hand.

In olden days such a boy was always bought by one or other of the quarters and presented as a slave to the Juju. Afterwards he might never enter the compound which bought him, but could go to beg food from others. Sometimes, when he has grown big enough, he makes himself a

[1] At the Etche town of Okudu Mba there was an Mbari house erected in honour of Ajala (Aja ground or mud), 'a brother of Ale.'

little house in one of the corners of the Mbari. Then people bring yams to him. Sometimes too the Juju asks for chop for him. If the Juju loves him very much, it will also ask one of the chiefs to give him a slave wife; but such a boy may never marry any free-born girl of the town. The same rule holds for girl orphans bought with money and given to the Juju. They may take slave husbands, but never marry a free-born man.

Another figure to be seen in every Mbari house is that of the ape Ogbango. This is the kind into which the souls of bad Ibo go after death.

In the Western Etche country these temples are generally called 'Mgbe houses. Umoyo, the principal place hereabouts, is a queer little town—or rather two towns—through which runs a single long street, fenced in on either side by a palisade of posts and palm leaves. The houses lie well back, often out of sight from the main road, in gardens which bear luxuriant crops. At the end of the street stretches a line of cacti to keep out evil influences.

The head chief Wobilo was friendly to Government, and we had hoped to gain from him a considerable amount of information regarding the origin and rites of this singular cult. By an unfortunate accident, however, some of the principal men of the town had lately been drowned in the Juju water formed by the sacred Otaminni River just below its junction with the Ogochi. No sooner were the sad tidings made known to relatives and friends than the whole town turned against the head chief, saying that the deaths lay at his door, because he had induced them to undertake the journey which resulted in their untimely end.

Fig. 9. Shrine of Otaminni, Opioro

In consequence, Wobilo found himself outcast in his own town and, when on our next visit we asked a few questions concerning the figures in the local 'Mgbe house, the chief refused to run the risk of increasing his unpopularity by giving away information, and we were everywhere met by the answer: ' I do not know. We did it for no reason. Perhaps our ancestors may have had knowledge of these things ; but, as for us, we have long since forgotten, and only copy the customs taught by our fathers because we believe that by so doing we shall draw prosperity upon our town.'

The only information we could get ran as follows:

> Mbari or 'Mgbe is our Chineke, also our Juju. People from Orata built the house. At certain seasons girls dress themselves and come before the shrine, there to dance, eat and drink.
>
> Amad'ongha is a great Juju, but our people do not worship him much. His proper country is over the other side of the Otaminni River.

When an Mbari house was to be erected in Etche country, a medicine man was consulted as to time and place of building. Thereupon he brought out a human skull—in the old days that of a slaughtered victim, but since the coming of white rule one sought amid the ' bad bush ' near his town. Round this were set out the Agu images—always, be it remembered those typifying fatherhood and motherhood, together with representatives of the animal kingdom, including ' dog ' who brought fire to earth. A cock was killed and its blood sprinkled over the skull and the little images. Then the magician gave utterance to the supposed wish of the Earth Mother or Sky Father with regard to the building to be erected in their honour, by means of which, it was thought, prosperity of farm, byre and marriage bed might be secured to the town.

At Opioro stands an Mbari house built in honour of the spirit of the Otaminni River—the only one known to us throughout the Division. The image of Otaminni is set in the centre of the front side, with his 'big relation' Ala to his right and his three wives Ogori, Ocham and Wujere in a row on his left.

On the opposite side of the house, in the seat of honour, sits the Earth Mother again; while, near her, groups of women are engaged in pursuits set apart by custom as purely feminine. For instance, a midwife ushers a babe into the world; cam-wood is ground, etc. All the characters, with which one had grown familiar in other houses of this type, were here reproduced with one exception, that of ape. An enquiry into the cause of his absence brought the surprised reply: 'Ogbango is here, sir! He stand for middle place at other side of house.'

A visit to the spot indicated revealed no sign of what we were seeking—only an unseemly group such as is to be found in nearly all such buildings, the woman bending forward at right angles from the waist, her head resting upon the square base of one of the roof pillars, while the male figure behind her was unmistakably engaged in the Geschlechts Akt. The present head priest of Otaminni, Amade Onyeche, was at the moment anxious to be appointed to the post of warrant chief in the place of his late brother. This

Fig. 10. The Chief of Opioro, head priest of Otaminni

made him not only willing but eager to impart information. His disclosures were, indeed, on certain points rather embarrassingly full. He stated, and his account was afterwards borne out by those of other Ibo, that the male figure was not that of a man but of the very Ogbango whom we had thought absent. In proof of this statement the priest pointed out that, in its right hand, on the left shoulder and beneath the left arm, the ape held a round ball, representing those hard fruits which, according to widespread native testimony, it is his habit to fling at passers-by, thereby stunning, or even killing, them. This we had already heard from many parts of the country. At Obogwe it was added that so heavy were the fruits and so great the strength of this ape that it was thought he might even succeed in stunning an elephant therewith ! Amade Onyeche continued:

> It is customary among our people to take up the position of this couple for such a purpose, when there is no bed near at hand. It is forbidden to lie upon the ground, lest Ale should be defiled thereby. There are many of these great apes in our bush who, if they meet a woman alone, force her to bear a child to them.

The same belief, according to Amuneke of Umo Yekki, is held in the neighbourhood of Owerri. It is probably connected with the idea that the souls of bad men pass into ape form at death. It appears that the evil human spirit, confined in the animal body, is thought to take this means of providing a new form in which to re-incarnate.

III

MBARI HOUSES (*continued*)

In Mbari houses built in honour of Amade Onhia it is made perfectly clear, as is natural, that the Thunderer himself holds first place, while his consort is of secondary importance. In the shrine at Omo Dim, as previously mentioned, the place of honour, facing the entrance, was occupied by the figure of the so-called deified ancestress Mbafor—a bowl for offerings sunk into the ground at her feet and her daughter upon her knee. The face and form of the mother are bright yellow, the colour of the clay from which she is modelled as are those of Ala in all shrines yet visited; while the whole body of the child is dead white, like that of the Thunderer himself, the deified ancestor Njokku seated above his sky ladder, or indeed ghosts and ' sky people ' in general.

On the white of her body five coal-black crescent moons had been painted; one just above the shoulder, one on the top of the arm and three down the flank. All, save that on the arm, showed a protuberance in the centre, exactly in the place where the nose would come when children draw the face of the man in the moon. The point would not have been worth mentioning but for the fact that in each Mbari house visited a peculiar decoration was noticeable, only to be described as a screen of lattice-work, formed of

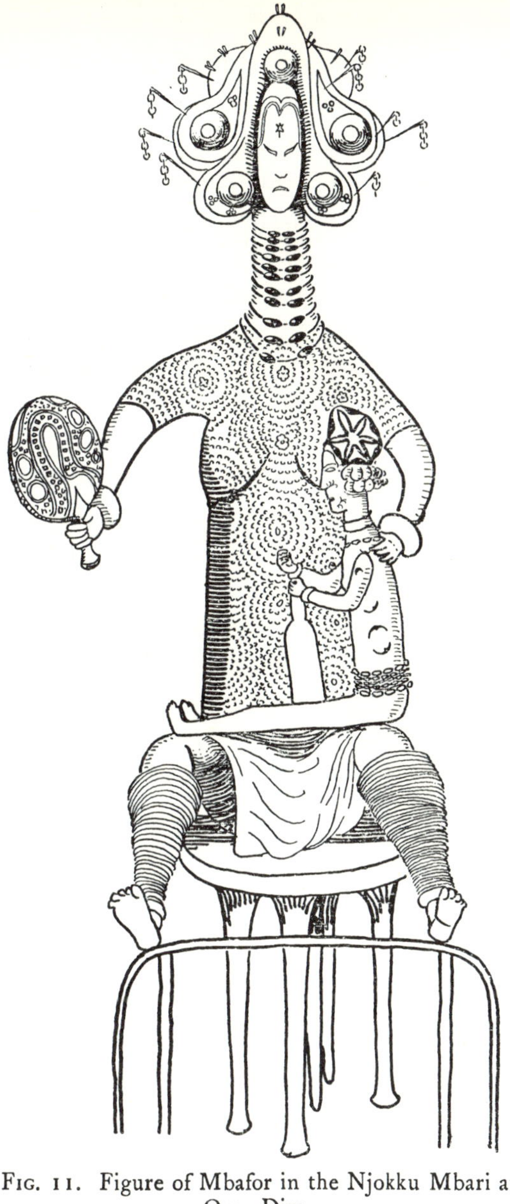

FIG. 11. Figure of Mbafor in the Njokku Mbari at Omo Dim

interlacing human figures. This was explained as representing the slaves sacrificed and flung into the grave—or laid there still living, but with broken arms and thigh bones—to form carpet and bier for the body of the dead chief. It may well have borne some such interpretation, but this would hardly explain the fact that, in each case which we came across, one row of figures, usually the centre one, bore faces the shape of a crescent moon, mostly dead white and outlined by a deep black rim. At Omo Dim, Okpala and Obogwe too there is a figure —which is duplicated with more or less fidelity in several other shrines and which for obvious enough reasons was named, by my companions, 'little moon-face'—of the same type as those in the human trellis work.

FIG. 12. "Little Moon-face," Omo Dim

Now the crescent moon is a sign of growth the world over. Ekoi women come together, beneath her faint beams, to carry out the rites which, according to their belief, will ensure fruitfulness. Ibibio and Ibo also hold that her rays are endued with fecundative powers, while pregnant women count the time to their delivery by her waxing and waning.

Some few weeks later, in passing through the town of Ebubu in the extreme east of Degama District inhabited by that strange and hitherto unstudied tribe, the Mbolli, we came across a shrine of a type such as we had never before seen. It is carved from a solid block of wood some four feet high, set in a carefully smoothed clay base, swathed round the bottom by folds of white cloth and surmounted by an inverted crescent. The name of this Juju is Obo Esa, *i.e.* in Mbolli dialect four hundred yams. The reason given for this name is that only full chiefs have the right to erect such a fetish, to which they must sacrifice each harvest-time baskets containing the given number of yams. It was explained that Obo Esa is a male Juju—a statement borne out by the appearance of the symbolic pillar—and to him, at the cutting of new farms and digging of fresh yams, living sacrifices must be brought and slain so that their blood is shed upon the clay base, whence it trickles down over the seven little moon-shaped depressions to the thirsty earth beneath. These small half moons may well typify the period during which the yams are confided to the bosom of Mother Ale—called Nkike by the Mbolli—while the great crescent, surmounting the pillar, probably represents that of the month of September during which the harvest festival is usually held.

Considering the close connection between the waxing moon and the powers of fertility, it is not without significance that personified representations of the crescent are to be found in each Mbari house, especially when it is remembered that the shrine of the Earth Goddess is always close by and that only after consultation with her priest is the building begun and carried through.

Again, although we were expressly told, as already related, that the chief figure at Omo Dim did not represent either of the principal deities, but only a deified ancestress, yet a man present volunteered the information—it is true, in a highly superior manner—that some old and very ignorant people held them to be those of Amad'ongha and Ale. So stupid, however, were such that they even believed the white child, on the knee of the Earth Mother, to be the moon! As if any but the most foolish could look upon the moon as a daughter of Earth!

In the Obogwe Mbari house—the only one which we have yet found built in two separate edifices—the first building was dedicated to Amad'ongha and the second to Ale, locally called Ala. Our informant, Omere Madu, was the son of the late head chief who therefore, *ipso facto*, was priest of Ale. He told us that this goddess was the dominant power in the town, and that she ordered her priest to have the two houses built in that place and form—one for herself and one for her spouse Amad'ongha. In both buildings he sits in the seat of honour, but in the first alone, while in the second she is seen on his left, in the same position as that of the figure at Obodo to which her name was first given, but which was later called Omu Ngwaw, the fruitful mother.[1]

[1] See p. 40.

In the temple dedicated to the Thunderer, on the left of the central figure is seen one, the name of which was said to be Eku Nechi—*i.e.* 'the big woman who cooks,' or more fully 'who gathers the children of others around her and cooks for them.' The figure is seated, supporting a boy and a girl against her sides; while another pair sits, one upon each of her outstretched legs. The most singular thing about this group is that each of the male children bears a crescent moon for face, while from the necks of the two girls is painted a cloth thickly covered with white dots. On the wall of the Ale shrine, a fresco may be seen on which a moon-faced boy is depicted climbing up the right hand side of a rainbow, painted in black, yellow and red stripes. In such a position he is supposed to be an envoy from the Earth Goddess, climbing the sky with a message from Amade Onhia, or, when descending, bringing word from the latter to the children of men. Beneath, on a black ground, a crescent moon and stars are shown—the stars represented by white dots exactly like those painted round the necks of the girl piccans of Eku Nechi. It is not

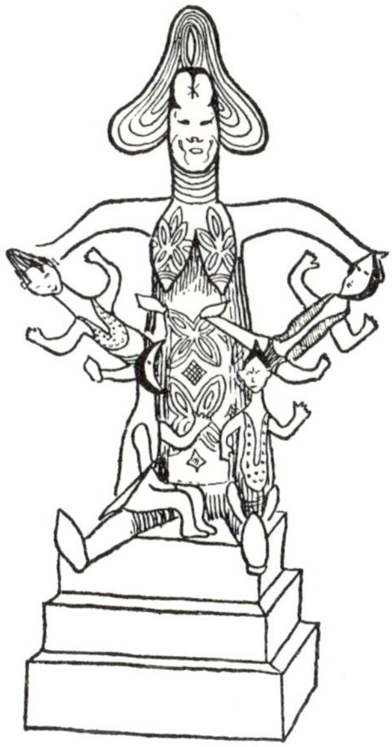

FIG. 13. Group in Obogwe Mbari house

impossible therefore that here again, in ‘ the big woman who feeds the children of others,’ we have another forgotten picturing of Ale, the Earth Mother, with her starry progeny.

A singular fact about all the Mbari shrines hitherto visited is that, in each, figures may be seen, obviously modelled with the express intention of depicting licence in its most blatant form. Primitive peoples the world over, however frank in picturing or mentioning facts treated with the greatest reticence by civilised races, are usually ignorant of real vulgarity or indecency, since the very simplicity of manner and treatment robs their statements of offence. The Ibo of this region, especially, have a code with regard to sexual matters which, however lax according to our ideas, is yet strangely strict in some directions. According to them four of the most evil things are:

(1) For man and woman to lie together on the earth, since this is thought to defile Ale. Among Kalabari indeed the idea is carried so far that no woman is allowed, under any circumstances, to seat herself upon the ground. In the absence of stool or convenient tree-trunk she must stand. As already mentioned, according to chief Amade Onyeche, the position adopted by Etche Ibo, when no bed, mat or cloth is available, is for the woman to stand bending forward at right angles from the waist, while her lover stands immediately behind.

(2) Connection is absolutely forbidden during the hours of daylight, or even at night time when a light

is burning in the room; also at any time in the bush or in a farm, where there is no house.

(3) It is the height of impropriety for a man to have relations with a woman who is not clothed in the prescribed custom.

(4) For a husband to attempt to view the genital organs of his wife is regarded as so serious an offence as to be considered valid ground for divorce. In a case brought before me in the Degama Native Court, the claim ran: 'To demand freedom of marriage on account of peeping.'

In every Mbari house yet visited, however, figures were seen modelled with the obvious purpose of expressing a breach of one or other of these rules. In most of the buildings groups were found in which the feminine figure was shown partially lying on the ground—in a position impossible to any human anatomy and therefore, it would seem, so posed as intentionally to express direct rebellion against the generally accepted rules of decency.

An official of high rank, who was the first Government representative to visit this region, described to me a shrine which he saw about twelve years ago, near Ingaw in Owerri District, where certain points were even more naïvely depicted than by those erected in the present day. Among the more noticeable groups were men in the act of copulating with a sheep and antelope respectively. As regards the latter animal, it is not without interest to recall that, according to several accounts from well-informed sources, ancient Yoruba custom ordained that, after the kill of his first antelope, a young hunter must have connection with the still warm form. Possibly some such rule obtained, or maybe even yet exists, in these regions.

The group of men and sheep seems to point to the existence of a like custom among Ibo as one learns, on good authority, prevails among the neighbouring Ijaw, with whom the chief feature of male initiatory rites consists in each boy proving his manhood, before a circle of elders, upon a specially selected sheep. Should he be unsuccessful, he must wait until the following year and is prevented from marriage until after having passed the test. From certain information it would appear that one of the principal centres, where this rite is carried out, may be found on a southern creek in the neighbourhood of Kula.[1] It was naïvely added that the sheep 'never go 'gree to this and always vex too much' when the rite was carried out. Later, a similar custom was reported from among the Ekkpahians of Ahoada District.

It is true that every Ibo or Kalabari who mentioned the subject was eager to state that Ekkpahians perform this rite 'merely out of badness; for no proper reason at all.' Yet, though it is unfortunately not permitted me to give a single name as authority, it would appear, after very careful weighing of evidence, that the practice has been exacted from time immemorial as a test of manhood. Both Ibo and Kalabari also

[1] In this neighbourhood are the principal shrines of Adumu, the head and father of all the snake cults of the region. The little village of Adum-Ama is its chief centre, while at 'Ngeri-Baw-Ama it was stated that 'only men may talk with him; for with his cult some of the most important of the male secrets are said to be connected.'

asserted that unnatural vice is extensively practised among this people, though rare with other races of the Division; but it is only just to state that the practice appears to be carried on not for the purpose of sensual indulgence, but, in some cases at least, from the idea, held among certain Australian tribes, that such customs increase the race by magical means.

That the practice is not held in as great detestation throughout Ekkpahian and neighbouring territory as among other tribes is proved by the more or less casual manner in which the matter was mentioned as well as from one or two Court cases. It will be enough to quote that heard at Omokku on January 20th, 1913, in which Atoma of Erema charged Okereke of Idu with indecent assault. In the course of her evidence plaintiff stated on oath:

> About three months ago accused came to my father's house to have connection with him. At that time I went to bed. . . .
>
> *Question by Court.* When he came to your house, where did he stay with your father to have connection ?
>
> *Answer.* Outside the house.
>
> *Question by Accused.* What date did I come to your house ?
>
> *Answer.* Orie day.
>
> *Question by Court (to father).* Was accused your friend ?
>
> *Answer.* No.
>
> *Question by Court.* Did accused ever come to your house and have connection with you at night ?
>
> *Answer.* Yes. He always come to my house and prosecutor saw him.

Among Ekkpahians and the Abuan, as well as with the Western Ikwerri, elaborate, two-storied buildings may be seen, upon which the wealth and utmost resources of the town have been lavished, even to stained- and patterned-glass for all the windows. My attention was drawn to these buildings by a man high in the medical service of the Protectorate, with the information that they were erected for the practice of unnatural vices. This was later confirmed from native sources with the addition that they were the homes of the Obukere Club and that the customs were of religious significance. The fact that such habits exist is, unfortunately, too well known to be worth mentioning, were it not for a few words dropped by one of the chiefs and intended in extenuation of the practice. 'It is true,' he said, 'that the custom is a very bad one; yet aged men tell us that it was taught in olden days as a very great magic *whereby our flocks and herds might be multiplied and made strong. Even, it is said, the crops in the farms are increased thereby.*'

The idea was confirmed by another chief who however insisted that it was only a tradition from the olden time—held by dead men, very far away—and he did not think that any such belief was prevalent nowadays. He also added, cautiously, that this form of vice was far less indulged in at present than was formerly the case.

The information fitted in with that already gleaned concerning the supposed efficacy of phallic shrines set up amid the fields in order to secure plentiful crops.

As a result, further information was sought concerning the cult of Obukere, one of the most interesting of whose lodges was discovered at Obelle Oduaha. An avenue, half a mile in length, every trunk of which bore a sinister-looking smear of cam-wood dye, led to the house. At the entrance to this grove it opens out into a cleared space, from the centre of which springs a clump of trees smeared with deep bands of red and hung round with white cloth. Behind these rises a giant ant-hill, while round their roots a mound of earth about five feet high was piled. Amid the rich mould and fallen leaves stood votive pots and bowls, among which bundles of young tombo palms just bursting from the parent kernels, were to be seen, mostly enclosed in wrappings of broad green leaves bound round with tie-tie. This clump of trees is regarded as the abode of Obukere himself. Here members of his cult assemble to carry out the rites. Before his dwelling-place the worshippers cover their faces and, thus veiled or masked, go in procession through the sacred grove—the tree trunks of which, down to the smallest sapling, have been fresh smeared with the symbolic blood-red cam-wood. In these regions Obukere is regarded as the great giver of fertility to all in air, water or upon earth—fish, animals, plants or men.

All lodges of this club as yet visited show a peculiar development in the highly conventionalised animal head-dresses which are worn for plays. In the Otu Obukele (house of Obukele or Obukere) a big shed made of solid wooden posts, at the Abuan town of

Okobaw, some head-dresses of unusual type were found; among them representations of antelopes, porcupines and the 'increase of the Sky people,' typifying the sky world above that of men.

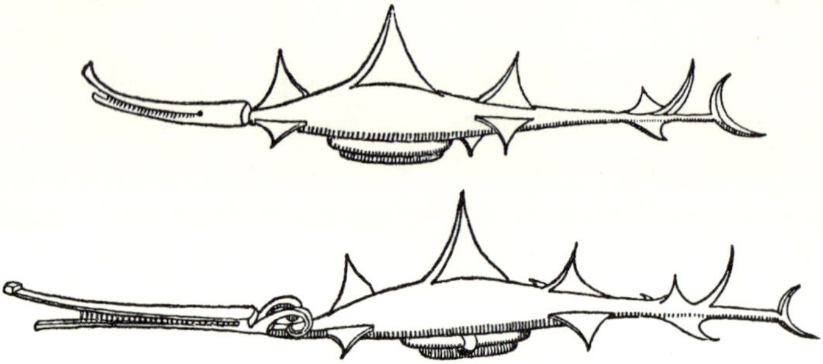

FIG. 14. Obukere Club head-dresses

Round the lodge at Obelle Oduaha were seven phallic shrines six of which were of the usual pillar type, while the seventh showed a featureless head, arms and legs indicated in the roughest manner, and only the distinctly feminine organs modelled with any care. The position of these shrines in close proximity to the house of Obukere worshipped with the avowed purpose of increasing fertility in man, animals and crops, can hardly be regarded as without significance. Within the house were two objects of interest—a xylophone in the shape of a canoe manned by eight figures, stated by the chief to have been specially designed to express 'joy' and raise feelings of pleasure in those who behold them; and an object which strongly resembled the Ajokko Ji or king yam shown to us at Oppe, separated by the sacred crocodile swamp from Alessa, and which will be more fully described later on page 99.

The drum used at Oduaha to call together the members of the Obukere Club was said to have been brought from Abua and to have been made for the Sekapu Club, connected with the spirits of fish, crocodiles and—in this part of the world—land beasts. It may be only a whim of the carver that the figure of the woman, depicted with rounded body as a sign of pregnancy, should be joined to that of the sacred crocodile. Drums of similar type were later found among Abaw Ibo.

FIG. 15. Sacred drum used to call together the Obukere Club, Oduaha

IV

MBARI HOUSES (*continued*)

In nearly all towns of importance in the Etche country, elaborate Mbari shrines are to be found, built in honour of the Thunder God. In most, just within the principal entrance, may be seen the seated figure of the deity, white from head to foot, and bearing in the right hand a sword, spear or bayonet, and in the left an imitation of one of the old stone axe-heads, thought by natives to be thunder bolts, or one of the long iron sceptre-rattles, or possibly another sword or dagger. By his side sits his consort, to whom various names are given, most of them apparently synonyms for the Earth Goddess Ale, Ala, Ana or Aja. At Ibodo we were told by one informant that the figure represented Ala—Bride of the Bladed Thunder. The more general Ibo idea as to her identity was confided by the head priest, Achongwa by name, to chief G. A. Yellow: 'That,' said he, 'is Omu Ngwaw, wife of Amad'ongha.'

Omu Ngwaw is literally 'the children (or young leaves) of the tombo palm tree,' *raphia vinifera*. Now, when a woman has given birth to a first or second babe, the days which she spends in seclusion are often called by the same name, while the word for fruitfulness itself, or giving birth, is Omumu. The connection thought to exist in primitive minds is the probable reason why young palm leaves are in such evidence

Fig. 16. Figure in Mbari House, Umoyo

Fig. 17. Wrestling scene ('Mba) in shrine of Amade Onhia and Ale. Shrine drummers on the right

before the shrines of all beneficent Jujus; the half-unfolded frond stands as type and symbol of fruitful motherhood.

On floor and walls, serpents twine and twist ; hippopotami hold men half devoured in their mouths, leopards stand over new-slain goats, elephants wave long trunks or fall to the guns of hunters, apes climb or swing, and fabulous creatures disport themselves on every hand. A clerk counts his money on a little table. Two wrestlers may be seen locked in one another's arms [1] and a native doctor anoints the womb of a woman patient with a feather dipped in oil. In short, so far as in them lies, the whole life-history of the people is here reproduced with infinite pains and care. As in the Owerri Mbari houses, the head-dresses of the women are most elaborately rendered, while the modelling of a ram's head and of one small monkey which sat devouring a corn-cob were extraordinary samples of artistic skill. Again, a peculiar feature of several of these were figures obviously modelled with the intention of expressing the feeling of joy. It is probably only a coincidence that so many of the figures of Ale show much enlarged navels—the ὀμφάλος of the Earth Goddess.

In all these shrines the mural decoration is not painted, but applied to the walls like a gigantic piece of Cloisonné—clay, tinted with various dyes, being filled in between strips of raphia palm which serve to

[1] The wrestling scene depicted in every Mbari house generally represents the ceremonial wrestling 'to help the crops grow' described on p. 112 *et seq.*

outline the design exactly as does the brass edging the enamelled leaves and flowers of the above-mentioned ware.

One of the most interesting of the temples visited lay some two and a half miles off the main road near Ibodo and was approached first by a narrow bush-path and later by a broad way over-arched by great trees, the branches of which interlaced overhead to form a clear translucent twilight even at noonday. As we passed beneath the fern-fringed, orchid-decked boles, the sky was overcast and the sun already low in the west, while the voice of the Thunder God might be heard in the distance—a low, threatening note in the twilight.

When the village of Omako was reached and we approached the shrine, the sun was just setting. Blue smoke rose from amid the strange figures, over which flames flickered and danced from a little fire tended by an old, old woman, who among such uncanny surroundings was quietly cooking her evening meal. She was the 'slave of the Juju' who had sought his protection as a refuge from oppression untold moons ago. Her whole life is spent amid the weird figures which she guards and serves, lighting fires during the rains that the soft clay may not be melted nor the roof and wood-work rotted by damp and mould—though, strangely enough, it is strictly forbidden to make the slightest attempt at repairing when cracks appear in figure or wall, however much care was expended on the building of the shrine.

So near to one another are the figures that the little sleeping mat of the attendant could hardly find space

FIG. 18. Clay figure of Amade Onhia in an Ibo Mbari house

to be stretched out in between. Their eyes were set with fragments of looking-glass, which twinkled and gleamed in the most life-like way, as the flames rose and fell. How many years the gentle old slave, with her soft voice and deprecatory gestures, had served the Juju, none could tell. She herself seemed to have lost all memory of any other life ; but the dim eyes brightened at the gift of tobacco leaves and the gentle voice followed us, still calling Ndeawo—the common word both for 'thanks' and for 'greeting'—as we went away.

In every case which we have seen as yet, the Thunder God wears a sharply pointed black beard. In many instances little rattles hang from his neck or are attached to a spear or staff held in his hand, while a cluster of bells is slung from a rope usually passing over the right shoulder and resting on the left hip. In one place his feet were set upon a curved bar of iron which had once been gaily painted and was said to represent the rainbow. It is with the rattles that he produces the roll of his thunder, while the bells strike together to form the clash and bang of each separate peal. The type of figure was identical with that of the so-called deified ancestor Njokko, seated at the top of his sky ladder upon each rung of which 'air people,' *i.e.* birds, were perched.

It is perhaps not without significance that, upon either hand of his throne, two slender pillars the shape of an elongated torch and each bearing a bird, are set.[1] These are small and vaguely modelled, but it is

[1] Cf. The Bird and Pillar Cult of old Crete.

possible that they once represented the eagles of Zeus—which, among Ibibio, are still sacred to Obumo, the Thunderer.[1]

At Ibodo, on either side of the door of the central shrine—the ' holy of holies ' which only the priest can enter unscathed—we first noticed the two strangely shaped figures which are also to be seen guarding the inner sanctuary of the Owerri Mbari houses. They were thus explained to us:

' These are the servants of Amad'ongha. Their names are Omogwa and Otamelli. The first '—with spread tresses—' is calling up the tempest by striking on her mouth.' (This action was later described, at another shrine, as ' cleaning her teeth with a bush stick! ') ' The second is about to loosen her hair which floats around her in the storm-wind darkening all the earth '—a possible picturing of the rain-bearing clouds.

> Omogwa's left hand is stretched out to warn intruders from entering the chamber which she and her sister Alose are set to guard, lest thereby the wrath of Amade Onhia should be drawn down upon the trespasser.
>
> In former days, when men had offended against the law of the Juju, they were brought by the priests and shut up within the shrine. Then, in the night time, came some fearful thing to torture them to death, perhaps by beating, perhaps in other ways. At any rate the body of the offender was always borne forth at dawn and shown to the trembling people as a sign of the fate which would overtake any who dared disobey the law of the Thunder God or the commands of his priests.

[1] See *Life in Southern Nigeria.*

FIG. 19. The Guardians of the Shrine, Omogwa and Otamelli

As already mentioned on page 20, this custom also prevailed among the people of Owerri. Near the two Alose, on each side of the inner entrance, are small holes in which offerings of kola are placed when people come to ' bless the shrine ' or ask for special favours.

In the neighbourhood of Ibodo and indeed all over the Etche country, according to the testimony of chief Achongwa, it is customary before cutting palm-nuts to offer sacrifice to some specially tall trees, one of which will be found in every compound. These are named Amad'ongha's palms, because the people say that those, which reach very high, are nearer to the deity. Men who neglect this rite find that their palm-nuts do not produce much oil. Later, we found that the custom was also practised by Aro and a row of the trees—here known as the palms of Kamalo, the name given by this people to Amad'ongha—was shown us in the compound of chief Ogunda at Azu-Miri near Nkarahia. In an Aro compound at Ozoaba each tree had a tall palm-leaf tied against its base, the top leaflets cut off straight and surmounted by a scarlet parrot's feather, an egg, etc.

At Ibodo, from the Thunderer's shrine to the corner of the rest-house, stretches a sacred grove beneath the shade of which native pots and other offerings may be found. Here, during the dry season, a number of small mats of plaited palm were seen, each bearing an offering of goat's flesh. It is perhaps worth mentioning that, among Ibibio, curtains of plaited palm-leaf are hung before holy pools and groves or round the trunks of sacred trees. The plaited part is said to represent the rainbow, while the long fringe from the lower edge typifies the rain itself.

In the grove at Ibodo beneath one of the trees, peeled, short-branched wands—the symbol of lightning—were still standing, and we were told that formerly many such had been set up in other spots. When these rods decay, the power of the Thunder God is said to pass from them into the nearest tree. Once drawn within the many-forked branches, the 'mana' of Amad'ongha fades not with the fading of its first frail tenement, but is drawn into the vegetation around, growing and spreading with each new season's boughs.

At the far end of the sacred grove stands a tree such as we had never seen elsewhere, of which the crowded panicles of single petaled flowers, deepest crimson in colour, swayed to and fro in the breeze amid dark quivering leaves, or fell earthward in showers, like drops of new drawn blood.

One night, at the beginning of the tornado season, we were sleeping in the neighbouring rest-house, when a storm arose with the appalling suddenness usual at this time of year. The wind tore at the frail palm-leaf roofs, while rain lashed in through open window- and door-frames, flash after flash was followed, with scarce an interval, by crash and roar so deafening that for a long time all other sounds were drowned in the awful tumult. As the storm began to pass away, another sound made itself heard in the lengthening intervals. Each lightning gleam was followed by a burst of trumpeting, as though the followers of the storm god had come together undaunted by the force of the tempest to hold a play in honour of their great deity. It is impossible to give any idea of the impressiveness of this act of worship. From out the impenetrable darkness, between long lines of rain, like a sword from its scabbard leapt the dazzling flash. The branches of the sacred grove moaned and swayed, bitumen dark against this more than daylight brilliance; while, from beneath their shade or from the neighbourhood of the shrine, each burst of flame was answered by a blare of savage trumpets, the sound of which merged into the roll of the sequent thunder.

So long as the storm lasted the strange music continued, broken now and again by the cries of the terrified cattle, which rose in chorus from countless byres and were hardly distinguishable at times from the rude horns blown by their owners.

Save for the fact that the outer colonnade, which gives accommodation to further groups of figures in Owerri Mbari houses, is absent, wholly or in part, from many of the Etche shrines, the buildings are practically identical in type. Many groups are to be found, save for the smallest of details, exactly reproduced in each, and it is owned that freedom of intercourse between the sexes is allowed in the cults of both Ale and Amade Onhia at certain seasons, with the idea that this will have the effect of increasing fruitfulness not only among the human inhabitants of the town but also in farm and byre.

The connection between the two cults was indicated by a practice which still obtains at Omo Chuku, a quarter of the town of Ibo near Okomoko inhabited by Etche Ibo. The principal chief of the place, Ababua by name, is also head priest of the Thunder God and, by the local law of the cult, is only permitted to eat in a hut which stands by itself in the middle of his compound. In this, all the dried yams and seed-corn are stored and there too is his Ajokko Ji or king yam, here represented by a basket filled with yams and skulls.

Each wife cooks in turn, and the one who has prepared the meal serves it and is permitted to partake. Should the priest so will, son or daughter may be invited to join in the repast; but none may do so without special permission. The chief himself sits upon an elaborately carved stool, but the others place themselves humbly upon the ground or on small logs. The doorway is curtained by a fringe of young palm-leaves which are never allowed to wither.

The son of chief Ababua, who accompanied us for some distance, stated that his father might never eat of the new season's yams for at least two months after this was permitted to ordinary men. As chief priest of Amad'ongha, Ababua was also obliged by ancient law to perform certain ceremonies to his personal god as well as to the special protectors among his ancestors—the shrines of which are placed just within the threshold of his Obiri (reception room)—before allowing any portion of the new season's yams or corn to pass his lips. It was explained that, by taking his food amid the seed set apart for planting, the priest was thought to endow these with special fertility by the power of the Thunderer whom he served.

Not far from the little dining hut, a small, highly decorated mud house was to be seen, consisting of a dark inner chamber opening from an outer porch-like one. The chief explained that this was the local Mbari house and that they built it each year—making the mud walls gay with shells and brightly coloured plates because their fathers had bidden them do this in order to draw down prosperity upon their people. He added, somewhat hastily, that no special rites were carried out and that the structure got its name only because the word means 'fine' or 'decorated'—probably from its decorations or, perhaps, from the gay robes, beads and brass ornaments worn by the women when gathered together there.

All round the compound the much-branched, peeled wands sacred to Amad'ongha are to be seen. Beneath one of these, two pottery drums were placed, one half embedded in the ground and one above. By the principal shrine before the main entrance a curious adjunct was noticed. From a sapling, cut so as to form a fork, hangs a large oval calabash. Between the prongs a farm hoe is held, while beneath it two tortoises are impaled. The explanation of this given by the chief was that one night his god ordered them to be placed beside the shrine. The combination of objects, taken in conjunction with the fact that this priest of the Thunderer may only eat amid the seed corn and yams, suggests that this is another of the many Jujus for augmenting the fertility of the farm. It is not without significance that, beside that of

FIG. 20. Burial scene in Amade Onhia shrine, Okehin

Amade Onhia, the only other shrine of importance in Omo Chuku is dedicated to Ale.

At Okehin, the Thunderer, instead of occupying a whole building, is only given the front verandah of a house. At one end was to be seen the figure of a mother with a new-born babe in her arms; at the other, a group representing a corpse laid in the grave with a pot of offerings beside it and a pet monkey watching at the foot by the seated figure of a woman. The pot of offerings usually contains a small plate, knife, pipe, tobacco, snuff and bottle of gin, rum or palm-wine. Between these two groups representing birth and death stands the figure of a medicine man, a magic horn in his right hand and a Juju knife in his left.

In niches cunningly contrived in the rear wall, or upon the low clay ridge which separates the verandah from the road, carefully modelled birds sit upon nests of interwoven twigs, containing eggs, tinted or speckled in close imitation of nature. Small monkeys climb the pillars, dogs mount guard, while the phallic serpent twines and twists between all.

V

SKY GOD AND EARTH GODDESS

AMONG Etche Ibo, especially those to the west of the Otaminni River, Amade Onhia has practically usurped the place of Chi, the Creatrix, and reigns as supreme deity. For months after our arrival, we were invariably told by natives of all parts of the Division that the Thunderer was distinct from his brother Igwe, Lord of the Bright Sky. Later on, while collecting information concerning rain-making by magical means, it transpired from the words of the invocation used that the two originally symbolised different aspects of the same personality—Zeus of the thunder, lightning and storm cloud, Lord of the dark sky as well as the bright. Now, though most people regard them as separate deities, the old idea has not yet died out, especially among rain-makers.

Formerly, it is said, Igwe was more generally worshipped than at present. This was explained as due to the fact that the God of the Bright Sky only gives advice by his oracles and does not ensure wealth, health or special good fortune to his votaries; while these additional gifts may be obtained through prayer to Amade Onhia.

In January 1915 good fortune led us to Ozozo, where stands the greatest of all shrines of the Thunder God—a temple not made with hands—the sanctity of which is so great that pilgrims come thither from hundreds of miles. Until now its existence had been carefully guarded from the knowledge of Europeans, and the chief priest had so far avoided coming into contact with any white man of the few who had visited the neighbourhood.

Early next morning we set out to seek the place of pilgrimage. The way led through a part of the bush set aside for the reception of the corpses of the unburied dead. At intervals the road was strewn with cowries, while ghost-offerings such as pots, broken that their astral forms might be set free for the use of the shades, and lengths of cloth, faded by sun and rain, were to be seen in the bush on either hand. Here and there, too, a long, narrow crate formed of palm stems was passed, half covered by the dense undergrowth. In these the bodies of the unblest dead had been borne to their last resting-place, thence to be flung forth for vultures, ants and other carrion-feeding creatures to work their will upon—leaving but a handful of bleached bones for the luxuriant vegetation to cover with its charitable mantle.

Through these ill-omened shades we hurried, only stopping to pluck a new flower, the white cups of which together with masses of their strangely flattened calices had been found strewing the pathways of the beautiful Oban District, but hitherto it had been impossible to secure any leaves owing to the height of the trails, which had eluded discovery amid the network of giant branches to which they clung. Here, in the glade of the unburied dead, the path was festooned from side to side with spray upon spray, rich in flower, fruit and leaf.

Thence we crossed the market-place and, by a net-work of many mazy paths made apparently for no other purpose than to mislead chance-comers, reached an open space shaded by giant cotton trees and heavy-scented Monodoras. In the low bush round about sprang great aroids, said to be connected with the worship of the Thunder God's children. It is possible that the idea is due to the phallic-like appearance of the central spike, the long, thin, basal flowers of which give it somewhat the look of the Schlange im Schilf—the Pangwe description of the phallus.

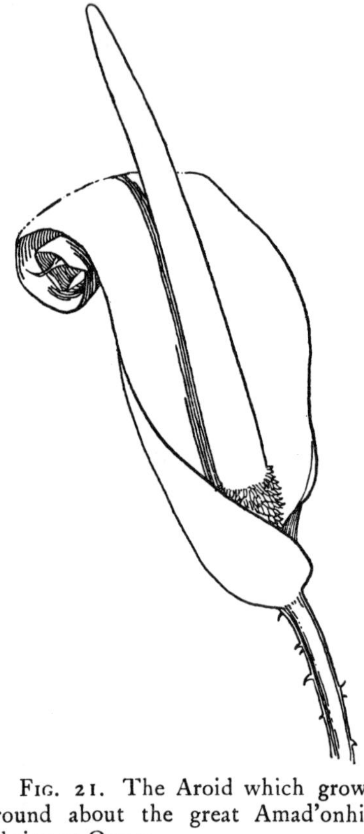

FIG. 21. The Aroid which grows round about the great Amad'onhia shrine at Ozozo

At the further end of the space lay the compound of the head priest, its open sheds full of cult objects but deserted; for the priest and all his family had fled at our approach.

Towards the near end of the cleared space two paths branched off, one on either side of a great clump of trees, the gnarled roots of which stretched right across as though barring the way. These two paths join later by a second group of no great size, which has sprung up round the riven base of a forest giant, the remains of whose trunk, lightning-scarred, may still be seen stretching far out into the bush beyond. Some few yards away a palm-leaf screen is placed across, shutting off the cleared space from the priest's compound. In the midst of the screen a little erection like the door-frame to a miniature house may be seen thickly plastered with the blood and feathers of sacrificed fowls. For about seven feet before this the ground is broken as though continually disturbed, and here and there in the soft sand depressions may be found as though round-bottomed water-jars had been set therein. This was explained as follows:

> When pilgrims come hither bringing the appointed gifts, the priest first makes sacrifice and afterwards calls aloud the special favour which the worshipper has come to ask. Should Amad'ongha be favourably inclined, so soon as the prayer is finished, the roll of his thunder begins to sound, no matter how clear the sky. Then, with a great crash, a ball of stone about seven inches across falls from the blue overhead. This is the sign of the god himself, come down from his home in the clouds to bless the earth folk.

In vain we looked upwards, expecting to see branches which might serve to hide these mysterious missiles. Nothing was to be seen above but slender twigs tossing a delicate tracery of scarce open leaves against the blue.

On the far side of the fence, however, stretched part of the high priest's compound; so, if the means by which the seeming miracle was worked baffled discovery, the probable agency, at least, was not far to seek.

Later we learned that the name of the priest was Chioma Madume, and after some difficulty we succeeded in overcoming his dread of meeting a white man—a matter which had hitherto been considered as tabu. He was even persuaded to come with his two assistant priests to visit us. He proved to be a strange and somewhat pathetic figure, borne on a rude litter, thin, pale and with only one foot; the other, according to his own account, had 'rotted away and dropped off.' The skin of his two attendants was of that peculiarly vivid red occasionally met with in these regions. This appears to bear out Sir Harry Johnston's theory of an original red stock, but is explained by Ibo as showing that man or woman so marked out is a child of Amade Onhia. Both among the last named people and the Kalabari the law of the Thunder God ordains that all such shall be devoted to his service and become 'slaves of the Juju' unless ransomed by their family for a heavy sum. A sister of chief G. A. Yellow was thus chosen on account of the redness of her skin but was afterwards ransomed.

Chioma Madume gave the following account:

> I myself have been priest of Amade Onhia for seven years.[1] Before me my father, Madume, held the office for

[1] No information could be obtained as to whether the priest 'died' at the end of the seventh year of his office, like the priest of the Aya-Eke cult at Elele, *vide* p. 103 *et seq.*

about the same time and before him my grandfather, Odu Kerin, ruled—I cannot tell for how long.

Our god is a very great god and is the only one throughout this region who gives a visible sign of his presence. When he wishes us to sacrifice or perform ceremonies for him, we ask a sign whereby we may know that this is really his will. In answer he sets a rainbow in the sky. When he descends into the shrine before the screen of plaited palm, the rainbow comes down also and hangs just above the place, thereby showing his presence. Many thunder stones fall there and the holes in the ground before the shrine are caused by something which falls from the sky, denting the earth; but it is invisible. No man has looked upon its shape.

(This assertion is in direct contradiction to the statements of pilgrims, who declared, as above related, that the holes were caused by stone balls, roughly speaking, seven inches in diameter, which fell down from above. It was, however, explained by one of the chiefs present that it was probably unlawful for the priest to describe the mysterious missiles—the outward, visible sign of the Thunder God's power.)

Chioma continued:

Amade Onhia, like Ale and the Aro Chuku Juju, is against all those who act contrary to native custom. The Thunder God sends down his bolt to strike such sinners; so, when a man is killed by lightning, people always know that he has done some bad thing. Witches and wizards specially dread his power and never dare to go out during a storm.

It was explained, in all seriousness, that the reason Amade Onhia so often sends his lightning to strike tall trees or hill tops is because he is jealous of all things which seek to raise themselves near to his kingdom. Only the birds may venture safely into the sky realm.

The children of earth should keep close to the breast of their mother. The idea seems contradictory to that held among some Etche Ibo and Aro as to the efficacy of sacrifices made to the so-called ' palms of the Thunder God ' mentioned on p. 46.

With Amafa Ibo this jealousy is thought to be developed along curious lines. Among this people it is forbidden for a woman to climb to any height, up a tree trunk or even over the top of a wall or fence. So strictly is the tabu enforced that ' civil war ' actually broke out among this people because the late chief Oosi, father of the present head chief of Amafa, built himself a ' story-house,' *i.e.* a two-floor building raised above the ground upon a foundation of piles—and allowed his women to go up and down the stairs. That this superstition obtains also among Isokpo Ibo is shown by a complaint brought before me by two men of Nkarahia as to the treatment accorded them by the chiefs of their town who were enraged because they had ventured to build themselves a ' story-house,' to the top rooms of which they allowed their women to climb. The chiefs declared that this endangered the safety of the town; for, should Amade Onhia hurl his bolt at the offending structure, peradventure he might punish the whole people for this disregard of his laws by two of their number.[1]

At sacred places, such as the shrine at Ozozo, the grove at Young Town or the sacred bush at Ngeri-Baw-Ama, no leaf may be picked nor branch broken.

[1] The tabu among Okoba and Ale Nsaw Ibo against climbing palm trees is probably due to the same idea.

FIG. 22. The shape, surrounded by skulls and draped with blood-stained linen, which represents the earth goddess Ale in the shrine at Ewafe

To every one of the great Jujus slaves can run throughout the Ibo country and become its servants, after which no man has power to take them back without paying a great sum of money to the priest. In some cases even this is forbidden. In many parts of the interior such slaves can go into the market-place and take anything they want without payment; for no one dares touch them. After living for a long time with the Juju, they might sometimes go free; but could only go back to their native town at their own risk, for there their masters could recapture them. Amad'ongha and Ale have special power and their shrines are often placed near to one another, because this is pleasing to both, since they work together.

Perhaps the central part of Degama District may be looked upon as that where the worship of Ale holds chief sway. One of the strangest of her shrines lies at Ewawfe, in friendly nearness to church and school. Between them, more to the rear is a great, open shed, with elaborately fringed, corrugated iron roof. Beneath this are several clay pillars of the Ibudu type, before one of which some beautifully wrought torque-like bronze manillas lie amid a heap of smaller ones. A few yards off stands a small mud hut containing a figure of Ale indescribably gruesome with its strangely-shaped skull, its folds upon folds of blood-stained linen and the streams of blood poured and splashed over the supporting logs and the skulls and clumps of feathers thickly strewn around.

At this town it is customary to store all seed yams, etc., in the huts built for carrying out the rites of the ancestors—to whose care the germs of the new season's crops are thus entrusted.

Indeed, amongst many peoples here, the dead are thought to be more powerful even than Ale for the granting of fertility, especially as regards the crops, which is not surprising since they are supposed to live under the ground between incarnations on earth. In most parts, however, the fertility of the marriage bed, of the byre and of the crops is deemed to be chiefly due to the great Mother Goddess of the Earth. The duty is usually delegated to some of her subordinate tribes of Jujus and it is the members of one of these who are responsible for placing in the womb of the mother the spirit of the being about to be born on the earth plane. There is no ignorance here as to the necessary part played by the human father and mother, but their action would be fruitless and conception impossible without the help of the gods or jujus.

At the neighbouring village of Ogbokoro the chiefs were anxiously waiting to speak of a serious trouble which had befallen them. One of the schoolboys had broken the fence round the principal Ale shrine and stolen therefrom a quantity of manillas out of the mass of such which were to be seen, half smothered in feathers and congealed blood, upon the mud altar. On being assured that such desecration would be severely punished, the head chief answered:

> This is a good word for us. We feel this thing very much. Ale is our mother and our god; all that we have comes from her, and without her gifts we must indeed be lost.

As already mentioned, it is indicative of the reverence in which the Earth Goddess is held, that only the head chief of a town can aspire to be her priest. It is not without significance that the same rule holds with regard to the principal shrines of Amade Onhia. Only after pilgrimage to Ozozo may subsidiary lodges be erected, while the shrine of Ale is usually found nearby.

Where Amad'ongha is paramount, he appears to arrogate to himself the functions of Igwe, the Ibo sky god proper,[1] thus following in the footsteps of his Grecian prototype, 'Zeus, God of the bright sky,' who is also 'Zeus, God of the dark sky'; and it is in this capacity, as Lord of the drenching rain-storm, that he fertilises his consort the Earth Goddess.[2]

Of these mystic spousals of Earth and Sky perhaps the most beautiful picturing of all is to be found among the Ekoi of the South Cameroons and of Oban, Southern Nigeria.[3]

A curious link between the worship of Ale and the bearing of babes came to light one morning just as we were leaving Isokpo water-side, a market town of some importance on the banks of the upper New Calabar River. A long, shadeless march, by roads as yet practically unknown to white men, lay before us. We had risen at earliest dawn in order to place the first miles behind before the sun should add to the burdens of the carriers, when, just as we were setting forth after seeing the last load safely started, a complainant arrived with a letter appealingly held out in both hands. It was entitled 'To his Majesty the District

[1] Cf. p. 52. [2] *Zeus: A Study of Ancient Religion*, by A. B. Cook.
[3] Vide *In the Shadow of the Bush*, p. 14.

Commissioner. *Re* Wansumu *v.* Egeom. 17th February, 1915,' and ran as follows:

> Sir,
>
> I have the honour, most respectfully, to lodge this my humble complaint before your kind worship. . . .
>
> I am living in the defendant's town because it is my mother's city. Deceased is my brother. . . . His death took place in that month during which it is forbidden to die. By our native custom, should any one disobey this law, heavy expenses used to be paid before that person might be buried. Defendant knew that the place I am residing in is a mother city, yet he allowed me to perform all the ceremonies on behalf of the deceased Wawesi without assistance. . . .
>
> Leaving this for your discretion
>
> I have the honour to be,
>
> Sir,
>
> Your obedient servant,
>
> WANSUMU (his X mark).

On reading this document, it struck an ignorant white man as somewhat strange that there should be any month 'in which it is forbidden to die.' On this point the complainant stated:

> The man died in the seventh month of the year. Now according to our native law and custom no unmarried man may be buried during the seventh moon of the year. Should any die at that time, none may take notice of his passing and no relative may show sign that a death has taken place; for the seventh moon is the month of our mother Ale and by her law it is forbidden for anyone to die during this holy time. Most of all does she forbid the death of the unfruitful, whether man or woman. The bodies of such must be thrown away with all secrecy and may not be buried. The only exception to this rule is in the case of a man belonging

> to a very rich family. Then, in consideration of the property left, some of the relatives may undertake the expense necessary for carrying out his funeral rites. Should a man die during the holy month of Ale many purificatory ceremonies must be gone through. This law extends over the whole of our country lying round Isokpo part.

When questioned on the subject, chief G. Yellow owned that a similar 'rule' exists among Kalabari, but is only enforced during the day on which an Owu play is given. He added that the prohibition as to burial applied also to those who die of certain diseases. 'When such people die,' he said,

> a certain mark is visible upon the body. The flesh of such an one looks decomposed, whereon people say 'Ale has forsaken him!' Such bodies must be carried far from the town and, if buried at all, it must be a long way from the haunts of men. When a woman dies in childbirth, her death is concealed for the same reason, since to pass away before bearing a babe is displeasing to Ale. In such a case, a corpse must be carried forth at night secretly through the back door of the house. Young maids and pregnant women may never see the body of one so accursed. By native law all the property of the dead must be destroyed by fire, lest the ban of sterility should pass to any who might afterwards make use of such things.

Among Okrikans, during the seven days on which the feast of the Earth Goddess, called by this tribe Elechu, is held, a similar rule obtains. Should a man die, he may not be buried but must be flung away into the 'bad bush' set apart for such outcasts. Only if the family be rich enough to support the cost of the purificatory ceremonies necessary before the goddess can be appeased, may the dead be laid to rest in the breast of the Earth Mother—thence, like sown seed, to spring forth to new life. The spirits of the accursed corpses flung into the place of ' bad bush ' on the other hand become Akalagoli or Ekwensu and on such the gate of reincarnation is closed for ever. They haunt waste places and lonely creeks, seeking to harm those who still dwell in the sunshine. Specially at noon or midnight is their evil power most to be dreaded.

Should pot or bowl be let fall, or wooden implement broken, during the feast of Elechu, the sherds must be piled in a heap upon which is flung the body of any animal which should die during the festival. So large had these mounds grown in many cases that they formed a serious menace to the health of the town and proved no inconsiderable difficulty in the way of an official with leanings towards sanitation. It is to a mixture of good fortune on the one hand and reasonableness on the part of the Okrikans that the trouble is now, for practical purposes, a matter of past history.

Among Ibibio the burial of women dying in childbirth is also forbidden. These were borne forth, through a hole purposely broken in the house wall, to be flung away in the bush, lest their barrenness might have ill effect upon the fruitfulness of the Earth Mother.

VI

IBUDU

To those who pass through the country with open eyes it is obvious that the phallic cult is very strong among Ibo. Where the Ibibio had contented themselves with a plain mud pillar, set as emblem amid the farm, Ibo take special pains in modelling not only a personification of the symbol, but in showing unmistakably that the circumcised phallus is intended to be represented.

Among Ibo, as with the ancient Egyptians also, the feminine, as well as the male, genital organs are worshipped. Both are rudely depicted under the title Ibudu—a name which embraces the chief protective Jujus[1] erected in town or compound, the primary purpose of which appears to be the granting of piccans, though most also act as protector in general to the family or village of which they are the fetish, and bestow fertility on farm and byre. The feminine part of the Juju is usually in bell shape, instead of the pot or calabash form found among Ekoi and Ibibio. It generally shows the high coiffure only permitted to Ibo women after the birth of a babe. The nose is often joined to the base of the hair ridge and the

[1] Many of these would now be classified by me as symbols of 'medicines' or charms, not 'jujus.' Vide *The Peoples of Southern Nigeria*, vol. ii. p. 153.

impaled tortoise, already explained as a feminine symbol, is as a rule seen in the foreground.

Perhaps the most convincing testimony to the efficacy attributed to the feminine genital organ is a carefully carved representation of the labia, which was explained as having been one of the most sacred objects in a great Andoni Juju house, whence it was taken by a man who had no idea of its significance. In course of time it came to my notice and was subsequently added to our collection.

An example of the simplest form of phallic pillar may be found in a compound next door to that of Ababua, head chief of Omo Chuku. Save for two roughly modelled feet at the base, no attempt was made to add limbs to the column, down either side of which a row of rough wooden pegs had been driven. It was explained that each man of the compound inserted one of these on taking a wife, so that the Juju might have a constant reminder of the need to send 'plenty of piccans' to their hearth.

In another quarter of the same town, in front of Omo Alipo compound, an Ibudu may be seen of which the pillar represents a body from the loins upward—the hands, so roughly modelled as more nearly to resemble feet, resting upon the circular base as though in the act of lifting the upper part through from the earth beneath. The figure is headless; only the end of the central pole and the twigs and tie-tie forming the core, round which such images are modelled, protrude from the broken rim. It is perhaps worth remarking that this pillar, like some to be mentioned later,

Fig. 23. Obelli Oduaha Ibudu juju for granting many piccans

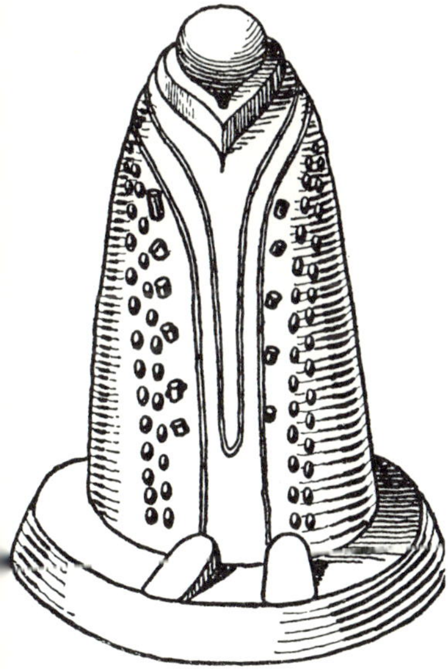

Fig. 24. Ibudu in compound next
ɔ Chief Ababua's, Omo Chuku

Fig. 25. Headless Ibudu in Omo Alipo compound, Omo Chuku

combines both male and female attributes, somewhat in the style of the Indian Linga.

Perhaps the most highly conventionalised of all such images is one to be found in a shrine built in a prominent position on the main road, just outside the Omo-Ofo quarter of Ndelle. This represents the male part of the Juju. At the other end of the shed a smaller figure is to be seen, bell-shaped and showing feminine symbols. This is typical of most of those intended to represent the feminine creative power, though one of a type more nearly approaching the male form of Ibudu was found, later on, in Chief Wokogg's compound at Omo Akani, Owerri District.

Just beyond the shed containing the two phallic pillars, a couple of shrines may be seen, one on either side of the main road. That on the right is built in honour of the Juju Onru-Ji (farm yam). This was explained as ' one very big woman spirit, all same Ala.' In the ground were many knives and pieces of iron, said to have been placed there by order of the priest who declared that the Juju needed them.

A little further, on the opposite side of the road beneath an arbour-like cutting made in the thick bush, was a piece of white baft stretched between two posts. This is set up in honour of Onru Ka'n Ala, stated to be the husband of Onru-Ji. The chief of the quarter explained:

> Both of these Jujus are strong too much. Therefore we never swear a man on their name, because, should he even hesitate to tell the truth when brought before them, the spirit of one or other would strike him dead at once, giving

Fig. 26. Ibudu at Ogaminni, near Ndelle

no time for repentance! It is a very strong rule for our part that both Jujus must be dressed by the people of Omo-Ofo before they may eat new yams.

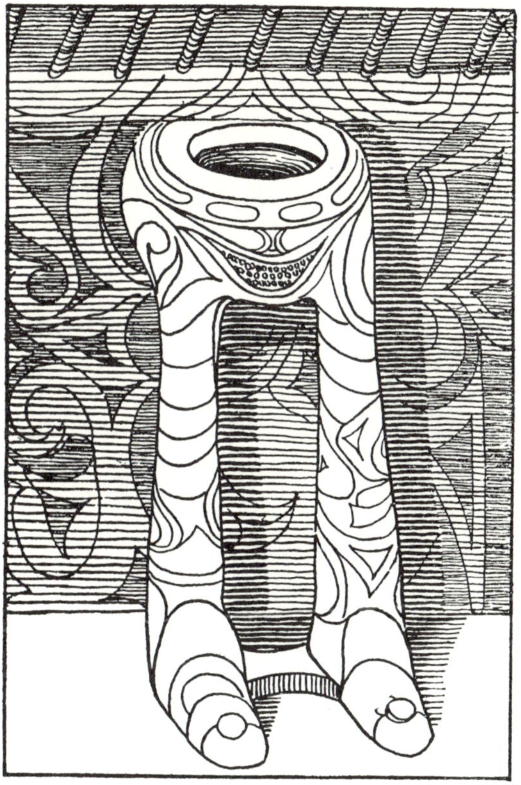

FIG. 27. Ite Uru Ibudu

See page 71

At Aloa, a town in the centre of the Division, a shrine is to be seen containing a fetish, the like of which is not, to the best of my belief, to be found elsewhere in these parts. It is in the corner of a room set apart as sacred to Chineke, the Creatrix, in the compound of Chief Wegu, and consists of an oblong block, terminating in a carefully modelled representation of the male genital organs, raised upon three steps. To this the owner makes sacrifice every month, usually at the time of the new moon, in order that ‘ plenty piccans ’ may be born to those of his house.

A somewhat similar fetish was found among the Ale Nsaw Ibo in the shrine of Chief Idu of Oborotta

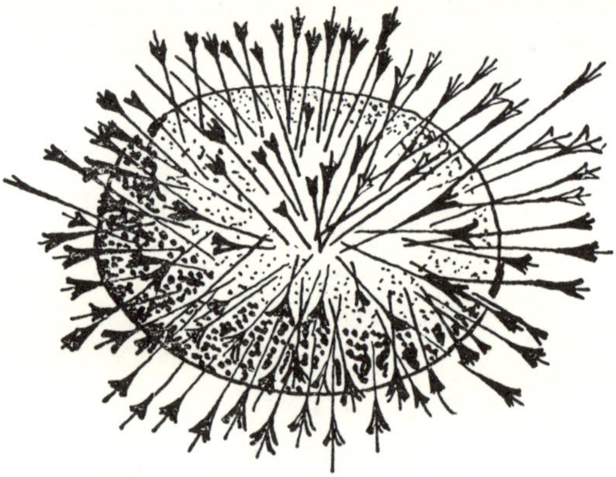

Fig. 28. Charm
See page 71

raised upon a clay step in the angle of the wall at the right hand corner. This consisted of two small round pots fixed neck-downward into the clay, while between them protruded a piece of wood, roughly phallic in form, on the upper surface of which two miniature Offor sticks were bound lengthwise and side by side. The object of this fetish was to bring prosperity in general and, in particular, many children to the compound.

A Juju, intended to represent a woman's body from the waist downward, was found among the same people. This was called Ite Uru, *i.e.* pot of gain, and was supported at the rear by the wall and in front upon two roughly modelled legs. It formed the principal cult object in the shrine of Chief Okuroji of Obokoffia and was set up by the grandfather of the present head of the house, but had been freshly decorated (Fig. 27).

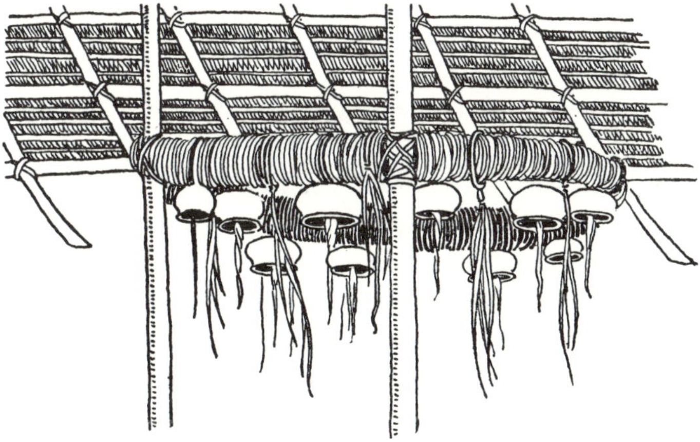

Fig. 29. Ibudu Nwa

Another Juju for bringing 'plenty piccans' to the house and for making them grow up fine, strong and tall—also for giving long life to its owner—was hung up to the roof over the main door of the head chief's house at Ndelle (Fig. 28). The arrows were planted so thickly that one could not see of what the oval groundwork was made.

At Ale-Barada, a charming town to the west of the Upper New Calabar River, never before visited by a white man, and which, as its name denotes, is under the special protection of the Earth Goddess, a Juju is to be found, called Ibudu Nwa, *i.e.* Ibudu for children. This occupies the centre of a rectangular shrine and is set beneath a canopy of tie-tie, attached to the roof, from which depend inverted pots, the shape of a shallow bell, each with a twist of gay-coloured cloth swinging, clapper-wise, from its centre. Beneath these hang fringes of palm-leaf, so long, in places, as almost to sweep the market-basket placed upon the neck of the strange, headless figure beneath (Fig. 29).

On marriage, before going to the bridegroom's house, each maiden of the town is brought by her friends to this shrine and, bending before the image, dips her hand into an earthen pot filled with 'medicine' which is placed there in readiness. Then she rubs her hands over the Juju, after which she laves them in a small bowl filled with pure water. Again she passes her left fingers over the image and afterwards over her own body; 'for' as the head chief explained, 'Ibudu Nwa is a very strong Juju in our town and will surely grant fruitfulness to all those who carry out these rites. So we were taught by our forefathers and this we believe even to-day. Should any man doubt, he has but to look round and see the many piccans which are born to our town.'

Between the upraised arms, resting upon the place where the head should be, is a market basket, full of dried roots, seed yams, etc. Outside the shrine, each protected by a small shed, were two unusually large phallic pillars, to which bridegrooms bring offerings.

Across all, from post to post, rising like Venetian masts, were long chains made from linked rings of creeper, from which hung, at intervals, inverted bowls with gay-coloured strips of cloth waving to and fro in the

Fig. 30. Ibudu Nwa at Ale-Barada

breeze, like those decorating the canopy of Ibudu Nwa. To the left stood a great tree, its trunk hung round with white cloth, the reputed home of a powerful and beneficent nature spirit. Before the principal shrine sprang little saplings of the bush which Ale first brought when she came swimming through the wide waste of waters to form the first abiding place for her children—men, beasts, trees and flowers.

Altogether Ale-Barada is a charming spot and the manners of the sons of the soil were unusually gentle and friendly. They willingly answered every question, in striking contrast to the inhabitants of the next town, Oduaha, where a Juju of somewhat different type is to be found. This was sullenly explained to us as without name and only used for protection—'not to give piccans.' The canoe upon its head was likewise stated to have been put there 'only to look fine. Not for any purpose.'

At Omo Hume, a quarter of Omo Dioga, another Ibudu was found, which was said to be intended as a representation of the Earth Goddess, here called Aja. In a little clearing to the right of the main road stood a shrine of unusual size, sheltering two phallic pillars. The smaller of these, placed in front and a little to the left, was obviously female and smeared with blood from the breast downward. The rear figure bore no name save 'Husband of Aja,' or at least none other was confided to us. So tall was this that it filled the whole space from floor to roof, looming, colossal and with a certain impressiveness, from out the shadows at the back of the shrine. Between the two, on either side, lay a piece of plaited palm-cloth, black and white, such as widows wear in some parts; while two deep fringes of palm-leaf were hung before the entrance, screening the strange, rude deities within from the glances of passers-by.

It was explained that the cloths were those of barren women, and had been laid at the feet of Aja and her spouse in the hope that, when resumed by their owners, the ban of sterility, imposed through the hate of some rival, might be broken by the power of the fertility-bestowing Earth Gods.

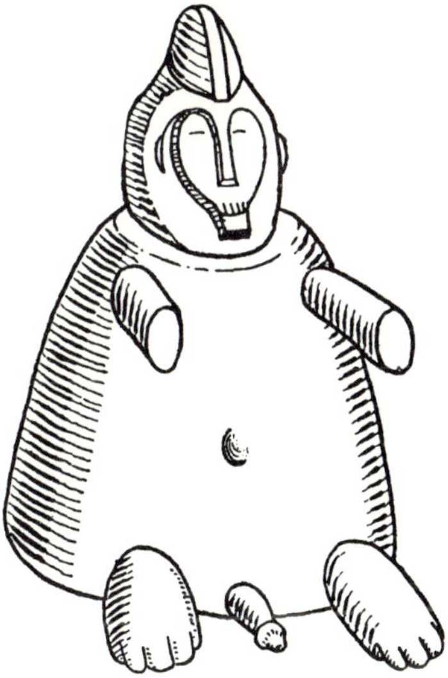

FIG. 31. Ibudu at Digiriga

At Bush Digiriga again, a small town to the east of the Sombreiro River inhabited by Abuan people and never before visited by Europeans—a Juju 'for the obtaining of piccans' is to be found, which in many ways resembles the Ibo Ibudu. About this particular fetish, however, there are certain points which we never met elsewhere. In addition to the high coiffure—a recognised symbol of femininity—the head is provided with a square beard in shape like those false ones worn during certain dynasties by Egyptian rulers, especially queens reigning in their own right. It is perhaps worth noting that, while the arms of the figure are mere stumps, without any attempt to reproduce hands, and the feet are so rude as to be almost shapeless, the phallus is modelled with the utmost care, showing that in the minds of its makers this detail was of very special significance.

Outside the entrance to the Omo Dara quarter of Akpani, an Ibudu of unique type may be seen, one looking-glass eye twinkling in the middle of its head beneath a ring of feathers set crown-wise in the clay. Before it, to a four-branched post, a medicine-pot was bound.

FIG. 32. Ibudu placed before the entrance to Omu Dara quarter of Akpani

In the midst of the quarter, beneath a little palm-leaf hut, stands a group of Ibudu. The largest of the pillars represents the female, the smaller the male, attributes. They are modelled seated back to back—a prostrate leopard lying to the left and a crater-like mound, containing a pot for Juju medicine, to the right. Chief Woke Abara, head of the quarter, gave the following explanation:

'Formerly it was very hard for us to get children. Nearly all our women were barren, so we raised the two Ibudu, one male and the other female. Since then we got plenty piccans in our town.' He added that the 'leopard spirit' helps the Juju to prevent the deaths of children. The small cone in the foreground and the headless animal lying in front of this were the work of the few children then existing.

With regard to the figure of a leopard, it is perhaps worth remarking that the ancient kings of Benin were wedded, in mystic spousals, with a leopard bride. Also, among thòse Ibo dwelling in the group of towns round Igrita, the spirits of the righteous dead often take

FIG. 33. Ibudu at Akpani

up their abode in leopard form while awaiting a new term of earth life, but those who enter into crocodile, ape, or bush cat, are regarded as for ever accursed.

Amid a branch of Kalabari settled at Oguta in Owerri District, a type of Ibudu is to be found, not, so far as our knowledge goes, to be met with in other parts. Each of these emblems consists of two sphinx-like figures, one male and the other female, facing different ways but joined together by a ridge of clay, which forms, as it were, the back of the sphinx.

At the Ibo town on the far side of the beautiful Oguta lake, we came across another phallic pillar combining the figures of the dual personality, male and female, of the Ibudu Ezum Mezum. As in the case of the Ale shrine, described on page 74, the consort was nameless, bearing no designation save that of husband of Ezum Mezum. The figure representing him held the place of honour at the base of the column which symbolises the joint attributes of the Juju; while, at a height almost double that of the husband, towers the face of the wife. On either side of the pillar, out-topping the male figure from the neck upwards, climb two great crocodiles; while placed here and there, at irregular intervals, human heads stand out in high relief.

Chief Onomonu, the owner of the shrine, told us:

> The Ibudu Ezum Mezum is mostly worshipped at Amaii in Abaw District and priests came thence to build this shrine for us. It was made at a time when a great sickness was raging in our town, in the hope of staying this scourge, granting protection and prosperity in general and especially to help our people in the bearing of piccans.

At its installation, about twelve years ago, the Abaw doctors held a great ' smelling out,' and, in consequence, decreed that the epidemic was caused by the witchcraft of the six *richest* women of the town, who must therefore be put to death and their property be made over to the medicine men! When informed of their doom, the victims refused to acquiesce and were therefore beaten to death in the market-place. The number of heads, modelled at irregular intervals over the pillar, corresponds to that of the victims thus slaughtered at the inauguration ceremonies—four at the back and two in front, between the sacred crocodiles. All are liberally smeared with blood poured upon the heads and trickling downward. This is the only example known to us at the time in which an Ibudu is so represented as to show the dual creative forces, male and female, combined so as to form a single pillar. Many Ibudu were later seen among the Abaw Ibo of Kwale District, where this particular type of symbol would seem to have reached its greatest development.

The phallic figures, above mentioned, are, however, by no means the only examples met with in West Africa of the mingling, in one object, of male and female symbols. For instance, the emblem of the greatest of all Ekoi Jujus, Eja, unmistakably combines the two. Here, the phallus, represented with the uttermost pains and fidelity, is the sign of the harvest god himself, while the bowl-like object to which it is attached represents the womb of his wife Ekumoke. The united symbol stands upon a base formed of wide-open human jaws.[1]

Among the Ekoi, both in the South Cameroons and Southern Nigeria, as indeed throughout the greater part of the West Coast generally, a pot or calabash is regarded as a feminine symbol, and it is of considerable significance that traces of male semen have been found

[1] *In the Shadow of the Bush*, p. 76.

in no inconsiderable number of the pots set before Ibudu images and in other Juju shrines throughout the Ibo country. This fact is vouched for by a medical officer.

In the ritual chant sung by Ekoi at the festival of Eja, which is also the feast of the first fruits, the names of the combined deities are always invoked :

Man Eja! I am staying with you.
O, I am staying with you!
Ekumoke ! I am staying with you.
O, I am staying with you !

Of these two deities it was expressly stated: ‘ Eja is male and the most strong. Ekumoke is less strong than Eja; nevertheless without her help he can do nothing.’

During the annual rites a woman was formerly sacrificed and the genital organs cut out and laid in the sacred pot, which contains the ‘ medicine ’ of the cult. Since the coming of Government it has naturally become increasingly difficult to obtain this necessary ingredient, and it was a matter of grave anxiety on the part of the priest lest the power of the Juju should decrease in consequence.

Amidst some of the eastern Ibo sub-tribes and the northern Semi-Bantu, the ancestors are represented by small clay pillars or mounds, clay balls or round or pointed stones, before which sacrifices are made and prayers offered for the granting of fertility, especially at the two great festivals of the year, the planting of farms and the harvest.

In those parts of the country where rock is available, *i.e.* among the northern Yoruba and Semi-Bantu, many stone monoliths may be found, some of which are unmistakably phallic, while others are used not only for this worship but also as ancestral memorials. In fact, the two cults are inexplicably mixed, as is natural when it is remembered that amongst these peoples fruitfulness is, to a large extent, attributed to the forefathers. Some of these memorials date back many hundreds of years; a fuller description will be found in Chapter XVII, vol. ii, of *The Peoples of Southern Nigeria*.

In the club-houses of the great Ekkpe secret society the sacrifices are made before a phallic monolith, which represents the former members of the club as also the tutelary deity, while in, or near, its base are generally placed rounded pebbles, the symbol of the Earth Goddess. A similar monolith is worshipped amongst many of the Bantu and Bafumbum-Bansaw as a representation of the supreme deity.

VII

EKU

All over the western part of the District a strange rite still obtains which is obviously only another manifestation of the phallic cult. As there are local differences it will be necessary to describe separately the peculiarities of each centre.

By the roadside near Umo Abale, a quarter of Omo Dioga, half hidden amid grass and creepers, we came across a crowd of figures formed of sun-baked clay, cone-shaped and painted black. Further on, in front of almost each compound, smaller groups were to be seen, usually arranged at the base of some Juju tree, or round a sapling of the sacred Ogrisi (*Dolichandrone* sp.). In several cases circular moulds of baked clay, much like an old-fashioned spittoon in shape, lay nearby. It was explained that upon these the girls of each compound, after undergoing the initiatory ceremonies preparatory to marriage, set the food cooked as an offering to the Eku, as the phallic figures are called. This word is also used to designate the cones of baked clay used to support cooking-pots. Should any girl, after arriving at the age of puberty and being inducted into the feminine mysteries, neglect to set up such an image each year, about the time of making new farms, until she becomes a member of her husband's house, no babes would bless their

Fig. 34. Eku at Umo Abale quarter of Omo Dioga

union. In one or two cases a slight amount of decoration, formed by lines drawn with the fingers in the soft clay, has been added; while here and there an attempt was made to surmount the cone by what was explained as a representation of the high head-dress only allowed to Ibo women after the birth of a babe. Mostly, however, the images showed nothing more or less than a simple attempt at depicting the phallus.

About a month later, at the house of Chief Ugwa in the Oturu quarter of Akpani, Eku of a still simpler type were found, together with clay pot-rests of much the same shape as those already described; while just outside, in the bush by the roadside, we came upon some thirty or more phallic figures, the tallest and frankest yet seen. Some stood on circular, some on rectangular, bases; but on each the membrum virile was modelled with especial care.

It was explained that every year, when making the more elaborate pillars, each betrothed girl fashions several of the plainer type, a foot to a foot and a half in height. These are said to be used as 'strong Juju on which to swear people.'[1] Three of these are borne by each maid to her bridegroom's compound, there to be presented to the chief woman of the family, by whom they are set together to support the pot in which food is cooked for the future husband. When ready, this is poured into a native bowl and placed upon the clay ring. After marriage, the bride comes to the new home and herself cooks her husband's

[1] It is perhaps worth remarking that among Mbolli all fire brick is used for the same purpose.

meals upon the same three pillars prepared by her own hands.

It is not without significance that the trinity of cone-shaped pillars, with cup-like depressions, raised before the Kalabari Nduen Fobara (ancestral shrines), into which libations to the forefathers are poured every eighth day, are of almost identical type. At Oru-Sangama, an ancient town on a creek leading into the San Bartholomeo River, we came across two of these small cones modelled within a circle, also of clay, beneath the palm-leaf roof of a tiny hut. So like were these to the Eku emblems that we took for granted that the little shrine was but another dwelling-place of one of the manifold representations of Ibudu Omumu, *i.e.* the Ibudu of fertility. Long sojourn in Africa should, however, teach caution even to the most careless enquirer, and we therefore, as always, took the precaution to keep our ideas to ourselves and asked the significance of the symbol. As a result we were told that they represented the Nduen Fobara of a neighbouring house. Our informant added:

> Some men make three, some two, small pillars for the pouring out of libations to the spirits of their dead. Some again make only one such emblem for the reception of drink offerings. Here no carved images are shown as is usual in rich Kalabari towns; the cones themselves represent the ancestors, except in the case of men of distinction.

Considering the peculiar powers thought by many tribes to attach to the phalli of the dead, especially those of warriors or others who excelled in strength or power, as also the Egyptian legend of the birth of

Fig. 35. Pillars, carved tusks, and bronze torques. Kalabari Shrine of Awome-Ka-So

Horus—that seed of life, snatched by the widowed Isis from Death himself—it is perhaps not too far fetched an idea to imagine that the likeness of symbol was intended to signify a connection between the physical body of the new-born and the astral shape or ethereal mould, supplied in most cases according to general belief from the ghost realm, where the ancestral shades await reincarnation—by preference in the bodies of those about to be born to the family to which they themselves formerly belonged.

Sir James Frazer, in his wonderful *Golden Bough*, tells of sacrificial victims whose phalli were beaten with twigs—not out of cruelty, but with the idea of increasing the powers of virility. Among the Ekkett Ibibio sacred boughs are drawn over the pudenda of warriors while parts are even cut off and buried secretly by the marriage bed, in the byre or on the farm. In this connection it is perhaps worth mentioning that one of the most dreaded of West African tortures, employed upon captives of distinction, was the continued flagellation of the phalli.

Chief Igo, of Omo Nelu, gave the following information:

> We start to make the Eki—as they are locally called—at the time of cutting the undergrowth for the new farms. Then, when we have carried out the images and set them up by the roadside, we begin clearing away the top branches. The ornamented pot-rests are used for cooking chop for the Eki.
>
> Chief Chuku's quarter cooks for two weeks (*i.e.* sixteen days). Amadi's and my quarter cook for thirty days. It is the young girls who make these things—both the cooking ones and the others. For twenty-five days we hold the first

festival, that of the low round Eki, which we call Eki Mother. Every evening at about five o'clock time the girls cook. On the twenty-fifth day each girl starts making one of the high Eki, Ada Eki (eldest daughter of Eki), which is worshipped for five days before carrying it out. When my father was alive, the ceremony always started in his compound; for he was

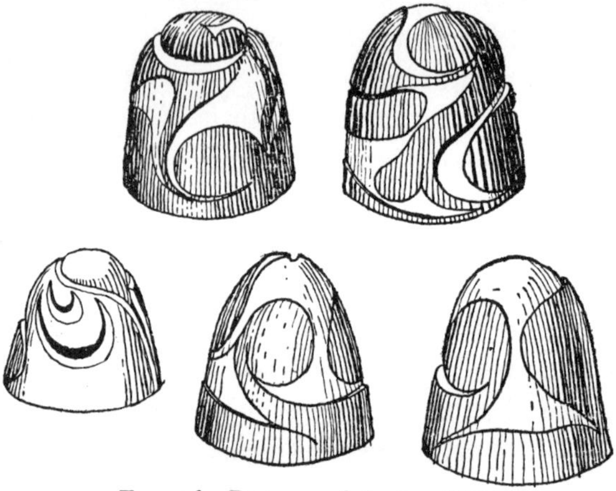

FIG. 36. Patterns of the low Eki

the head chief. After he had made festival for eight days, all the other compounds joined in and continued till thirty days were finished. Then all men took notice and said: 'It is now time to start the new farms.'

With us also the young girls go and get ant-hill earth before they make the Eki, but they do not use it for these, only keep it in their houses for three months and afterwards take it with them to the market-place, where they dance and play round it and then finally throw it away.

Egu 'Nde 'Nwayin is a woman's festival held at the time of digging new yams. It was my father, the priest of Ale, who set the time for this ceremony also. At this time the women dress very finely, wearing many beads round their ankles.

On another occasion, just after leaving Ndelle en route for Rumoji, we found, by the side of a bush path beneath the spreading branches of a Berlinia, a hut, the long, low, palm-leaf roof of which was covered with the fragrant white-petalled flowers showered down from above. Under this shelter was a platform of clay some twenty feet in length, carefully smoothed and with gaily coloured plates set at intervals along its edge. Upon this a double row of strangely-shaped finely-decorated figures were to be seen, formed of sun-dried clay, much in the style of the Eku already mentioned, but far more elaborately modelled and painted. On the bright yellow clay, ridges and lines of shining black, vivid blue and white were to be seen, while each was surmounted with an attempt to represent the elaborate styles of coiffure affected by girls of marriageable age.

Each had been brought thither by a maiden of the neighbourhood after undergoing initiatory rites in company with her 'age class.' The ceremonies are conducted in places set apart, under the leadership of elderly women of the town. The time chosen is after the planting of new farms when the seeds first germinate. At this season all little maids who have reached, or are approaching, the age of puberty—for the 'age class' includes those born within three years of one another—come together to be instructed, by matrons chosen for the purpose, in all that it is thought necessary for them to know as a preparation for marriage. Later, the neophytes return to their parents' house and there model the figures shown in the photograph. When all are ready they go, together with their instructress and a band of relatives, each bearing one of the Eku upon her head in procession to the spot chosen by priest or instructress. Here a platform of clay, decorated with insets of plates, pieces of looking-glass, etc., has already been prepared. The celebrants in turn place thereon the queerly shaped image which is supposed to be necessary in order to draw down upon the girl, who offers it, the blessing of fertility.

Beside those newly initiated, older maidens, to whom the mysteries have formerly been revealed but who are as yet unwedded, also take part in the rite, bearing a fresh Eku in the procession, year after year until the whole, or at any rate the main part, of the dowry has been paid, and they leave their parents' house for that of a husband. The elder girls offer images often over a yard in height, while the new initiates bring smaller ones, proportionate to their size.

At a little distance from the places set apart for the principal images, fish racks may occasionally be seen by the roadside and on, or between them, the smallest figures of all are to be found. These are said to represent 'the slaves of the Eku.' Each girl, after modelling her own symbol, makes at least one such little attendant, so that her image may be well served.

Near Ndelle waterside a somewhat different arrangement obtains. In front of the long line of Eku, a separate group may usually be found set round a sapling of the sacred Ogrisi tree. The central figure is dedicated to the principal girl of the town, while

Fig. 37. Group of Eku, near 'Ndelle

the smaller ones grouped round her represent her attendants. Near the centre, springing out of the clay base, was a small sprig of the bush which Ale brought with her when she first formed the earth.

At the same time of year, when the seed corn and yams lie awaiting rebirth in the womb of the Earth Mother, the unmarried girls of Elele carry out a ritual similar in many respects but with certain points of difference. Here the images are modelled from clay supplied not by the parents, as is usual in other parts, but by the bridegroom. These must be rubbed and smoothed for seven days and each is surmounted by a head, the coiffure of which is carefully copied from that of the girl herself. Every evening, food offerings are carried to the place where the Eki are set up, while the girls dance and sing before them. The bridegroom must provide from sixty to a hundred Awarawu manillas during this time, which are accepted by the parents as part of the dowry.

Often these strange images are modelled with breasts in addition to the male emblem. Is it an unwarrantable assumption to think that this may possibly be intended as a primitive attempt at picturing the ideal marriage, in which male and female attributes play equal parts? This peculiarity is not confined to the Eku but is even more marked in many Ibudu, as for instance the one already mentioned at the Umo Alipo compound, Omo Chuku.[1]

Some time after all the Eki have been set up in the farms, compounds and bush round Elele, preparations

[1] See p. 66.

are made for the carrying out of a further ceremony, called Nwan Aja, *i.e.* Child of the Earth, which is said to be closely related to the festival already described. For this, the unmarried girls of Elele go out to the bush and search round until each has found one of the great mounds thrown up by termites. 'With the help of relatives she digs down into this until she comes to the heart of the cave, named in our speech

FIG. 38. The Wekwe Eruru

Wekwe Eruru.' The floor of this looks like a mountain range in miniature. Breathless with excitement, the little maid counts the number of peaks; for just as many as there are of these, so many babes she will bear. With infinite pains, that not one may be broken off, she cuts round, then lifts the flat, roughly circular mass to her head and carries it home. This is a time of great anxiety; for, should any part break away during the process, the number of fallen points denotes —alas!—the still-born babes which fate will send her.

In some places all the girls of the quarter join together to seek out an ant hill and dig up the part in which dwells the queen ant. 'One of their number is appointed to carry this thing, which is then borne back to the town and set down on the road near some of the principal compounds. All stand watching to see in what direction the ants will go; for the way they take points out the compound in which the girls are to live until the time of the new yam harvest. There they must stay in seclusion, grinding cam wood and preparing for the approaching festival. Thither their future husbands come bringing palm-wine, yams and fish, together with six Awarawu manillas as dash for the owner of the compound.'

From many indications we had long suspected that the magic powers of the ant hill proceeded, in part at least, from its phallic resemblance. This was borne out by the number of Ibudu shrines, avowedly raised for the increase of children, before which these curious structures, known in these parts as 'Bush-men,' were found. In several, one of these lesser ant hills had been set up amid the special 'servants of the Juju' modelled on either hand of the principal image. Such an one is to be seen in the shrine of Ezum Mezum, erected within the compound of the Aro chief Ogunda of Azu-Miri near Nkarahia. On each side of the pillar stand her 'servants.' The nearest, a conventionalised phallic pillar surmounted by a head and with a little doorway in its tower-like base, through which one of the small elongated chalk cones—offered by every woman of the compound after conception—is seen, half in and half out, so as to appear in the act of entering. Next to this, but further from the image, is a natural ant hill, daubed with paint, against which leaned several of the lesser symbols.

These chalk cones or images, though more roughly moulded, bear considerable resemblance to those carefully modelled in clay and suspended over their father's shrine by each 'true daughter' of an Ibibio chief in the Mkpokk region to show that they were the

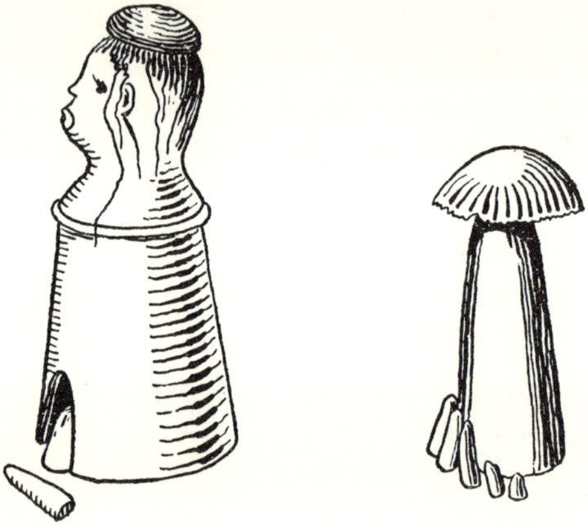

FIG. 39. The 'Servants of Ezum-Mezum'

legitimate offspring of the dead man, not of slaves, or of 'widows' born to the house, of whom he was only titular parent.

At the end of their period of seclusion in Nwan Aja's compound, the girls of Elele put on new cloths and gay ornaments, then sally forth to market (Eke Oma). This is a sign that the play is ended for the time.

Every other year a special play is given. According to Mr. D. Braid: 'This cannot be carried out more often, on account of the great expense incurred therein by the bridegroom. The name of this play is Ajiji'—

in some places Adidi or Adadi—' and it is one of the best of all plays for girls and ladies. It looks grand whenever they start same. They dress with brass ornaments, corals, etc., on their feet, all which expenses are run by the husbands, with the exception of the anklets for one foot which the parents are expected to provide. The brass ornaments are prepared by the blacksmiths, from nine Awarawu manillas for growing up ladies and four to five for younger girls. All go in procession round the town until they come to a place in the Omuneta quarter called Ebu, where there is a great tree in which dwells a certain powerful Juju. Here fowls are sacrificed and cut in such a manner that blood falls upon the feet of each girl. After this has been done, they sing all kinds of songs, dancing with great gladness for some hours.'

Both on the way there and back those girls who are about to marry rich men are carried in decorated chairs, with a canopy

fastened above them. Bearers are hired for this service by the future husbands. During the Ajiji ceremony many ghosts flock into the town. In olden days, these would strike the girls as they were borne by; because spirits are jealous of any mortal whose feet are not set upon the ground. A bride thus struck always sickens and usually dies within the year. That is the reason why, nowadays, each girl holds a picture before her, so that the ghosts may strike at this and let her go by unharmed.

On reaching home a feast is given by the parents and next morning all the girls take chop to the husbands' place. This food is distributed to all in his compound, together with rewards of money. The bridegroom is expected to do the same in return and all the expenses incurred by him at this time are counted as dowry. The play generally lasts for seven Ekes, *i.e.* about two months.

In October 1916, just outside Elele, on the Nkarahia road, a group of specially interesting symbolic images was found. It consisted in roughly modelled male and female figures, arranged in pairs and lying outstretched at the base of a great cotton tree (Akpu). The bays, formed by its buttress-like roots, were separated from one another by giant snakes moulded in clay, which, arranged in irregular loops, usually with the tail of one against the tail of the other, served to fence off the sacred enclosure from the wayside. Within the various bays thus formed smaller serpents twined and twisted, often placed between the male and female figures. In one case the phallic serpent was shown in the act of entering the body of a woman.

Dotted over the slope, forked sticks were seen driven into the ground or raised on little clay mounds. From these depended strings of great snail shells (*Acatina marginata*) or empty fish racks, in shape much like the head of a Badminton racquet.

This group, the name of which was given as Akpu Ogbe Ajiji, had been modelled by maidens of marriageable age belonging to Chief Woyike's compound as an additional means of increasing fertility.

Just beyond Elele Aliminni, on the Ndelle road, a great tree may be found to the Genius of which the unmarried girls of the neighbourhood go and pray during the Ajiji—locally called Adidi—ceremony. Three circular clay steps are built, one above the

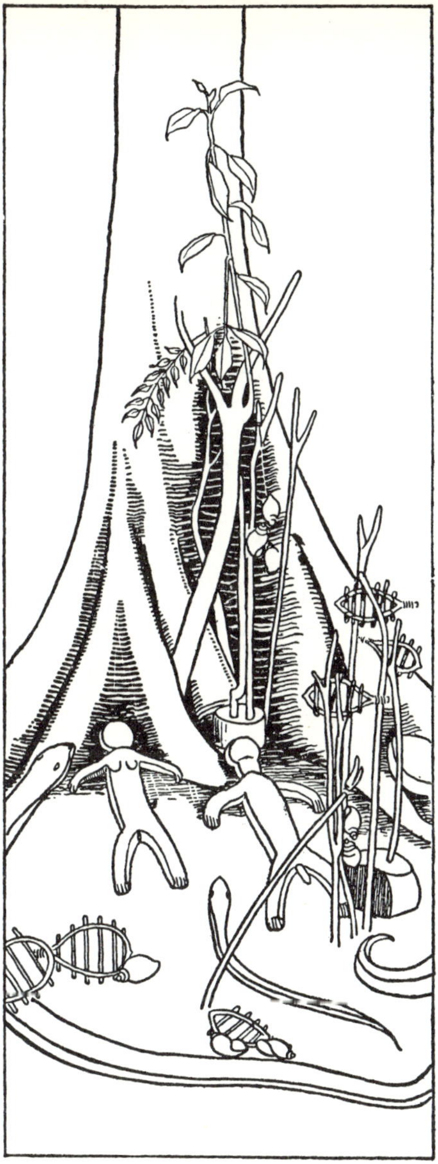

FIG. 40. Clay figures at base of cotton tree near Elele

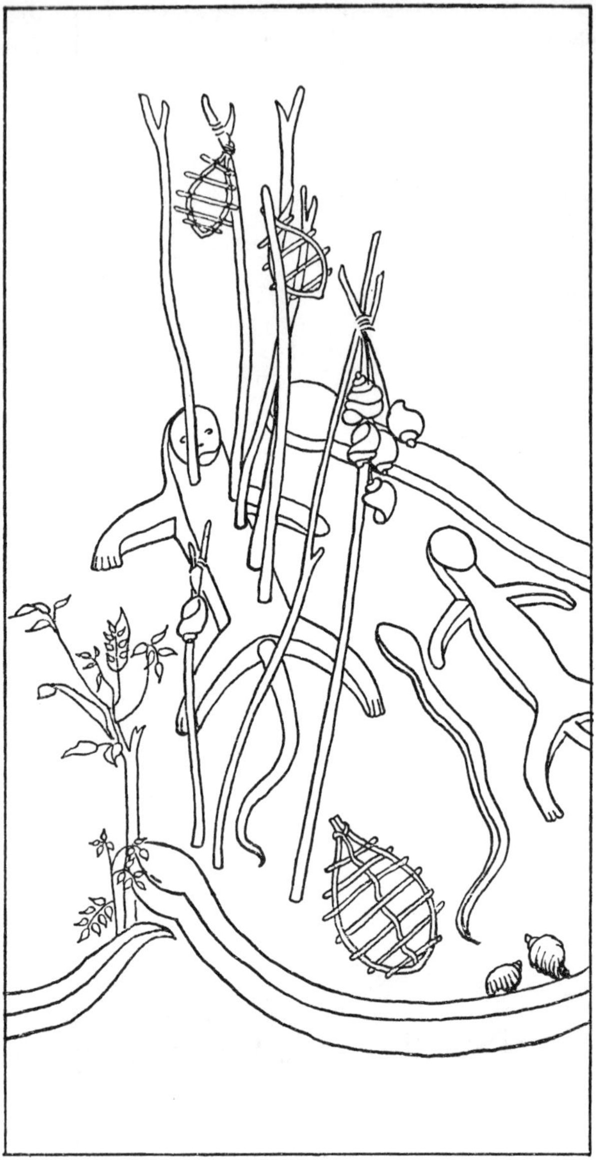

Fig. 41. Figures at base of cotton tree near Elele
See p. 94

other, round the base of the tree and reaching about four feet up its trunk, forming a rough altar upon which piles of *Acatina marginata* shells and empty fish racks (Paka Eji) were laid. A few yards further, in front of the compound of Chief Ofonda, a large terminal bud of the banana flower-spike, pierced with four slivers of wood was set up on a tall palm stalk. This bud is called Eni Awsoku, *i.e.* navel of plantain or banana. It is natural enough that these two trees should bear

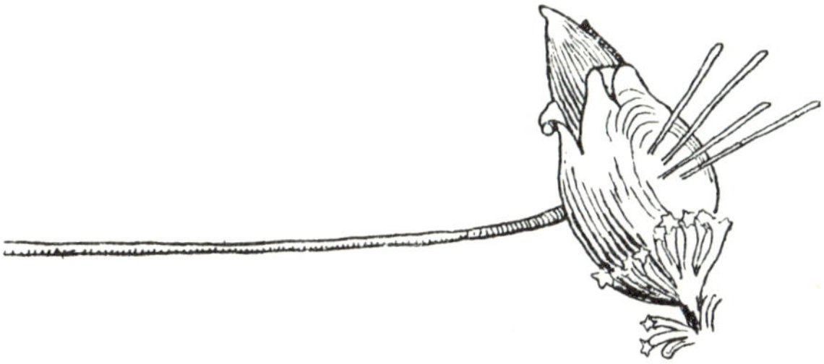

FIG. 42. The Eni Awsoku

special significance in the fertility rites. The combination of phallic-shaped fruit and terminal bud with its oval form offers an obvious symbol of the male and female reproductive organs.

After building the Adidi altar and setting up Eni Awsoku, the celebrants go in procession round the town, their faces rubbed with chalk of a pale café au lait shade and their hair covered with bright yellow paste. From a distance this colouring gives them a curiously European look. At the back, hanging round the waist, they wear a kind of apron of large glass beads, arranged in alternate squares, usually green and brown in colour, the whole fringed with little brass balls.

After a girl has been given in marriage and has gone to live with her husband, she may never again take part in the Ajiji play. At the end of the series of Eku ceremonies, which last, roughly speaking, from the ending of farm planting to harvest time, the whole town of Elele goes to Chief Eleche's compound for the feast of new yams which is held in honour of the great Juju Aya-Eke. On this occasion every man, woman and child bears a gift to the priest. Even little babes, too small to stand alone, are borne before him. The mothers press a gift into the tiny hands and then hold them out towards the chief that not even the smallest should fail to make offering.

The name Ajiji, given by Ibo to the greatest play in the series, would seem to be derived from Aja (sacrifice), which is also in some parts the name of the Earth Goddess herself, and Ji (yam).

VIII

THE YAM CULT

At the cutting of new farms most Ibo chiefs make sacrifice to Ale and again before harvest. Beside offerings to her, some should also be made to the Ajokko-Ji[1] or Njokkoji—the king (or Juju) yam, the biggest one of all the crop in which the yam spirit is thought to take up its abode. This is always set aside from one season to another, and when bird or beast is slain in sacrifice to the Genius of the farm, the blood is thrown upon the Ajokko-Ji.

> Should a man find that he has more yams one year than in the seasons before, he brings the richest sacrifice in his power and offers it in thanks to the Farm Spirit for giving increase and doing good to him. The word Ajokko means Juju, but it is also used with the signification of 'great' and 'mighty.' This king yam, as it is sometimes called, is kept throughout the whole year until next harvest comes round. Either fowls' or goats' blood should be poured out in libation upon it. Formerly a spirit dwelt within, which protected all the yam racks in the farm. Now, owing to the dying out of such beliefs, people are not afraid to steal from these. In olden days they never dared to do such a thing for dread of the yam Juju.

While visiting Oppe, a farm settlement just outside Alessa, we were shown a 'strong Juju' connected

[1] The Ajokko-Ji, the Yam Spirit, is further described in *The Peoples of Southern Nigeria*.

with the worship of Nkike, the Mbolli Earth Goddess. This was formed from a collection of skulls, yams and other roots, bound round with tie-tie into the form of a gigantic yam and then attached to a stout stake, the end of which was sharply pointed for driving into the ground. This symbol was said to take, for the

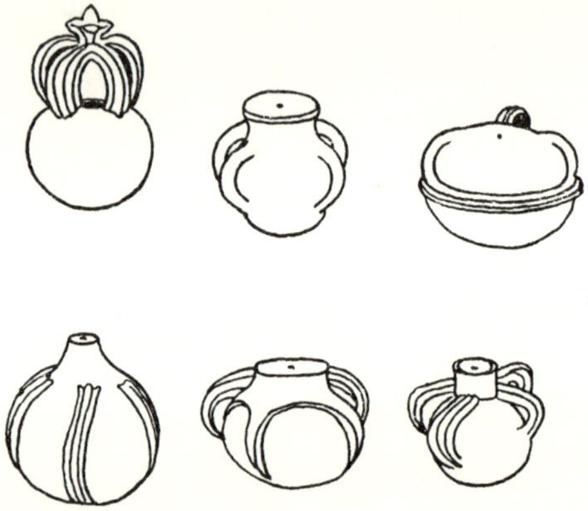

Fig. 43. Ife Ja Okko or Ife Ajokko at Ogu

Mbolli, the place of the giant Ajokko-Ji to which Ibo offer sacrifice.

A more elaborate substitute was found at Ogu on the Niger—a town occupied by a sub-tribe of Ibo, allied to those of Onitsha. There, in the house of one of the secondary chiefs, a row of small pots was seen, set in the clay floor, along one side of the verandah. These were explained as the Ife Ajokko—called Ife Ja-Okko by some—which for this tribe take the place of the Ajokko-Ji. There were nine pots of different shape; the number was explained by saying that, as each chief succeeded to the headship of the house, a new Ife

Ajokko was made. Eight, therefore, were those belonging to the ancestors.

Among Mbolli the phallic pillars are of a peculiar type mostly carved from wooden blocks instead of being built in clay. Of these, the one in the Juju house at Obudu may be taken as typical. Such bear the name Obo-Esa—the four hundred yams—and are specially raised as a means of increasing the crops.

When a fresh farm is cut, a special ceremony is carried out to induce the yam spirit to transfer its abode from the old farm to the new. The basket in which the great yam is contained, or post to which it is bound, is usually kept near a sapling of the tree which over the greater part of the West Coast is regarded as most sacred of all. This is a variety of Dolichandrone—strangely named considering the functions ascribed to it by natives—called by Kalabari Odumdum and by Ibo Ogrisi.

Among Ekoi, Efik and Ibibio, this beautiful tree with its glossy imparipinnate leaves and great clusters of pinkish-mauve flowers, is known as 'The Mother of the Town,' and a sapling of it is planted in nearly every compound. The finest specimen ever seen by us was found in one of the town playgrounds at Ikotobo in the Eket District.

Within the hollow trunk stood native pots filled with offerings, for to it come wives, young and old, to pray that 'plenty piccans' may be sent to bless their hearths. Hither, too, come ancient women to beg a like boon for their children and grandchildren. Should lightning shiver the ancient trunk or tornado strike it down, loud would be the wailing of those who had grown up beneath its shadow.[1]

It is unusual that trees of this species grow to such a size; yet very few compounds in the Ibo country are without a sturdy sapling, for not only its fertility-bestowing but also its purificatory powers are held in the utmost reverence. Should a Kalabari woman meet with vexation which causes her to shed tears while cooking her husband's food, it is thought that this will have ill results upon him unless, before serving it, she plucks some of the sacred leaves, draws them over her body and then strikes them upon the ground round about, that the evil effect of her tears may be negatived and her husband not suffer therefrom.

Not only is the Ajokko-Ji usually kept beneath the shelter of these sacred boughs, unless confided to the care of the ghosts in some ancestral shrine, but the Ogrisi itself becomes a symbol of the yam spirit. It was principally in this capacity, as emblem of the chief crop of the year, that at the death of each chief important enough to own an Obiri (reception room)—*i.e.* every head of a family of standing—a slave was killed as a sacrifice to the sacred tree.

Such unfortunate members of the community were well fed for several days, during which everything was done to cause them to be of good cheer and in perfect condition. Then they were robed in gay apparel and led forth to the sacred tree, where their throats were cut in such a manner that the blood flowed to the ground, fertilising the earth about its

[1] *Woman's Mysteries of a Primitive People* (Cassell), p. 81.

roots. No portion of such victims was ever eaten; their bodies were buried near by that thus Mother Ale might be enriched and induced to grant plentiful crops to those who brought her the offering.

The following information concerning the great Elele yam cult, Aya-Eke, was gleaned from Mr. D. Braid, for several years Native Court clerk of this town:

The compound where the Juju is kept is called Omo Kpurukpu and there, from election until death—at most seven years later, even should the full term of office be completed—the priest dwells, carefully guarded by all his people and never crossing the threshold unless called forth by some grave emergency. The reason for this restriction is that up to a few years ago any man who succeeded in killing the holder of this office would reign in his stead.

The whole prosperity of the town, especially the fruitfulness of farm, byre and marriage-bed, was linked with his life. Should he fall sick, it entailed famine and grave disaster upon the inhabitants, and there is reason to believe that, in such a case, facilities were offered to a successor. Under no circumstances did the term of office last for more than seven full years. This prohibition still holds; but since the coming of Government it is said that another of the same family, who must always be a strong man, may be chosen to take up the position in his stead. No sooner is a successor appointed, however, than the former priest is reported to 'die for himself.' It was frankly owned that, before Government came—*i.e.* some dozen years ago—things were arranged differently in that, at any time during his seven years' term, the priest might be put to death by one strong and resourceful enough to overcome him.

In answer to the question as to whether, in view of the fate known to follow after so short a period, it was not difficult to find men willing to succeed to the office on such terms, Mr. Braid answered in a somewhat surprised tone: 'Oh, no! Many wish for the post, because so much wealth is brought them at the annual festival that they become very rich—past all others in the town.'

Our informant also stated that, during his own term of office, Chief Eleche has only once been known to pass beyond the compound walls. The occasion was as follows:

A fellow townsman accused him of making a Juju to kill the complainant. The case came into court and, all unconscious of the excitement which such a proceeding must cause, the chief was bidden to attend and answer the charge. He arrived, accompanied by nearly all the townsfolk, who not only filled the court-yard, which is a very large enclosed space, but thronged the market-place outside. They came, in a state of great anxiety, to watch over the sacred priest and guard him, so far as in them lay, from any misfortune the effects of which, it was believed, would at once react on all the countryside.

Doubtless Mr. Braid would have been less ready to impart information of this nature, had it not been that he was about to leave the place, in all probability never to return, and had therefore nothing to fear from the townspeople. So soon as other official work allowed, I returned to Elele to adjust some difficulties which had meantime arisen, and also with the hope of gleaning further knowledge concerning Aya-Eke and its priest.

First I looked up the case in the course of which Eleche was summoned to appear. This was recorded under No. 353 and was heard on 7th December, 1914. It runs, in substance, as follows:

Yenanu, the plaintiff, stated on oath:

About two years ago I fell sick and the native doctors told me that people of my compound were trying to kill me. I therefore called a family meeting, in which the big men decided that Juju should be sworn for me. Eleche performed the ceremony, calling upon the Juju to slay anyone guilty of trying to bring about my death before new corn time. If this happened, they agreed to pay me four hundred manillas, four demi-johns of tombo, a basket of yams and a bottle of gin. Should no one die, it would prove that the accusation was untrue and I myself must pay the like amount in compensation for bringing a false charge. The time fixed upon had not expired when one of the men died, but I did not ask for payment.

Nine months after swearing Juju, the accused called me at Oka's compound and informed me that it was now young corn time; yet no one had died, therefore I must pay the amount agreed upon. This I refused to do since one of them had been slain by the Juju. Then they conspired together and gave orders that I should be killed; also they put Juju in my well to prevent me and my people from getting water. Certain Jujus were also hung on the road to my farm by Eleche and Okuku. On this I went to Chief

> Chioma and related the whole matter. He advised me not to eat any yams from the farm near which the Juju was placed. After this they ordered me to clean a portion of the road, but seeing that they were seeking to kill me I refused and went to work with Chief Chioma's people. After the road was finished, I was called before a meeting at Woda's house, where they ordered me to break down my compound and take all my properties to Chioma's quarter.

Oluene, witness for plaintiff, stated on oath:

> I was present at the family meeting when the accused consulted together and made a rule that anyone who saw Yenanu should kill him ; nor did any of our people allow him to take fire, etc., from their houses.

The case was dismissed, but the complainant died soon after. Next Eke day, Eleche, wearing his Juju hat trimmed with seven eagle's feathers and the tail of a parrot, sallied forth, followed by all his people, to hold a progress throughout the town, while his attendants triumphantly proclaimed that Aya-Eke had slain the man who dared to summon her priest before mortal tribune.

On arrival at Elele our next step was to seek further information from the head men of the town, when these came to salute us. At first, the result was distinctly disappointing. No one had ever heard of the Juju or its priest! In fact, on the authority of all the principal inhabitants, no institution even remotely resembling Aya-Eke existed in the neighbourhood. Only after the case above quoted was shown to them did a light dawn upon the chiefs. Ah yes, they said, in very ancient days they believed there was some such

Juju in their town, but the memory of it had long since died away. As for Eleche, now they came to think of it, the priesthood had been in his family and possibly even he might hold that the office had descended to him. Since Government came to their country however—this with the most ingratiating smile—people had no use for such old superstitions, which had therefore fallen into utter neglect and forgetfulness. It was eagerly stated that there were other customs in their town much more worthy of the notice of the District Commissioner—for instance, Odo's Juju, the head priest of which was immediately found and brought forward. It would indeed be a pity, they added deferentially, should our time be wasted in enquiries into matters of so little account as those with which Eleche was concerned.

It was quite obvious that one and all were anxious to prevent further investigations and the result of the interview was naturally to send us hot-foot to the Omo-Kpurukpu quarter of the town, which is separated from the main section by some half mile of road. Here, in a house formed of elaborately carved wooden panels—to the best of my belief the only dwelling of its kind throughout the whole Division—lived the priest-king Eleche. Before the house stood a rude figure, formed of a stout post bound round with cloth, crowned with a cap and with two sticks extending arm-wise at right angles from near the top. This represented the late priest Eyinda, a brother of the present holder of the dignity, said to have died about two years ago.

Eleche himself wore a similar hat of office, its crown bound with a strip of white cloth, into which the seven emblematic eagle's feathers and the parrot's tail were fastened. He explained that he could not yet wear the full Juju dress of white baft, because he was not entitled to don this until after the third year of his priesthood, which period would not be ended before next harvest. His predecessors in the office, so far as his personal recollection went, had been named Eyìnda, Omeneyin, Wana and Azunda. He himself had been a small boy when Azunda died. 'These,' said he, 'were great men of our house. Now of them all I alone am left to carry out the rites of the Juju, which is so powerful that death falls upon every man who offends against its laws.'

> The rule of this Juju is very good, much like the law of the white men. By it, it is decreed, that no fighting or quarrelling, no seizure of property—above all, no shedding of blood—may take place upon Eke day.[1] No priest of Aya-Eke may eat of the new season's yams. All the harvest must be garnered and the festival held. Then, though others may eat, I may not until all the new farms have been cut and planted. Only when the last of the seed yams has been laid in the ground do the people bring me those which yet remain over in the yam racks. These I eat, calling the first of them 'my new season's yam' though, in reality, it was garnered at the last harvest about seven moons before.

Our visit chanced to be paid at the beginning of April, and Eleche told us that nine days earlier he had eaten his first yam of the year.

[1] Eke day is one of the four days of the Ibo week. It is market day at Elele. Eke is also the name of the great python. See p. 7.

'All the people of Elele bring offerings to me,' he said. 'When the yams finish they bring plantains and I begin to chop those. Also they bring me much tombo. It is a very strong law of the Juju that no yams, save such as are old enough to plant, may be eaten by a priest of Aya-Eke. None has ever broken this rule; for, should it be disobeyed, the seed yams would die in the ground, bearing no increase. All the great men of our family have kept the law faithfully. Now no more big men are left in our house; but I, though but a small boy in comparison with those powerful ones, also hold to this rule.'

Hereupon one of our party asked if he himself had power to appoint a successor, or in what way one was chosen. No sooner was the word 'successor' uttered than Eleche raised his arms over his head twice as though to ward off threatened danger, while his head wife, who kept close to him throughout, shrugged her shoulders violently over and over again, repeating in an agitated voice: 'Mba! Mba! Che! Che!' (Let it not be! Let it not be!) Meanwhile the crowd of retainers took up the cry, low but angry, like the rumble of distant thunder, waving hands outward as if to drive off the ill-effects of such ominous speech. Eleche answered excitedly, the words tumbling over one another in his agitation:

'No successor is needed; for I shall never die! It is forbidden even to mention such a word! In the beginning of things, when I came out of the world, it was arranged that I should not be as other men but should live very long—looking after my people and bringing them prosperity. The fate of common men is not for me!' Thereupon, like a Greek chorus, came the response of the crowd: 'Oda! Oda! (Forbid it! Forbid it!)

The head wife, who had seated herself so soon as her husband did so, although all the others remained standing at a respectful distance, was a youngish woman evidently holding a position of more than usual importance. Later, we learned that it was customary for this head wife to die 'about the same time as her husband'; but all attempts to extract more definite information were met with professions of ignorance.

The most important ceremonies of the cult are held at the time of the new yam harvest, when a great sacrifice is made and, as already mentioned, every man, woman and child of Elele brings a gift to the house of the priest. Before leaving, we asked whether no other rites were observed in honour of Aya-Eke and were told that early in May, *i.e.* at the beginning of the rainy season, all the inhabitants gathered to witness a wrestling match held in the open space before Eleche's house. This is continued on every big Eke day, *i.e.* each eighth day, for about three months until the new yam festival, during which the feast of the ancestral spirits is also celebrated. Later, all go to Chief Woyike's compound in the Omopo quarter and there wrestle in honour of the new corn Juju, Mbara (Lord of the Town), of which he is priest. After his festival is over, all wrestling finishes for the year.

No sooner had we learned this than we set out for the new shrine. Here, at the opposite extremity of the town, lies the compound known as Obakere, inhabited by Woyike, priest of the rival Juju. The chief received us with simple friendliness and seemed

FIG. 44. Chief Eleche with his head wife, standing by memorial pillar of the late Head Priest of Aya-Eke

willing for a visit to his shrine. Nor, after the first shyness had worn off, did he show any reluctance to speak of the Juju, concerning which a few carefully-careless questions brought out the following information:

> When the wrestling at Eleche's is finished, all men come here to witness mine; after which the whole town must cease from such contests, which may not be held again till the next season comes round. We think that this ceremony will help the crops to grow strong, overcoming evil influences and bearing much increase. The reason why the wrestling is held first at Eleche's place and then mine, is that his Juju Aya-Eke is wife to my Juju 'Mbara. The first is feminine and looks after the yams; mine is male, the spirit of corn. When the first green shoot pushes through the soil, I make ready and, on the coming of the young cobs, my Juju proclaims a four months' peace. During this time no one may fight with another nor seize any person or property. Should a man offend against this rule six manillas and a goat must be paid to revoke the Juju for him, otherwise he would die.
>
> When the time comes round, I go forth and announce that if anyone does anything to annoy the Juju I will not allow him to take part in my ceremony. To me no gifts are brought like those borne every year to Eleche; but when the season comes round I make a great feast for the people, giving them much food and palm-wine in abundance.

The priest was old and somewhat worn looking. Round his shrunken ankles were bound little bones, pierced through at either end and fastened by black cord in three rows. These, he said, were a powerful medicine to keep off rhcumatics and other ills which beset the aged, but had nothing to do with his Juju.

'How indeed could such a thing be possible,' he queried,

> since 'Mbara is a male Juju and the bones are those of Tortoise, who, as is well known, is proper only to feminine cults? By the place where I usually sit a tortoise was impaled years ago for protection; then, when it was decayed enough, I took the little bones out from the shell and, after they had been cleaned, strung them into these anklets, as you see. There are three Ale shrines in our town, by each of which Tortoise is impaled. Also before the shrine of Aya-Eke a shell may naturally be seen.

Towards the middle of May we found ourselves back again in Elele and enquiries brought out the fact that the first wrestling of Aya-Eke was to be held about noon on the morrow. The hour seemed a strange one to choose for such a purpose, under a tropical sun; but before mid-day drums began to beat in the distance, summoning the people with the unmistakable rhythm only used for such occasions. So soon therefore as court was over, we set out to follow the call.

It was 15th May and a day of blazing sunshine; yet crowds had already collected and sat, the elect in a circle many deep round the compound, while the rest almost blocked the road along its front. Three sets of drums were playing; first Eleche's household band, secondly one supplied by a neighbouring quarter, and thirdly, just before the shrine, that which bore the proud name of 'The Juju's Own.' This consisted of six drums, three tall and upright, three long and oval.

Opposite the door of the principal shrine a little group of offerings was to be seen, backed by the branched sticks of the Thunder God. Questioned as to this, Eleche said:

> Amade Onhia is kin to my Juju. In many towns the biggest Jujus have the habit of sending to request him to come and stay by them. Aya-Eke did this and ordered that his shrine should be placed opposite to her own, saying that when ceremonies were made in her honour they should be performed for him also. On being asked as to when the wrestling would begin, Eleche answered, with true African placidity, that this depended upon the arrival of the combatants, who would probably not appear until the sun sank lower in the heavens. He explained that he had told us the play began at mid-day, because by ancient custom the summoning drums must start at that time.

Now, according to widespread West Coast belief, noon and midnight are the special times at which ghosts walk abroad. Among Ibo and Kalabari little children are warned never to throw sticks or stones when the sun is high overhead, lest they should inadvertently injure one of these wandering spirits and thus draw down its wrath upon themselves. With Mbolli and Etche Ibo—as usually in the Ikwerri country—seed yams and corn are stored in the shrine of the ancestors, *i.e.* beneath the guardianship of these beneficent friends, much as was the seed-grain of ancient Rome within the sacred Mundus. Chief Eleche also told us that the Egu Nda Madu, the festival of the forefathers, is always held at the same time as that of the new yams and, were these rites neglected, the ghosts would cease to exert a protective influence upon the next season's crops. It is probable, therefore, that the reason the drums must start to play at noonday is to call the attention of the ancestral shades to the fact that the ritual wrestling is about to begin.

First, one or two youths stepped out, at long intervals, from the ranks of patient spectators, to dance round in wide circles, always from left to right—in the contrary direction to the hands of a clock. Later, as the shadows lengthened, more and more joined in the pastime, till from twenty to thirty were dancing almost continuously. Nearly all raised eyes and hands to heaven at a point, roughly speaking, halfway round the circle. Most of the performers wore necklets of knotted palm, while a considerable number bore in addition a single vivid bloom of the scarlet Akpane Besin—the old Ekoi wrestlers' challenge—stuck in their black locks.

In the midst of the circle danced a strange figure, wearing a tail of skin behind and a long strip of blue native cloth falling before. Round his waist was a girdle of brass bells; a band of cowries, three deep, was fastened beneath the knee, while a cloth of leaf-green silk was tightly bound round the loins. In his right hand he bore a horn, black and twisted like that of a bushbuck, the open end filled with a tassel of long fur. This, when stationary, he sometimes drove point downwards into the earth or, while circling round with the other dancers, bore it raised over his head. Chief Yellow explained that such was the traditional wrestlers' costume.

During the dances several 'masters of ceremonies,' bearing bunches of palm-leaves, went up and down, keeping a clear space—driving back the circle of

Fig. 45. Wrestling to make the yams grow. Chief Eleche's place, Elele

spectators by striking these on legs and feet. Suddenly the performers scattered, leaving two of their number alone in the centre. These bent and touched the ground with their fingers, then almost immediately gripped and after a struggle, which caused the wildest excitement among the spectators, the taller and slighter of the two flung the other to earth and seated himself firmly astride the prostrate form—to be lifted upon the shoulders of a friend and thus borne round amid the plaudits of the multitude.

So it went on, couple after couple struggling till one was overthrown. Occasionally, if they were deemed ill matched or thought to be growing angry, friends rushed in, as is usual in such contests, to separate the combatants. What struck us as unusual was the short time allowed to each pair. Should one not succeed in throwing the other after the first few minutes the spectators flung themselves between and bore them apart by force. This was explained to be 'lest they should become exhausted,' and was possibly done with the idea that such a result might, by sympathetic magic, have an ill effect upon the crops.

These wrestling rites are carried out amongst nearly all the Ibo in the Division, though held in greatest importance among the Ikwerri. The same ceremony is customary with the Mbolli, whose head chief told us: 'When the season comes round for the festival of Mbiencha,[1] we make sacrifice to her of fowls and goats. After the sacrifice has been made, we start wrestling. We do this for children, farms and health.'

[1] Mbiencha is the child of Nkike, the Mbolli Earth Goddess.

One evening, during our stay at Elele, we heard the sound of a far-off tom-tom, beaten with a queer insistent call. The method of playing was new to us, so without a word to any one we set out to investigate. There was no need to ask the way, since it was easy enough to follow the beat of the drum. This led through the market-place along the Omo Dioga road; then, after a sharp turn to the right, we found ourselves in an open space, upon one side of which trees tossed dark branches against a sky of scuttling cloud.

The moon, nearing her third quarter, was climbing up the heavens, shedding a cloud of misty silver radiance upon the scene beneath. By a fortunate chance our shoes fell soundlessly upon the soft sand; so we stole in unnoticed, shadows amid a multitude of shadows which flitted to and fro 'now in glimmer and now in gloom'—in swaying, everchanging lines of a dance impossible to describe.

My companions were wearing white, as was nearly every woman and most of the men present. The latter mostly wore long flowing Hausa robes, bought or imitated from the fashion set by Chief Ododo, the enterprising Hausa who, following in the steps of a mighty elephant-hunter of his race, settled here and made himself chief of the town.

At once, on realising what was going forward, we slipped into a pool of shadow, cast, it seemed, expressly for our convenience in a spot where we could see everything but ourselves passed for a while unnoticed.

Men and women danced in separate lines, approaching and retreating. To our surprise we saw that many of the latter wore not only white robes but white coiffures as well; for their crisp, dark wool was covered with a dressing of native chalk or pale-tinted clay, while the faces were often streaked with white lines, giving them an appearance indescribably ghost-like. To and fro, backward and forward, co-mingling at one moment and the next in clearly defined lines, moved the dancers to the monotonous tom-toming of their strange orchestra, which somehow managed to suggest things beyond the power of words—the fall of the first rains upon the parched earth; the enfolding of soft mists, from whose gentle embrace springs a stirring and quickening, changing her barrenness into fruition; the swelling of grain and root crops in the dark ground; the first feeble upward striving of young shoots, later to spring into radiant verdure in the free air above; the passion of pride, of life and strength and love—all that is poignantly felt but can seldom be expressed save perhaps by the monotonous beat of the tom-tom, the strange soughing of elephant horns and thrumming of savage lyres on such a night as this.

Only one air evolved by a northern musician gives any idea of the effect of these weird African melodies—that is the Braut March in *Lohengrin*, which, written on so few notes, yet beats with a strange persistence on certain fibres of the human instrument. In this, too, the theme is much the same—the bringing of the Earth Bride to the arms of her mystic bridegroom. Each thema, monotonous in itself, changed imperceptibly into another equally monotonous but built on different notes and shadowing forth a very infinitude of meaning.

In and out among the dancers crept strange shapes, elaborately coiffured and with whitened faces, much in the style of some Ibo masks, at the time of unknown origin, which wandered into our collection several years ago. These have since been explained as typifying the moon, much after the manner of the so-called Isis masks of the Pangwe Moon Goddess So; or again as representing those strange wanderers from the ghost realm, the spirits of beneficent ancestors who watch over the harvests of their descendants.

Hardly daring to breathe, we watched the strange phantasmagoric figures pass to and fro in the intricate mazes of the dance—the lines merging and separating in oozy triangles, squares and circles such as those woven by Ka for the perdition of the Banda Log.

Suddenly a change came over the scene. The tom-toms sounded a series of sharp insistent strokes. The moon, emerging from friendly clouds, shed a brilliant light upon the place where we had hitherto remained hidden in shadow, and the crowd, grown aware of our presence, began to scatter. We withdrew with all possible speed since nothing further was to be learnt by delay. After our departure the mystic dance began once more and continued, as could be heard from the far-away drumming, almost till the first rays of dawn.

On 26th July chance led us to pass by Chief Eleche's compound while a ceremony connected with the Aya-Eke cult was in progress. Under the Obiri shed, a band of various drums, together with a particularly sweet-toned xylophone formed of cork-wood slabs laid upon fresh-cut plantain stems, was playing. To the sound of this music danced the chief of Elele Aliminni (Ale by the water) with his three principal wives. Two points were specially noticeable in the performance; first, the intense solemnity of the dancers, and, secondly, the way in which their oneness of purpose was emphasised by gesture. This is the only West African dance witnessed by us in which the performers continually linked arms, or twined these round one another's shoulders and waists.

When Chief Eleche was questioned as to the meaning of the ceremony, he said that it was performed in order to draw down the blessing of the great Juju Aya-Eke on the chief of Elele Aliminni, his family and crops, before beginning to dig the first yams of the year.

A few weeks later came one of the greatest disappointments of our tour. By means of much planning it had been made possible, though with considerable difficulty, to arrive at Elele on the day before that fixed for the great yam festival, which we were anxious to witness. As ill fortune would have it, however, a runner came in in the late afternoon to bring tidings of trouble which was thought likely to break out in a far-off corner and to prevent which the presence of the white man was needed. To hesitate under such circumstances was of course naturally impossible. So the crowning ceremony of the year, the Aya-Eke harvest festival, was perforce missed.

IX

ALE AND THE ANCESTORS

ANOTHER link between Ale and her human children may be found at Ogu, a town inhabited by Okrikans, in the extreme east of the District. Here marriage is only solemnised once a year, immediately before the making of new farms. The Earth Goddess, locally called Amakiri (Earth of the town) is the principal deity, and not far to the rear of her shrine stands that of Ababa, the protectress of marriage. The spot sacred to the latter is an oval enclosure, fenced round by a wall of rough logs. Within this grow many Odumdum—the tree which, as previously mentioned, is looked upon almost all over the West Coast as bestower of babes, protector against evil influences and purifying agent, as well as in some cases the symbol of the yam spirit and that of the Earth Goddess herself.

Thither, before the cutting of new farms, go all the brides of the year to take the vow of faithfulness to their new-made lords. Libations of rum and palm wine are poured out, while the blessing of the indwelling Genius, Tenye Te'en, is invoked upon the faithful and her vengeance called down upon any woman who should prove false to her wedded vows.

In the local shrine of Obaji (or Obazi) the god of the

sea, we came across a representation of multiplied, or limitless, birth—eight frogs carved from a solid strip of wood. Several other slabs showed designs of the sacred crocodile with human beings laid out before it in sacrifice.

A frog is often depicted—with probably the same reason—in the carved tablets known as Nyama Ahia or sometimes Ahia Osimiri (the river market), which are hung up as ghost offerings in Ikwerri Ibo houses in order to remind the ancestral spirits of the need for constant activity in increasing the prosperity of their descendants. In one found at Elele, the sacred crocodile and the phallic serpent are shown together with the hoe, the symbol of fruitful Ale. Again, the central figure has its tail joined to another hoe, while the tail of the serpent touches that of the crocodile and is thereby linked with the hoe.

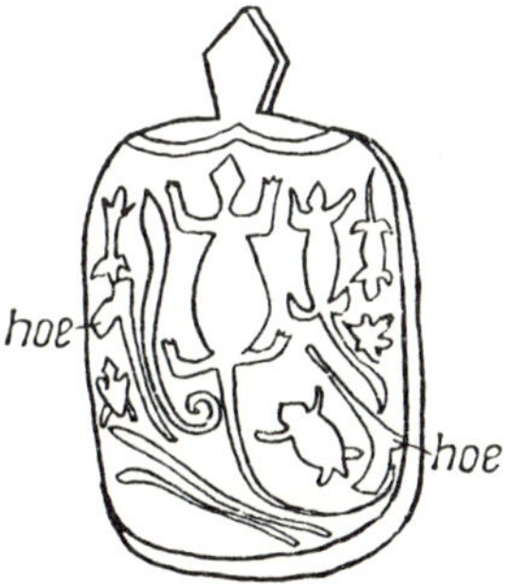

Fig. 46. Ancestral Tablet

During the making and planting of farms among Mbolli and Abuan—both tribes of particular interest and distinct type—the rule of strict chastity must be observed. No man may approach his wife until his share of the work is over. The labour apportioned to the males of the tribe at this season consists, first, in cutting and firing bush, after which women clear away the charred branches. Men again usually dig the holes into which it is the task of maids and matrons to lay the yam tubers. Nowadays, however, both the last mentioned duties fall to the lot of women. Till every ' seed of Proserpine ' has been laid in the dark ground, however, neither wife nor maid may yield to the prayer of husband or lover; for should the strictest chastity fail to be practised during this period, the farm of the frail one would yield but scanty increase.

Among Mbolli, in the words of the Chief Igwe of Ogali:

> We worship our ancestors (Okwenji). We sacrifice to them fowl and fish. Rich men give goats at such times. The sacrifices are made three times a year—at the harvests; first at the new corn month, next one month later again and then five months later, when we start digging yams. We hold this festival in the tenth month (November) and go to cut farm again two months later. We start to count months from putting the crops in the ground till we begin to dig—*i.e.* ten moons.
>
> At the feast of the ancestors we pour out drink, saying:
>
> | | | | | | | |
> |---|---|---|---|---|---|---|
> | 'Ebe | atena | 'mgbom | ami, | ami | 'mgbo | nan mwi.' |
> | 'As | (my) father | got | me, | (let) me | get | other child.' |
>
> We have already lived two moons in the farm—October and November. We shall stop another five. While we stay in the farms, we may not have connection with our wives; for such a thing we must come back to the town, sleep for a night and then go back. Otherwise we should offend 'Nkike, who would not let our crops grow well or send plenty children.

Among the Ale Nsaw Ibo a strict rule as to chastity was imposed by the direct command of the Earth Goddess. On this point Chief Osu of Obiakpo stated:

Fig. 47. Shrine of Ojuku juju at Woji

Our people are generally known by the name of Ale 'Nsaw (Ale's tabu or the land of the tabu) because in our ancestors' time there were many forbidden things in our part. All our women were sacred to Ale, therefore in olden days no man might reach out a hand to touch a woman's leg or foot. Should a man meet a woman going to bush, he must at once hide his eyes or pass by another way. In those days it was a very terrible sin for any man to commit adultery. Should one fall into this crime, he was not only heavily fined but at once made outcast. Never again was he permitted to join any 'company.' Never again might he drink or eat with others. As regarded his own family, because he was of their kin they would help to collect the fine, but after this was paid off they would have nothing further to do with him.

Among the Abuan, who live to the west of the Sombreiro River, the law of the Earth Mother as to chastity is even more strictly enforced. Like the Mbolli, this people on starting the new season's farms early in January, take up their abode in little huts built on their plantations. There they spend the space of three months, after which they return to their town for about four weeks, and then go back for another three months, weeding the crops and tending them till they grow strong for harvest.

During all that time strict continence obtains. It is absolutely forbidden for any man to approach a woman, *even his own wife*. Should desire prove too strong, the pair must leave their farm and seek their town dwelling for the purpose. Any breach of this law is thought to have disastrous effect upon the crops.

Again, while, as already mentioned, it is regarded throughout the whole of the region as a grave sin against the Earth Mother for a woman to yield to the embraces of any man, whether lover or husband, while lying upon the ground, the crime is of yet deeper dye if committed upon farm land than in the depth of the bush. In olden days a couple convicted of such an offence would have little chance of surviving the wrath of their outraged townsfolk. Even now such a charge would bring down upon the accused the invocation of some reputedly fatal Juju. For instance, in a case heard at Abua Court (No. 116/14), a woman named Ugenni stated as follows:

> All our townspeople laughed at me, saying that I was having connections with men under plantains. So I said, whoever accused me of having connections under plantains, the Juju Obuku of Amingbokko must kill that person.

The same law against intercourse in the bush—and in some parts in a canoe—prevails throughout almost the entire Niger Delta. Among the Jekri it is so strong that in a recent murder case (Rex versus Iyeabor) it came out that the dead woman had such belief in the strength of this tabu—and an additional one which enjoined chastity during pregnancy—that she had no hesitation in going into the bush with her murderer, a man whom she knew to be desirous of her.

Case No. 297 tried in the Ijaw Native Court of Nembe in January, 1925, gives the procedure which was adopted in order to convert a ' bush ' place, where cohabitation was not allowed, into a village, where this could take place with impunity.

> Igoin and his people sometimes stayed at this newly discovered place for two months, but no cohabitation was to be conducted there. One of the main reasons why they used to return to Nembe was because no husband was allowed to use his wife as regards sexual intercourse there.

Finally an envoy was sent to the Long Juju (that of Aro Chuku)—a journey which would have taken at least several weeks—' to ask for the necessary ceremony to be performed on the village, so that one can have connection with his own wife. Alegi returned from the Long Juju and told Ogede the rites which should be carried out. Ogede performed the necessary ceremony. The ceremony he performed was first he let a cock and hen cohabit at Ewelesuo. He brought one thing called ' Ovo ' (Covenant) from Long Juju, one ' Odo ' (a red round stuff) and a round white lime and gave these to the juju to appease the jujus and prayed that the village should become an inhabitable town and that one can have connection with his wife. Before this ceremony was performed it was forbidden for a woman to urinate in the village (Ewelesuo). On this account one place was chosen and called ' Sanpogu ' *i.e.* (Waterside for urine).

' Egula and Ogede were friends. After the ceremony had been performed Egula went after his friend and settled at Ewelesuo. Egula was dancing a juju called ' Akpana.' This juju Akpana and those at Ewelesuo made a covenant and Egula then ' danced ' juju at Ewelesuo. Eugla is a native doctor. Ogeda asked the juju, when Egula was dancing it, why they are not allowed to remain at Ewelesuo in November month. The juju asked whether he will be able to do so. He said 'Yes.' The juju then told him that, if people wanted to remain at Ewelesuo in November month, the people should keep a watch-night in the town and when the water ebb, they (the people) should take all jujus to the water edge and let the water soak them—which signifies that all the juju has gone out of the town (Oru iderimo). Then when December came the whole inhabitants should man one canoe, beat the tom-tom and sing a song and go to a creek called 'Orumokolo.' A prophet native doctor was to be in the canoe who will say to the people in the canoe that the jujus had come in. Then the canoe is to return to the town (Oru iwomo) and a juju called Ogoni is to be danced. Ogede agreed to perform all these. They (the people) were then to dance on three consecutive days after these jujus have been performed.'

In many parts of the country there is likewise a strong tabu against the commission of adultery, particularly in the husband's or adulterer's house, and against a woman cooking food for her husband when she has just returned from her lover.

No sooner is farm work finished, however, than, as already stated, scenes of licence are not only permitted over the greater portion of this region, but even enforced in certain parts; for, just as the priestesses of some temples of old Greece were obliged to offer themselves to strangers, so excesses, regarded as most reprehensible at other periods, are encouraged at this.

Among certain of the Brass Ijaw adultery is openly condoned under certain conditions. It is the custom, for some towns that are friendly together, to make an agreement that no man will take an action in Court against any other of their inhabitants and claim damages or punishment for adultery.

This plea was raised in case No. 253/25 before Amassama Native Court and an action for damages was dismissed in view of a covenant to this effect between the towns of Amassama and Agoro.

The cult, in which religious prostitution was perhaps most openly and extensively practised throughout the Ibo country, was that of Ife-Ala (literally 'thing of Ala' or 'that which concerns Ala').

To those few Europeans, who have hitherto had knowledge of this cult, it appears to have been known as the Ifallum Juju. All natives questioned on the subject, however, including Chief Gabriel Yellow, stated that the real name was as above given. The headquarters of this particular cult of the Earth Goddess were at Nguru, a town to the North of Okpala in Owerri Division:

> All people from neighbouring lands went there and lodges were also set up in nearly all important towns throughout Degama District. Many men and women, who could not be cured from trouble by native doctors, went there to pray

for help, but the priest refused to invoke the aid of the Juju unless the suppliant brought him a virgin as gift. The priest then took her as handmaid and she was kept in the temple and hired out by him to worshippers—especially to sterile men who came to pray for increased virility. Such 'slaves of the Juju' were marked out by a shaven patch at the top of the head.

There were about three hundred of these girls at Nguru but to none of them was it permitted to rear a babe, because by native custom they would have been obliged to refrain from the company of men for the two years during which they were suckling their offspring—and this would naturally have greatly diminished their earnings. So soon as a babe was born, therefore, the law of the Juju ordained that it must be disposed of in one of two ways; either must it be clubbed on the head and flung away, or laid in one of the big earthen jars and deposited in the bush beyond the town.

The Nguru lodge was suppressed about 1913 by Mr. J. M. Binny, District Commissioner. Great was the joy of the three hundred women thus set free to rear the babes born to them, instead of being forced to slay these at the harsh behest of the covetous priest of Ale.

A belief in the efficacy of sacrificial blood in order to purchase the favour of the powers of fertility is world-wide; but perhaps nowhere in past days did this dread libation flow in such streams as in West Africa. It is true that now the vigilance of Government and missionary effort have succeeded, to a great extent, in substituting that of slaughtered fowls, sheep and goats, for the costly ichor drawn from mortal veins; but in many a hidden shrine on the banks of unexplored creeks or in the depths of the silent bush—wherever indeed a chance occurred to do so in secret—human victims were till lately offered up. Especially was this practised at the season when the yam vines first send forth tender shoots to clothe the poles with green—as a means towards strengthening the new crops—and at harvest, in gratitude to Ale for her bountiful gifts of garnered grain. At such times it was dangerous for any unprotected wayfarer to venture forth beyond the borders of his own country, since strangers were very liable to seizure for such a purpose. Kula, the centre of many strange and terrible cults, bore an ominous reputation in this respect, until its evil practices drew the attention of Government and, as a result, the principal shrines were destroyed.

> In May of one year, a chief stated, they chanced to sacrifice a Brass woman. I do not know how she managed to disappear from her own town, but the Kula people caught her for their Juju. Always they made sacrifice when the new yams were coming up from the ground. Every Juju of every nation demands a victim at that time of year. News of the sacrifice of this Brass woman was brought to Mr. Binny when he was D.C. of Degama; so he went down and destroyed that Juju house. Word went forth that it was to be burnt to the ground, whereon the people came to him and said: 'May we not take the sticks of which it is made to mend our own compounds?' Therefore he gave permission and the townsfolk pulled it down themselves. In the shrine were found many skulls carved from wood in

exact imitation of real human skulls. There too were human figures, finely painted; some like those modelled in clay in the 'Mbari houses and others like the 'Nduen Fobara (ancestral images) in Kalabari shrines.

Yet another link between ancestor worship and that of the Earth Mother Ala is to be found at Omo-Ala (children of Ala)—a town in the south-eastern part of the Division which proved to be a great centre both of the cult of the Earth Goddess and of the forefathers.

Here, as in most other Ibo towns, nearly every compound has its sacred tree which is usually a specimen either of Ojji (*Chlorophora excelsa*) or Oil Bean (*Pentaclethra macrophylla*). In this the souls of the departed are thought to dwell while awaiting reincarnation. So long as the least fragment of the tree lasts, the faithful shades cling to its ancient trunk or branches or even retire into the furthermost rootlets. For this reason, when one of these giants falls beneath Time's axe, the family to which it belongs marks the place where it formerly stood and no farm may be made thereon again. Were this not done, it is thought that the ghosts might be imprisoned for ever since they could not break through the earth to return to the light of day, lest, by so doing, they might injure the sown crops of Ale.

Before the last rootlets of the 'ghost trees' return to the dust of Mother Ale, the spirits announce to their family through the mouth of some medicine man that a new tree must be chosen for their dwelling-place. The homes of such ancestral shades are obvious, even to the most careless passer-by, from the earthen pots or bowls and the freshly-offered plantains, etc., which may always be found amid the roots.

At the planting of new farms the members of each compound assemble beneath the family tree and give a great play. At such times they bring gifts and dance and sing, robed in their best, praying the ancestral shades to guard the seeds laid in the bosom of Mother Earth and help them to come to fruition. Again, at harvest time, another play is held to thank the ghosts for their share of the crops. A part of the increase is always set aside in gratitude to these beneficent spirits.

There is an interesting point to be noted about such 'ghost trees.' In this part of the District only the souls of good men are thought to await reincarnation in these peaceful dwelling-places, gladdened by sunshine, quickened by gentle dews or warm fertilising rain and refreshed by soft breezes. It is a matter of firm belief that, however fiercely tornados may rage around, these are spared. The branches of such trees are never rudely torn nor dashed together, while no thunderbolt has ever been hurled against their sacred trunks.

The ghost of an evil man would in vain seek admittance within the shelter of the family tree, but would be driven forth by the shades of his blameless kin to await, in animal form, a new term of earth life.

Young brides, therefore, often linger beneath those trees in which dwell the souls of gentle ancestors, in the hope that one such may choose her as his Janua terrae. Among Owerri Ibo, however, a different belief is held; only the ghosts of those foully slain, whether by force or witchcraft, are thought to seek refuge in the tree tops, there to wail and cry throughout the hours of darkness and in time of storms with a pitiful sound 'like a small chick or a piccan but a few days old,' until the guilty cause of their untimely death has been brought to justice.

It has already been mentioned that ghosts, who have taken on brute form while awaiting reincarnation, sometimes fall upon women who chance to pass through their haunts. By means of the animal body, which they temporarily inhabit, these evil spirits force their unfortunate victims to bear a babe, into which the sinful soul may enter—thus procuring an earlier return to mortal state.

From a case heard in Degama Native Court it also transpired that, among some Kalabari at least, the belief is held that the spirits of dead husbands are not altogether cut off from earthly joys but, when bound by specially ardent affection for the wives they have left behind, may on occasion return for the purpose of once more embracing the object of their desire. That such a proceeding is supposed to be not without danger to the woman thus visited will be seen from the statement of Ogoloba H. Horsfall, who summoned her brother-in-law, Charlie H. Horsfall, for accusing her of witchcraft. Complainant stated on oath:

> Three months ago the defendant accused me of witchcraft. This was on the Government beach. He stated that several people had died in the house owing to my having bewitched

them. My husband was defendant's brother. He died, and since his death has appeared to me in the night time and tried to have connection with me. I had to make medicine to stop this, as otherwise I might have died.

How deeply the longing for offspring is ingrained in the hearts of these people may be gauged to a certain extent by the horror of the means to which they will sometimes resort in order to overcome sterility or increase fruitfulness. For such an end no crime is too cruel; no magic rite too dark or revolting. For example, a case was reported from the Ogoni country on unimpeachable authority but seven years ago, in which the foetus was removed from a pregnant woman in order to be shared out among, and devoured by, others who believed this to be a sure way of increasing fertility.

In a land case, which had arisen between the Okrikans and the Mbolli tribe and came before me in April 1915, it was stated by Daniel Kalio, head chief of the former, that the disputed territory had been seized by his people in punishment for the terrible crime committed by their opponents.

In the old days, he said, the river formed the boundary between our land; but our women were in the habit of crossing over to attend the markets. One day, while thus peacefully buying and selling, the 'Mbolli rose and slew seventy-two of them at one time—forty-one at one place and thirty-one at another. Their heads were struck off and borne before the Juju; while the bodies of those who had been about to bear babes were slashed open and the small, small piccans removed and carried away.

It was suggested from another source that this last outrage was promoted by the same idea as that recorded among their neighbours the Ogoni and that the Mbolli sought, by this terrible means, to procure unprecedented fruitfulness to their own women. The suggestion, however, has never been substantiated.

The story of the coming of Ale was told by an Ibo named Obi Amara. It differs from the usual southern Ikwerri Ibo idea that Chi, or Chineke, the creatrix, was the great first cause from which all mortal men have sprung. He explained seeming contradictions by saying that to Ale the bodies alone were due, into which Chi sent down souls from the Spirit Realm.

> They make Ale play for this country at the feast of new yams and also give food to Ale when they want plenty yams, especially at the sowing of farms. Ale is the mother of all Ibo people. Her husband is called 'Ndiche.

Perhaps it is worth mentioning here that this was the only occasion on which any such appellation was given among the many local names for the spouse of Ale. Ndiche, or Ndichie, itself is the ordinary Ibo word for the forefathers, and the relationship here mentioned between the Earth Goddess and these beneficent shades is significant in view of the co-operation thought to exist between them, not only as regards seed corn and harvest but also fertility of the hearth. Further it may be noticed that the primary cause of the coming of Ale, as here given, was not to provide a home for the living but a resting place for the dead. To continue:

There is a big bird in our country named Ogbughu (hornbill). Its mother died. In those days Ale was not, so that the bird could find no place to bury his mother. He went round and round and at last had to bury her on his own head. That is why he bears upon his head a mound the shape of a grave to the present day. After a while, as he flew over the water, seeking a resting-place but finding none, he saw one fine woman and one man swimming in the water. As he watched, he saw they were making something and, in a short time, the first land began to appear. When it had grown quite big, Ale cried : 'When any man dies, let him be brought and buried here.' Her own body she stretched over the land; she it is who made all, both the earth and the earth-folk, whom she bore from her womb. When the dead are buried they turn to earth, so that our people say: 'We are of one body with Ale.' The trees too she brought. Ojji tree was the first that ever grew upon earth. The second was Agbo (or Akpu, the silk cotton tree) and the third Odala. Food is still given to this tree for every child which is born to a house and, if a woman wants a piccan, she brings a fowl to the Odala tree.

When a woman wants to become a mother, she lies down to sleep for night time after prayer to Ale. She dreams that Odala brings a piccan and lays it upon her breast. At daybreak she wakes and cries: 'Where is the piccan that was over my heart?' Then she takes a long piece of chalk,[1] called 'Nsu by Ibos, and lays it before the Odala tree, praying: 'Make my dream come true.'

The fourth tree which Ale brought was the Kola Ojji, the fruit of which is often set out in offering to the ghosts. At an Ale feast the women bring food and the oldest man of the town offers it up. After a man has eaten of such a feast,

[1] This offering is of the same shape, though apparently slightly larger than the small phallic symbols found before the Juju Ezum Mezum depicted on p. 92.

should he do any evil thing that day, Ale would surely kill him.

When a bad sickness comes upon a town, the old priest of Ale, who is always the head chief, beats upon the long drum to call all the people together in order to find out the cause of the trouble. Then Kola nuts are laid upon the place set apart for offerings. Each man in turn kneels down and picks up the kola with his lips, eats it and goes away. This is done until the guilty one comes. When a wizard bends down to take Ale's kola, the Earth Spirit catches him and he is forced by her power to confess how he spread the pestilence. Before all the people he must speak out, saying: 'I killed this man. I killed that man. That woman also I slew!'—until all his crimes are known. When everything has been told, his belly swells up and he dies. No man touches him. It is by Ale's power alone that he is slain.

This aversion to witchcraft is characteristic not only of the Earth Mother but also of her spouse the Thunder God; for, though certain magicians can raise a tempest by their spells, it is held to be extremely dangerous for witch or wizard to practise magic rites during the time of storms. When a man is struck by lightning, it is thought that Amade Onhia slew him on account of his crimes. Such men are never buried, lest the evil within them should defile Ale. The corpses are therefore flung away into the bush of the unblest dead. Similarly among Aro and some other Ibo tribes no tree struck by lightning can be used for firewood; since food cooked upon this would be accursed and even the light and heat given out by such logs would have a sinister influence on all whom it might reach.

With these peoples the bed-rock of religious ideas has perhaps been attained in this direction; and, unless the fascination of the subject has misled one with will-o'-the-wisp-like glamour, then surely in the cult of the Earth Mother, of the Sky Father, by whose fecundative showers her fruition is brought about, of the kindly ancestors, whose spirits still watch over their descendants and aid in the sending of rich harvests—lastly, and most intimately of all, by sympathetic magic through that mysterious link thought to lie between the generative organs, both male and female, and the fruitfulness of the animal and vegetable kingdoms—the innermost workings of primitive minds may, in a measure, be reached at last.

INDEX